For Monika,

With many thanks for
all your learned help
with my project — ?
an excellent photo!

Love,
Rob

# Jacob's Shipwreck

# Jacob's Shipwreck

*Diaspora, Translation, and Jewish–Christian Relations in Medieval England*

Ruth Nisse

Cornell University Press
Ithaca and London

First published 2017 by Cornell University Press
Printed in the United States of America

Library of Congress Cataloging-in-Publication Data

Names: Nisse, Ruth, author.
Title: Jacob's shipwreck : diaspora, translation, and Jewish-Christian relations in medieval England / Ruth Nisse.
Description: Ithaca : Cornell University Press, 2017. | Includes bibliographical references and index.
Identifiers: LCCN 2016047306 (print) | LCCN 2016048248 (ebook) | ISBN 9781501703072 (cloth : alk. paper) | ISBN 9781501708312 (epub/mobi) | ISBN 9781501708329 (pdf)
Subjects: LCSH: Judaism—Relations—Christianity. | Christianity and other religions—Judaism. | Intellectual life—Religious aspects—Judaism. | Intellectual life—Religious aspects—Christianity. | England—Church history—1066–1485. | Multilingualism—England—History—To 1500. | Hebrew literature—History and criticism—Early works to 1800. | Latin literature—History and criticism—Early works to 1800.
Classification: LCC BM535 .N58 2017 (print) | LCC BM535 (ebook) | DDC 261.2/609420902—dc23
LC record available at https://lccn.loc.gov/2016047306

For Willis Johnson
dear friend and teacher

An endless book can find completion only in
that of its unforeseeable prolongations.

EDMOND JABÈS, *THE LITTLE BOOK
OF UNSUSPECTED SUBVERSION*

# CONTENTS

# Acknowledgments

*Jacob's Shipwreck* has taken me a long time to complete and I have many people and institutions to thank. The project was supported by a grant-in-aid from the University of Nebraska–Lincoln, an ACLS fellowship, and National Humanities Center fellowship. I am grateful to Geoffrey Harpham, Kent Mullikin, Lois Whittington, and the brilliant, tireless librarians at the NHC, Jean Houston, Eliza Robertson, and Betsey Dain; my year there was a wonderful experience.

I offer thanks to the interlibrary loan librarians at the University of Nebraska and Wesleyan University for finding various obscure texts for me. The librarians at the Parker Library at Corpus Christi College, Cambridge, and the National Library of Israel kindly helped me with necessary manuscripts.

My editors at Cornell University Press, Mahinder Kingra and Peter Potter, as well as Bethany Wasik and Karen Hwa have been a joy to work with: I thank them and my valiant copy editor, Deborah Oosterhouse. I also thank the two anonymous readers for the Press, who provided many excellent suggestions for improvement.

An earlier version of chapter 5 appeared as "A Romance of the Jewish East: The Ten Lost Tribes and the *Testaments of the Twelve Patriarchs* in Medieval Europe," in *Medieval Encounters* 13, no. 3 (2007): 499–52. Part of chapter 4 appeared in "'Your Name Will No Longer Be Aseneth': Apocrypha, Anti-martyrdom, and Jewish Conversion in Thirteenth-Century England," *Speculum* 81 (2006): 734–53; and part of chapter 3 is forthcoming in *The Oxford Handbook to Chaucer*, edited by Suzanne Akbari (Oxford: Oxford University Press). I thank these journals and presses for permission to reprint the articles.

At the invitation of colleagues, I had the privilege of sharing my work with scholars at the University of Chicago, the University of Toronto, the University of North Carolina, Dartmouth University, the University of Connecticut, Harvard University, and Wesleyan. All of these generous audiences of medievalists and others changed my thinking in one way or another. The students in my seminars at Wesleyan and Duke on Jewish-Christian relations contributed to the same discussions.

It is a pleasure to thank my friends and colleagues whose support made it possible for me to write this book. Daniel Boyarin, Rita Copeland, Susan Einbinder, Miri Rubin, Michael Swartz, and Jocelyn Wogan–Browne encouraged me both by example and assistance. Suzanne Akbari, Monika Otter, Micha Perry, Fiona Somerset, and Magda Teter devoted time to reading drafts of my work and offering valuable comments. Sahar Amer, Stephen Cordoba, Sidnie White Crawford, Thelma Fenster, Cecelia Gaposchkin, Stephen Lahey, and Pinchas Roth are all experts who shared their expertise with me. I am fortunate to have colleagues at Wesleyan who could help me with all manner of things, including Michael Armstrong Roche, Matthew Garrett, Natasha Korda, Sean McCann, Jeff Rider, Michael Roberts, Amy Tang, and Stephanie Weiner.

My muse is my aunt Iris Shklar Ballon. Not only does she always amaze me with her erudition, but she keeps me laughing—and that is often difficult to do when working on some of this material. I owe Clarissa Campbell-Orr and Pegatha Taylor gratitude for their support in all situations. Rabbi Ben-Zion Gold, z"l was my spiritual guide, as he was for countless others. Finally, I dedicate *Jacob's Shipwreck* to my longtime friend Willis Johnson. Without his wisdom and encouragement, I would not have had the curiosity or courage necessary to begin.

# Abbreviations

| | |
|---|---|
| B. | Babylonian Talmud |
| CCSL | Corpus Christianorum Series Latina |
| CCCM | Corpus Christianorum Continuatio Medievalis |
| *CM* | *Chronica Majora* |
| *JQR* | *Jewish Quarterly Review* |
| M. | Mishnah |
| *NCMH* | *The New Cambridge Medieval History* |
| *REJ* | *Revue des Études Juives* |
| *SZ* | Eleazer ben Asher ha-Levi, *Sefer ha-Zikhronot: The Book of Memory; that is, The Chronicles of Jerahme'el*, ed. Eli Yassif (Tel Aviv: Tel Aviv University, 2001). |

# INTRODUCTION

*The Testament of Naphtali* is one of the rare extrabiblical texts that have survived in full medieval Christian and Jewish versions. While the two texts contain very different material concerning the patriarch Naphtali's advice to his sons, both offer a dramatic prophetic narrative. Naphtali recalls how he had two visions of the future of the twelve tribes and then recounted them to his father, Jacob. The first involves his brothers Levi and Judah seizing the sun and moon while Joseph rides a magical flying bull; the second is an equally fantastic account of the twelve tribes' experience of a shipwreck.

In the Greek version, Jacob and his twelve sons are standing by the sea when an unmanned ship filled with dried fish sails by inscribed as "the ship of Jacob"; they all get on board, but a violent storm begins and sweeps Jacob away from steering. Eventually the ship is broken to pieces. Joseph escapes in a dinghy and the others float off on ten planks—Levi and Judah share one—and they scatter to the ends of the earth. When the priest Levi prays for them, however, the storm stops and the ship reaches land as if nothing had happened. Everyone rejoices together with Jacob, and when Naphtali later tells his father about the vision, he proclaims that "these things must be fulfilled at their appropriate time, once Israel has endured many things." The point of this vision of the "last times" is that the scattering of the tribes will come to an end. Even though all of the patriarchs' children are destined to sin and to be punished with exile, the text concludes with the promise of a messiah from the line of Judah, and "in him Jacob will be blessed. Through his kingly power God will appear to save the race of Israel, and to assemble the righteous from among the nations."[1]

The medieval Hebrew version of Naphtali's shipwreck vision presents a more ambiguous future.[2] Jacob and his sons are standing by the sea and see a ship. Jacob tells them to follow him, so they all swim out to the vessel, which is carrying "all the goodness of the world" as opposed to fish. On a mast it is written that it "belongs to the son of Berakhel" (Jacob, son of Isaac, blessed by God). Jacob tells everyone to man some part of the ship, so Levi climbs up one mast and Judah another. Each of the other brothers takes an oar, but Joseph refuses. Finally he agrees to take the rudder from Jacob and steer the ship, and at that point Jacob disappears from among them. As long as Joseph follows Judah's directions from the mast and the two are in agreement, they sail smoothly. When the two brothers get into an argument, however, the ship hits a rock and breaks up. Everyone swims to shore, and Jacob has to scold Joseph for his jealousy of Judah and Levi; then he swims back out to sea alone to repair the ship. Jacob concludes with sorrow that "I loved [Joseph] more than you all, and because of the wickedness of my son Joseph you will be sent into captivity and scattered among the nations."[3]

The Christian text is part of the Greek *Testaments of the Twelve Patriarchs*, a second-century work that was preserved in Byzantium through the Middle Ages and later translated into Latin by Robert Grosseteste in thirteenth-century England. The Jewish text, translated into Hebrew from a Greek original, likewise probably traveled from the Byzantine East to the West; it was circulating in northern Italy by the twelfth century.[4] These visions capture two of the central themes of this book: the interplay of distinct Christian and Jewish temporalities, and the varying interpretations of Diaspora that emerge with the translation and circulation of various types of ancient writings. Theodore Korteweg argues that the Hebrew version, in spite of its late appearance, represents an earlier form of *The Testament of Naphtali* that simply predicts "doom and apostasy" without what he calls the Greek text's "happy ending."[5] Both visions are allegories of Jewish Diaspora, but they point to radically different ideas of past and future. The Greek text imagines the end of exile in a linear narrative that encompasses the twelve tribes' shipwreck of sin, dispersion, and, with the help of priestly prayers, the safe shore of messianic redemption. The Hebrew text, on the contrary, describes a potentially circular narrative in which any end to Diaspora is contingent upon Joseph and Judah's reconciliation. In the first, the shipwreck ultimately leads to universal salvation; in the second, the shipwreck could in theory happen over and over until an intervention from God. As an eschatological text, the Hebrew *Testament of Naphtali* exemplifies Gershom Scholem's concept of a Jewish messianism that "has compelled a life lived in deferment in which nothing can be done definitively, nothing can be irrevocably accomplished."[6]

In twelfth- and thirteenth-century England and northern France, Jews and Christians articulated their theological and temporal differences through the translation, rewriting, and circulation of ancient noncanonical or classical texts. Works understood as "external" or "apocryphal" in relation to scripture, for example, reveal how Jews and Christians challenge each other's authority.[7] In the dynamics of appropriation, authors claim to have recovered a text from the other religious group and then identify its origins as part of a larger imaginative narrative about history and language. The contest involves texts as diverse culturally as Jewish and Christian versions of Josephus's tremendously influential historical works, a midrashic Hebrew *Aeneid*, and the relatively obscure *Testaments* and *Joseph and Aseneth*, a Hellenic "romance" and adventure story about the patriarch's Egyptian wife. In the narratives that reinvent these works, Jews and Christians inscribe and erase each other by turns in a dialectic that operates beyond the exegesis of the Old and New Testament prooftexts that structure contemporary polemical genres. One prominent example of this kind of biblical debate, the late eleventh-century *Disputation between a Jew and a Christian* by the abbot of Westminster Gilbert Crispin, circulated so widely that it was read by twelfth-century European Jews as well as Christians. The author rehearses a familiar set of allegorical interpretations of the Torah and Christological readings of passages from the Prophets together with a new set of rational "philo-sophical" explanations of the Trinity and the necessity of God's incarna-tion influenced by his friend Anselm of Canterbury.[8] Written a little over a decade later, the *Dialogus contra Judaeos* (*Dialogue against the Jews*, ca. 1109) by the Iberian convert Petrus Alfonsi also became one of the best-known debates, in this case between the author and his former Jew-ish self, Moses. Petrus, who immigrated to England from Huesca, notably introduces rabbinic literature into the genre.[9] In particular he denounces the rabbis for the absurdities of *aggadic* (narrative or homiletic) texts in the Talmud, for example a passage that describes an anthropomorphic God weeping over the Jews' captivity.[10] In response, the twelfth-century bilingual Iberian polemicist Jacob ben Reuben wrote *Milḥamot ha-Shem* (*The Wars of the Lord*, ca. 1170) and addresses himself directly to both Gilbert's and Petrus's arguments. Jacob directly refutes the Gospel of Matthew—translated into Hebrew—for its errors about Jesus's divin-ity and quotes long passages from Gilbert's *Disputation* on the bible in order to defend Jewish exegesis and, in turn, to attack the irrationality of Christian doctrines such as the Incarnation.[11] The twelfth- and thir-teenth-century exchanges between Jews and Christians that I discuss, in contrast to these mutual accusations grounded above all in the bible, arise from discourses that encompass a sense of fictionality in the intersection of cultures. Alongside the familiar high medieval culture of debates and disputations, these alternate polemics provide crucial insight into how the two groups defined each other's secret histories and prized artifacts as well as their own.

Two formulations drawn from medieval compilations are useful for understanding how both Christians and Jews thought about different types of noncanonical, apocryphal, or extrabiblical texts as well as pagan literature. Vincent of Beauvais, in the preface to his massive encyclope-dia, the tripartite *Speculum Maius* (*Greater Mirror*, 1244–59), provides a Christian account of the hermeneutic role of the biblical Apocrypha and pagan texts within the writer's own design of textual compilation. The encyclopedia as a whole encompasses a *Speculum Historiale*, *Specu-lum Naturale*, and *Speculum Doctrinale*; over two hundred manuscripts containing at least one of these works survive.[12] Eleazer ben Asher ha-Levi's early fourteenth-century *Sefer ha-Zikhronot* (*Book of Memory*) and the two earlier Hebrew anthologies that he incorporated and used as his models, *Sefer Yosippon* and *Sefer Yeraḥmeel*, all speak to a hermeneutics of loss; for these compilers, the collection of nonbiblical texts is a recovery of Jewish memory and culture for the Diaspora.[13] Defining the texts themselves is more difficult. All are works outside the canonized Christian or Jewish Bible, patristic writings, and for Jews, often outside rabbinic literature; the writers themselves also offer theories that considerably expand these categories.

Vincent of Beauvais's preface to the *Speculum Maius*, known as the *Libellus totius operis apologeticus*, defines the Apocrypha as texts for which "there is no certainty of truth" and cites Paul's reference to Moses's enemies "Jannes and Jambres" in 2 Timothy and the reference to the *Book of Enoch* in the Letter of Jude (1:14–15) as examples.[14] In effect, the Apocrypha, unless openly heretical, illuminate historical and scriptural moments otherwise obscured. Vincent explains, "Thus I included a few apocryphal writings in this work, not claiming that they are either true or false; but just simply reciting them so that [those who believe in God] can read and believe them without violating their faith." He concludes his apologia by warning that "in no way should apocryphal, or likewise philosophical or poetical books, be read by any Christian except by keeping constantly in mind what the Apostle says: 'test everything, holding on to that which is good' (1 Thess. 5:21)." He adds, quoting from Jerome's *Letter against Vigilantius*: "My purpose and study in reading widely is to pick many different kinds of flowers, not so much as to save them all but rather to choose the ones that are good."[15]

The Jewish account emerges from a series of related medieval anthologies, beginning with the tenth-century southern Italian *Sefer Yosippon*, which includes, among other texts, a Hebrew translation and radical revision of two different Latin Christian versions of Josephus's *Jewish Antiquities* and *Jewish War* as well as an adaptation of 1 and 2 Maccabees taken from the Jerome's Vulgate Bible. The widely circulated *Yosippon* was itself anthologized in a larger mid-twelfth-century northern Italian collection known by the author's name as *Yeraḥmeel*. *Yeraḥmeel* brings together various late midrashic texts on Genesis including *The Testament of Naphtali*, a translation of the Aramaic parts of the book of Daniel into Hebrew, a peculiar and fully desacralized account of Jesus and his family members, and a specifically Jewish version of the widespread Christian apocalyptic tract, the "Fifteen Signs of the End of Days."[16] In addition to being an editor, Yeraḥmeel ben Shlomo was also a poet whose verses and riddles—most with signatures or acrostics—are preserved along with these other texts.[17] References in these poems to Rashi (R. Yitzhak ben Shlomo), the great northern French Talmud and bible commentator, and his grandson Rashbam (R. Samuel ben Meir) point to a personal connection with northern Europe.[18] *Yeraḥmeel* was known in some form to the French biblical exegete and anthologist Peter Comestor, most likely through his direct collaboration with Jewish scholars.[19] This collection only survives because the early fourteenth-century Askenazic compiler Eleazer ben Asher ha-Levi incorporated it, with numerous attributions to "Yeraḥmeel," into his own immense anthology. Eleazer bound all of the previous ancient works together with many more recent productions, including, following *Yosippon*, excerpts from the chronicles by Eleazer bar Nathan and Ephraim of Bonn of the persecutions of Jews during the First and Second Crusades. It also includes one of the Hebrew romances of Alexander the Great and the *Alphabet of Ben Sira*. All three anthologists describe their method as the recovery of texts almost lost to Jews through "scattering" or Diaspora; Yeraḥmeel directly quotes *Yosippon* that he has "collected things from the book of Joseph ben Gurion (i.e., Josephus) and the books of other authors who wrote about the deeds of our ancestors and assembled them in a single scroll."[20] Eleazer ha-Levi characterizes his motive for composing his collection as having "seen many scrolls of external books scattered about and I have set them down in writing for admirers of 'parables and poetic style' (*mashal u-meliza*)."[21] The book's editor, Eli Yassif, characterizes Eleazer's "external books" ("sefarim hiẓonim"), a negative term in rabbinic sources for apocryphal texts, as "unknown books or works not studied in Jewish educational institutions."[22] As the basis of his diasporic historical and literary project, Eleazer redefines the meaning of "external" from the nonbiblical texts rejected and even forbidden by the sages to the "lost" works worthy of recording for memory.

Vincent and the Jewish compilers, while relying on different discourses of scriptural and textual authority, are both interested in works that have a status between truth and fiction. Situated outside of scripture yet related in greater or lesser degree to sacred writings, these texts are usefully flexible in terms of interpretation. Vincent cautions the reader that his intention is not to assess the truth or falsehood of a given work but to pursue encyclopedic knowledge through the collection of as many sources and previous compilations as possible. In another apologia for pagan philosophers and poets, Vincent explains that he includes contradictory opinions of the philosophers so that the reader can choose among them; there is no definitive truth in such sources. The polyvocal aspect of the *Speculum* comes from nonauthoritative pagan writers as well as Christian and Jewish Apocrypha, anything indeed that can be "tested."[23]

For Yeraḥmeel and his compiler Eleazer, the similarly polyvocal "external books" are determined by the nature of Diaspora. With the fall of the Second Temple, innumerable texts that could add to the biblical stories and interpretations found in known rabbinic ʿaggadah and midrash collections or otherwise fill in the gaps in knowledge of "our ancestors" have been preserved but "scattered" geographically. *Yosippon*, translated and adapted from Latin, is the basis of the anthologizing impulse in the two later compilations.[24] Its version of Josephus's *Jewish War* balances the destruction of the Temple and the collective murder/suicide at Masada with the scroll's own project of the recovery of Jewish literature. Like its rabbinic counterpart *Midrash Lamentations Rabbah* ("The Great Midrash on Lamentations"), *Yosippon* emphasizes the terrible sins of the Jews that led to the destruction of Jerusalem (*ḥurban*). Alan Mintz writes of the rabbis' intertextual hermeneutic project of drawing meaning from the book of Lamentations beyond inconsolable loss: in the ruins of the Temple, "the text remained" and could be interpreted creatively through an "imaginative discourse" that encompasses both the sinfulness and lost virtues of Jerusalem. Mintz, by coincidence, likens the "nostalgic" rabbinic tales that recall the lost city to "debris from a shipwreck."[25] Eleazer, the editor of the *Book of Memory*, pointedly includes both texts about Jerusalem in his opus, staging a dialogue between the creative interpretations of classic midrash and the recovered category of classical historiography. In all of these compilations, as in many other medieval Hebrew texts, translation into the "holy language" is a diasporic mode, the way to recapture a Jewish culture lost amid the languages of other nations. Although these works are more properly adaptations than translations in the strictest sense, the transfer of language along with the hybrid fictions generated by that transfer are at their core. Naomi Seidman, in her study of moments of "Jewish translation" from Hebrew beginning with the Septuagint, characterizes the concept itself as "hard to categorize not only because it takes shape in a variety of contexts and periods, but also because translation is a term for doubleness and difference."[26] This doubleness is also evident in the negotiation between nominally Jewish and Christian ideas and representations behind the fiction of rescue in Eleazer's collection. Likewise, as much as Diaspora is characterized as loss, it is also productive in its "technologies of cultural transformation," to use Jonathan and Daniel Boyarin's term.[27] Eleazer, in this vein, signals the importance of fiction itself to his project. The gathering of "precious and worthy" books counters "the troubles and afflictions that our ancestors endured in their exile."[28] His "memory" is not only a response to the loss of imagined "homelands"—Jerusalem and also the pre-1096 Rhineland centers of Jewish culture—but also just a collection of parables and poetry, a source of literary pleasure for the present.[29]

Versions of all of the works at the heart of this book later ended up anthologized either in Vincent's widely disseminated *Speculum Historiale* or in Eleazer's unique *Book of Memory*. Yassif makes a compelling case for the *Book of Memory* as a "world chronicle" modeled in part on Christian encyclopedias.[30] Like the *Speculum Historiale*, which largely through excerpts from patristic and earlier historical texts, begins with the creation of the world and ends with the 1240s (including European encounters with the Mongol Empire), a first section of the *Book of Memory* organizes texts chronologically that, taken together, span a version of history from creation to the end of Temple and then the Crusades. Both extensive compilations end by looking ahead to apocalyptic programs and the end of history. In the broadest sense, Eleazer draws on the same historical thinking as late medieval clerics, although the thematic principles of the anthology—with *Yosippon* at its center—speak to different concerns. Vincent structures the *Speculum* on the idea of a providential Christian-Roman empire; Eleazer's guiding idea is the dispersion of Jewish writings within a hostile space very much like this empire.[31] The most prominent formal difference, of course, is that Eleazer continues his scroll after the end of days by collecting further imaginative texts in a sort of second section; the move suggests at the least an ambivalence toward the contemporary Christian idea of a "chronicle" or even a polemic against its temporal limits. Vincent includes, among the Apocrypha, abbreviated texts of the Latin *Joseph and Aseneth* and *Testaments of the Twelve Patriarchs*. He also includes an abbreviated version of Petrus Alfonsi's *Dialogue*, an index of the anti-Jewish polemic's influence. Eleazer includes *Yosippon*'s Hebrew adaptations of the *Jewish War* and the *Aeneid*, and then further on in the manuscript includes Berekhiah ha-Nakdan's late twelfth-century Aesopic *Mishle Shu'alim* (*Fox Fables*). All are appropriations from another tradition, and all are translations—or translations of earlier translations—real or imaginary. In their historical contexts, all use the resources of fictionality set out above to address the most difficult aspects of relations between Jews and Christians: martyrdom, Diaspora conversion, and eschatology, as well as the respective sacred and secular roles of the Hebrew and Latin languages.

*Jacob's Shipwreck* focuses primarily on medieval England in the "long twelfth century" (ca. 1050–1250) situated within the Angevin sphere and northwestern Europe more broadly, or in Jewish terms Ẓarfat and Ashkenaz (roughly France and western Germany). This historical and geographical context illuminates the transmission and circulation of Hebrew and Latin texts in cultural exchanges between Jews and Christians. Jewish–Christian relations in England have most often been defined by the Jews' role as financiers, the multifaceted dangers to coexistence like the notorious Norwich blood-libel accusation of 1144, and the conflicts that led to the massacre and mass suicide of the Jews of York in 1190. A century of persecutions and financial pressures under the Plantagenet kings ensued, culminating in the expulsion of the entire Jewish community in 1290.[32] This story is complicated, however, by the rich tradition of Christian Hebraism in England, in which Jews were hermeneutic rather than financial intermediaries. Beryl Smalley, Michael Signer, and others have thoroughly described the innovations of Hugh of Saint-Victor and his English student Andrew with regard to the study of the Hebrew Bible.[33] Returning to Jerome's principle of reading and translating the "Hebrew Truth" (*Hebraica Veritas*) rather than the Greek Bible, Andrew looked to Jewish informants, his "Hebraei," to reveal a truly historical level of scripture. The Jewish scholars he consulted were in turn influenced by their own innovative twelfth-century biblical commentators who focused on "literal" and philological interpretation: the "Northern French School" of Rashi and his successors, including Rashbam and Joseph Kara. For Andrew, the literal sense of scripture rooted in Hebrew study was the necessary basis of Christian allegorical exegesis; occasionally he scandalously favored a Jewish interpretation of prophecy over a Christian one.[34] Andrew's disciple Herbert of Bosham, secretary and biographer of Thomas Becket, acquired an even deeper knowledge of Hebrew grammar and rabbinic literature from his Jewish teachers in England and France. Bosham's revision of Jerome's Hebrew Psalter and his accompanying literal exegesis rely most frequently on Rashi's commentary on the Psalms and medieval Hebrew grammatical works.[35] In the mid-thirteenth century, Robert Grosseteste and a circle of scholars practiced another type of Hebraism, limited for the most part to England. A collection of English Hebrew manuscripts of the psalter and other biblical texts with new Latin word-for-word interlinear translations as well as glosses testifies to a "close collaboration between Jews and Christians, thus shedding a unique light on professional and intellectual exchanges."[36] The Jewish scribes of these pedagogical artifacts, working closely with their Christian counterparts, occasionally even wrote the Hebrew text from left to right to accord with the Latin words above. The inclusion in some manuscripts of glosses in French as well as Latin points to conversations between Jewish teachers and Christian students.[37]

Another, related, story of exchanges between Jews and Christians concerns the intersection of languages in the Angevin sphere. Whether in controversies over respective claims of the Latin and Hebrew narratives of the fall of Jerusalem or over *The Testaments of the Twelve Patriarchs*, which Grosseteste translated with the polemical intention of recovering a "lost" text from Jews who wanted to hide its messianic prophecies, Jewish and Christian scholars were engaged in an ongoing uneasy conversation outside of biblical exegesis. Peter Comestor's encounter with obscure extrabiblical materials on the families of Cain and Noah in *Yerahmeel*, for example, points to a different sense of scripture than the Victorines' "Hebrew Truth." Compiling as many sources to illuminate biblical history as he could in his *Historia Scholastica*, with Josephus's *Jewish Antiquities* as his favorite book, Peter was willing to track down Jewish texts beyond the Talmud and classic Midrash that everyone involved in the transactions probably understood as productive fictions, traditions outside of any canon.[38] Studying noncanonical works alongside scripture led both groups, among other things, to rethink Diaspora according to new models. From different perspectives, Jews and Christians conceptualized the spatial imagination of Diaspora in contrast to familiar linear models of power including *translatio imperii*, the transfer of empire from previous kingdoms to Rome and then to western European claimants.

It remains to consider Hebrew in relation to the other languages of Jews in this intellectual and political milieu. While not spoken outside of worship and liturgy, Hebrew was the written language of rabbinic scholarship and literature. It was the language of the bible and, in conversations between Jews and Christians, also the "original" language of the Vulgate Old Testament. Much recent scholarship has stressed the dynamic multilingual aspect of twelfth-century English literature. For Ian Short, it was a trilingual "polyglot"—French, English, Latin—Anglo-Norman culture supported by patrons with interests in all of these languages in a multiethnic England.[39] This vital literary environment celebrated the concept of *translatio studii*, the progression of learning from Greece to Rome to France and the Angevin sphere.[40] Language and culture, in this ideological construct modeled on *translatio imperii*, follow power. R. R. Davies proposes a very different account of the English twelfth century as a period of "island mythologies" in contest with colonized Wales and Ireland. The era was marked by the need for historians and poets to meet the political challenges of by far the most popular author, Geoffrey of Monmouth (d. 1154/55), who claimed to have translated his *History of the Kings of Britain* directly from the Welsh language. Some of the inconvenient aspects of this work that subsequent writers had to assimilate to Anglo-Norman or English identity were the descent of the Britons or Welsh directly from Aeneas through his great-grandson Brutus and the unifying figure of King Arthur, conqueror of the Romans.[41] Accounts of a multilingual and multiethnic England have become more focused in recent years on the repressions and elisions carried out by its authors. However much these scholars allow for fissures in an unduly positive view of Anglo-Norman literary production, they have nevertheless virtually excluded consideration of England's Jews as writers and readers.

On first glance, it makes perfect sense to leave Jews and their languages out of the Angevin literary narrative since their role within the English court of Henry II itself was solely as large-scale financiers; their sages' halakhic (legal) and grammatical writings were limited to their own community.[42] English Jews were best known to Christians in general as moneylenders to the crown, the aristocracy, and ecclesiastical institutions. The most familiar accounts of their history—both medieval and modern—stress how many Jews, protected and exploited as the legal property of the king, became immensely wealthy but frequently lived in a tense situation with their debtors. In a recent intervention, Judith Olszowy-Schlanger has considered the implications of the Jews' financial transactions for their basic literacy in Latin. She argues that through the mutual witnessing of Latin and bilingual documents—legal contracts for deeds of various sorts—Jews would have attained some knowledge of the Christians' administrative language.[43] While none of the many documents she cites involves Jews learning to read complex Latin literature, these interactions provide a way to approach the role of Jews in England's multilingual society. French was the Jews' spoken language, yet many Jewish men had frequent contact with Latin and English as well as Hebrew and Aramaic.[44]

Scholars have recently begun to make the case for the influence of French courtly literature on Jewish prose and poetry in twelfth-century Ashkenaz and Ẓarfat. Susan Einbinder has shown that the First Crusade chroniclers' representations of interiority and heroism demonstrate the new trends of romance with its "inner conflict and doubt." For example, Shlomo bar Samson's portrayal of Isaac the Parnas's "unfolding thoughts" about his delayed martyrdom bears a distinct resemblance to the *Roman d'Enéas*'s monologues or Chrétien de Troyes's interior debates in *Erec and Énide*. Romance was a form that described extreme psychological situations; the Jewish authors adapted the vocabulary to Hebrew.[45] Kirsten Fudeman, along the same lines, has argued from thematic elements that courtly conventions, specifically from Chrétien's romances, inform a bilingual Hebrew-French wedding song in its images of knightly prowess and "romantic" sexual violence.[46] Building on these works, Hanna Liss has made the bold claim that Rashbam wrote his biblical commentaries in dialogue with Old French courtly literature. She also demonstrates that Anglo-Norman glosses in his *peshat* commentaries reflect contemporary Jews' familiarity with particular idioms that appear in Wace's *Roman de Brut* and Gaimar's *Estoire des Engleis*.[47] These examples and others present a convincing case that learned Jews appreciated new fictional genres, had access to books, and were active participants in the literary world. In England, it would have been difficult for like-minded Jews not to be aware of Geoffrey of Monmouth and his narrative of the Trojan Brutus's arrival in Britain, whether through the Latin original or French translations. The *Aeneid*'s legacy of Troy and Rome and the ubiquitous elements of *translatio imperii,* the movement of the Roman Empire westward, were part of a widespread literary and political vocabulary.[48] For Jews, all of these were texts about "Edom," a rabbinic name for Rome that encompassed their traditional oppressors both pagan and Christian, but they were also sources of historical knowledge and reading pleasure. A more inclusive approach to twelfth-century English literature, moreover, would take into account Berekhiah ha-Nakdan and his works. Although he is unquestionably a unique figure in both Angevin and Jewish literature, not least as an author-translator who worked in both Provence and Northern Europe, his interest in the contemporary literary forms of fables and dialogues should be seen as a fully realized expression of a widespread cultural contact.[49]

The five chapters that follow address Jewish and Christian approaches to the problems posed by multilingualism, real and imagined. The themes of language, translation, and transmission are the basis for my larger argument about how certain texts defined as "external," "apocryphal," or outside these two categories demonstrate the fundamental conflicts between Jews and Christians over temporality and narrative—how to interpret the past and future. I am indebted in my thinking about these subjects to a group of recent prolific historians, among them Jeremy Cohen, Israel Yuval, Ora Limor, and Ivan Marcus, who interpret medieval Jewish–Christian relations in terms of the two religions' coemergence or ongoing exchanges of symbolic systems and cultural representations. Yuval's work, in particular, theorizes the possibility of recovering and reconstructing the always intertwined relations between Jacob and Esau, the "twins" whose identity shifts between Jews and Christians, Jerusalem and Rome. His deep analysis of these mutual counternarratives opens the way "to reveal fragmented images of repressed and internalized ideas that lie beneath the surface of the official, overt religious ideology, which are not always explicitly expressed."[50] A fragmentation of texts, scattered in the Diaspora and reinvented in medieval Europe, drives the narratives that I discuss here.

The first chapter concerns a constellation of texts that establish the terms of Jewish Diaspora through competing claims to Flavius Josephus's Greek historical works, available to medieval Christians in Latin translations and adaptations, and to their Jewish counterparts in a medieval

Hebrew translation and thorough reconception. The Christian texts are the essentially faithful patristic versions of Josephus's historical works, which focused interest on the *Testimonium Flavianum*, a brief account of Jesus's life and death, and the *Destruction of Jerusalem* or "Pseudo-Hegesippus" (hereafter *Hegesippus*) a late fourth-century patristic epitome of the *Jewish War* that transforms Josephus's text into a polemic about the supersession of Judaism by Christianity. In the early Middle Ages the influential *Vindicta Salvatoris* (*Vengeance of the Savior*) appeared, which further dispensed with history by transforming the Roman emperors Titus and Vespasian into Christians who avenge the killing of Jesus by slaughtering Jews. In response to this tradition, the tenth-century Italian author of the *Sefer Yosippon* sought to reclaim Josephus as a Jewish historian by translating parts of *Hegesippus* into Hebrew, adapting rather than entirely rejecting its Christian origins. During the crises of late twelfth-century England, Jews and Christians competed, in a sense, to control the remains of the Second Temple, real or textual. Using a range of sources, including biblical commentary, secular and monastic chronicles, and Hebrew poetic accounts of martyrdom from the post-Crusade era, I show how the various "Josephus" texts shape Diaspora in both the Christian and Jewish imaginations, particularly in ideas about conversion and resistance. Under the influence of a new scholastic interest in textual transmission and the ideology of the Third Crusade, English writers like Gerald of Wales and Peter of Blois used Josephus both to rethink crusader hagiography and to imagine Jews mistakenly as keepers of a Hebrew text whose account of Jesus they reject. With the revival of classical Roman historiography among Christians, Jews also laid claim to a type of classical text in *Yosippon* and make use of its understanding of the past of both Jerusalem and Rome. For the Jews surrounded by their murderers at the massacre of York in 1190, *Yosippon* provided a coherent narrative of the Masada martyrs, and one that fascinatingly retains crucial aspects of its Pauline, patristic, and Neoplatonic origins.

The Hebrew *Yosippon* is in a profound sense *about* translation, in which the original Josephus becomes the powerful military leader and writer "Joseph ben Gurion," a figure radically altered from both the author of the *Jewish War* and his intermediate Christian personae. *Yosippon* fashions Joseph into the paradigmatic translator, a cultural mediator—or traitor—both literal and figurative. He becomes, in other words, a version of his namesake, Joseph the "Egyptian" patriarch, negotiator between Jacob and his sons and Pharaoh. As in the original *Jewish War*, he moves back and forth between the Hebrew and Latin worlds as he negotiates with the Romans. With this emphasis on transfer, the medieval author inscribes himself—and his own cultural role in medieval Italy—into the text. The second chapter considers the bold act of translation with which *Yosippon* opens: a brief Jewish version of the *Aeneid*. Here the Romans descend not from Aeneas, who is the king of Carthage, but from his protegé and general, Zefo ben Elifaz the son of Esau. Whereas the first chapter relates how *Yosippon* challenges the Christian account of Josephus's Jesus, the second shows how the text likewise challenges western European legends of Rome from the Carolingian era on. Another popular text, the *Midrash Va-Yissau* (or *The Wars of the Sons of Jacob*), narrates a military defeat of Esau/Edom, speaking to a similar cultural dynamic. By the time *Yosippon* was circulating in northern Europe, the Hebrew "epic" would have stood out even more as a parody of the Virgilian histories produced for aspiring empires, exemplified by the Angevin courts of Henry II. This section of *Yosippon* functions as a midrashic counternarrative to Anglo-Norman literary works like Wace's *Roman de Brut* and the *Roman d'Enéas*: the Hebrew text undermines the basis of Rome and the linear ideal of European "translations of empire" through diasporic geography and the fictional recovery of a "lost" Rome in Jewish texts.

The third chapter continues to interrogate the classicizing culture of the twelfth century with the singular Jewish grammarian, biblical commentator, and philosopher Berekhiah ha-Nakdan, who produced two translations from Latin sources into Hebrew. Berekhiah explains his theory of translation as a "purification" of language in his earlier work *Dodi ve-Nekhdi* (*Uncle and Nephew*), a version of Adelard of Bath's *Natural Questions*. In his groundbreaking scientific text, Adelard claims to be following "Arab studies" in contrast to the old disciplines of the Paris schools and to draw upon observations from extensive travels. Rewriting Adelard's accounts of his journeys to the Middle East, Berekhiah emphasizes how his own diasporic, as opposed to European and territorial, view of travel and language radically changes the interpretations of natural phenomena that appear in the Latin text. His most famous work, the later *Fox Fables*, is a collection of Aesopic texts mainly

translated from early Latin sources. Several of Berekhiah's English contemporaries, including Marie de France and Alexander Nequam, wrote
collections of Aesopic beast-fables; Berekhiah uses the didactic genre to
engage in a dialogue with his fellow fabulists, but above all to transfer its
style of fiction into a new context. Berekhiah penned the *Fox Fables*, an
elaborate poetic text, as a scathing rebuke of his own Jewish community
for its greed and impiety. In a lengthy preface filled with quotations from
the Hebrew prophets, he warns his fellow Jews to return to a moral path
and then transitions to the lessons of the classical fables. Berekhiah takes
the term "Fox Fable" itself from rabbinic literature, and he shapes his collection, with twists and turns, as a cultural recovery of an original Hebrew
genre from Latin sources. In contrast to his aristocratic contemporary
Marie, who conceives of her translation of fables as a linear progression
from Greek to Latin to the "Romance" of the Angevin court, Berekhiah
figures his translation as exilic. In a corrupt world, the work itself nevertheless represents a purifying displacement of the imperial language in
favor of the holy language.

The fourth chapter turns to Christian authorship and shows how
*Joseph and Aseneth*, a first- or second-century Greek Jewish text, translated to Latin in late twelfth-century England, reemerges as significant
within a crisis over Jewish conversion. In the wake of persecutions during
the 1260s, some monastic chroniclers began to question the paradigm of
Jewish–Christian relations based on the narrative of the fall of Jerusalem, which inexorably led either to Jewish martyrdoms or to Jewish conversions of dubious authenticity. In the monastic chronicles' accounts of
contemporary Jewish converts, especially women, their interior spiritual
condition remains unreadable. At this historical moment, the romance
of *Joseph and Aseneth*, the patriarch and his Egyptian wife, provides a
more optimistic narrative of transparent interiority. The heroine, having
abruptly dismissed Joseph as a foreign slave, converts to Judaism mysti-
cally after being ravished by his divine beauty. The earliest manuscripts
suggest that the romance appealed to monastic thinkers who, influenced
by the heightened apocalypticism of the Crusades, were trying to work
out the eventual role of conversion itself within Christian eschatology.
Before she marries Joseph, Aseneth's transformation, read as identically
a conversion to Christianity, makes her a "city of refuge" or a haven for
all converts.

Robert Grosseteste's 1242 translation of *The Testaments of the Twelve Patriarchs* from Greek to Latin is the subject of the fifth and final chapter. The hybrid Jewish-Christian series of admonitions of fathers to their sons all conclude, like Naphtali's, with prophecies of crises that resolve in redemption. The translation appears at exactly the same time as another eschatological crisis was playing out: the invasion of eastern Europe by a Mongol army led by Chingiz (Genghis) Khan's descendants. According to the historian Matthew Paris, the Mongols were in fact the ten "lost tribes" of Jews, who had been locked away in Asia by Alexander the Great but were now free and being aided in their conquests by the Hebrew-speaking European Jews. For Grosseteste and his many readers, *The Testaments*, with its account of the patriarchs' acceptance of a Christ-like messiah, was a reassuring hermeneutic alternative to the present dangers of the ten Jewish tribes running rampant. Matthew Paris's vision of Diaspora as a force of world domination was in fact a construct that intersected with similar contemporary Jewish claims about the powers of dispersion. For example, in the *Debate of Rabbi Yehiel*, the Hebrew account of the 1242 Parisian "trial" of the Talmud, the author uses both the realities and fantasies of the Diaspora from the Muslim world to Asia to Ethiopia to dismiss the Christian judges' power. Likewise, several Jewish writers celebrate the Mongol invasions as the triumph of their kinsmen, imagined as forerunners of the messianic age. In response to the Jews' acknowledged powers of Diaspora, *The Testaments* offers a stable Christian linear messianism.

The chapters follow a trajectory from the fall of Jerusalem to the end of days as mediated by a series of appropriations and translations by Jews and Christians. In the interplay of languages, ancient texts become medieval polemics. Josephus's works, twice removed in their Hebrew version, restore to Jews a forgotten history of Jerusalem that defies the authority of its Latin counterparts; a Hebrew *Aeneid* steers Aeneas to a different shore, giving Rome a subversive new genealogy. Likewise, the Latin *Joseph and Aseneth* and *Testaments of the Twelve Patriarchs* provide Christians with a way to relocate contemporary Jews in narratives of universal conversion and salvation.

In "The Task of the Translator" Walter Benjamin writes of translation as redemptive of meaning in the "perpetual renewal" of language: "Translation keeps putting the hallowed growth of languages to the test: How far removed is their hidden meaning from revelation, how close can it be brought by the knowledge of this remoteness?"[51] Bella Brodzki, following Jacques Derrida's interpretation of the "survival" of languages in the essay, considers Benjamin's theory of translation more broadly as, "the mode through which what is dead, disappeared, forgotten, buried, or suppressed overcomes its determined fate by being borne (and thus born anew) to other contexts across time and space."[52] Medieval Jewish and Christian translators found the texts discussed in *Jacob's Shipwreck*, scattered around in various libraries, and adapted them to the new contexts required by their diverse polemical and literary aims. As might be expected, the newly employed languages occasionally brought out different and even contradictory narratives that had been buried and revealed. In some cases, the transfers, redeemed, offered possibilities for comprehending a fragmentary past or a messianic future. These stories reflect the unending conflicts between Jews and Christians during this period, yet they speak to less violent forms of cultural imagination as well. Even in their wary engagement with each others' languages to recover and repress meaning alike, the writers who produced and collected these works still often had words in common.

# 1

## Josephus, Jerusalem, and the Martyrs of Medieval England

In his treatise *On the Instruction of Princes*, the twelfth-century historian, royal clerk, and bitterly disappointed would-be archbishop Gerald of Wales offers a digression from his account of the reign of Tiberius Caesar, a story concerning English Jews. As he moves from Suetonius to Flavius Josephus to address the birth of Christianity as a new religion under Tiberius's tyranny, Gerald identifies the latter author's *Jewish Antiquities* as a source of "historical truth" about Jesus by an unbelieving Jew. He quotes the entire text known as the *Testimonium Flavianum*:

> About this time there lived Jesus, a wise man, if indeed one ought to call him a man. For he was one who wrought surprising feats and was a teacher of such people as accept the truth gladly. He won over many Jews and many of the Greeks. He was the Messiah. When Pilate, upon hearing him accused by men of the highest standing among us, had condemned him to be crucified, those who had in the first place come to love him did not desert him. On the third day he appeared to them restored to life, for

the prophets of God had prophesied these and countless other marvelous things about him. And the tribe of Christians, so called after him, has still to this day not disappeared.[1]

Recent scholarship regards this anomalous passage as either an early Christian rewriting of Josephus's own words about Jesus or an interpolation into the *Jewish Antiquities* from the period before it first appears in Eusebius's *Ecclesiastical History* in the fourth century.[2] For Gerald, as for all other medieval Christian readers, however, it was the passage that gave Josephus's two histories, the *Jewish Antiquities* and the *Jewish War*, their real significance as an account of Jesus's life and times by a contemporary nonbeliever, almost an eyewitness. The current-day Jews' reception of this text is the most scandalous evidence of their eternal treachery. Although Josephus is their own people's greatest historian—and they have his books in Hebrew, which Gerald takes to be their original language— the Jews refuse to accept the truth that he only reluctantly revealed. When confronted with the "Testimonium," they claim that the passage was never in their books and must have been added later.

According to Gerald, in one of his masterful anecdotes, the Jews' nefarious misrepresentations had finally been revealed by one of twelfth-century England's most learned scholars. Robert of Cricklade, prior of the abbey of St. Frideswide in Oxford (1141–ca. 1174), a man "not ignorant of the Hebrew language," had taken decisive action. A figure already known to the Jews, he obtained manuscripts of the Hebrew version of Josephus from several cities and towns with Jewish communities and found that in two copies the account of Christ was included in the text but had been recently scraped away; in others, the testimony had been omitted altogether. Robert then summoned the Jews of Oxford and confronted them with this fraud that clearly showed their hostility to the Christian faith. Gerald concludes with the observation, which he wrongly attributes to Jerome, that the Jews have been secretly altering and corrupting Hebrew texts since the time of the early church in order to prevent their own authorities from supporting Christian theology: when the Jews realized that the emperors were converting the entire world to Christianity, they essentially rewrote the terms of Judaism in opposition. Since at least Jerome's own era, therefore, Greek and Latin versions of scripture have always been more reliable.[3]

Gerald of Wales's multilayered narrative reveals, in an unusually stark way, the contest between Jews and Christians over the authenticity and cultural significance of ancient postbiblical writing as well as the bible itself. He appears to direct his ire not only toward Jews but toward Christians foolish enough to trust them, and like his contemporary Peter of Blois, he accuses the Jews of a willingness to alter their own scriptures in order to support their claims against Christians in debates.[4] These polemicists' target is perhaps the contemporary school of the Abbey of Saint-Victor, where Hugh and his student Andrew were studying the Hebrew Bible and rabbinic commentaries to use in their exegetical writings. Their reliance on local Jewish teachers was a return to Jerome's practices from his translations of the *Hebraica Veritas*.[5] Ironically, based on Gerald's own words, Robert himself appears to have been friendly enough with some Jews to learn Hebrew from them and to receive their books upon request. Gerald's fear, sparked by these Jewish manuscripts, is that no original Hebrew text can ever be truly authentic. The Jews' machinations can be discovered but not really undone even by the best of Latin or Greek scholars. In the case of Josephus, one of the most significant and often-cited ancient historians in the Latin Middle Ages, the history of the Second Temple beyond the Gospels is all potentially forever cast into doubt. Gerald's anecdote in this regard speaks to the dangers of manuscript transmission itself, the fragility of parchment and ink. With a stroke or two adding or subtracting words, the *Testimonium*, a document understood as central to early Christianity, becomes foreign, hostile, Jewish. The set of Josephus-texts that were actually at stake in Gerald's particular case, however, are so intertwined by translation and adaptation that the labels "Jewish" or "Christian" are at best dubious.

The manuscripts that Robert of Cricklade gathered were evidently copies of the *Sefer Yosippon*, a Hebrew version of parts of Josephus's *Antiquities* and *Jewish War*, along with various other ancient texts. Composed in the mid-tenth century in southern Italy, the work circulated widely among Jews in both Christian and Muslim Europe. The text's modern editor, David Flusser, shows that *Yosippon*, a hybrid created in most unusual circumstances, is actually in part a Hebrew free translation of the immensely popular late fourth-century patristic Latin epitome of the *Jewish War* known erroneously as *Hegesippus*.[6] Substantially faithful patristic Latin translations of both Josephus's Greek *Jewish War*, often attributed to Rufinus, and the *Jewish Antiquities*, from Cassiodorus's *Vivarium*, were equally readily available in western European libraries, in manuscripts that always included and often highlighted the *Testimonium Flavianum.*[7] However, the *Pseudo-Hegesippus*, as it should technically be called, is the work that initiates the Western Christian interpretation of the fall of Jerusalem in 70 CE that resounds throughout medieval theology and literature.[8] From its author's polemical introduction attacking Jewish unbelief to his reworking of the martyrdom of the last of the rebels, the text explains how the political events described by Josephus reflect God's punishment of the Jews for the crucifixion of Jesus. As a Jew, Josephus was ignorant of the meaning of his own words. The civil chaos caused by various revolutionary factions in Palestine, Josephus's own military defeat at Jotapata and his surrender to Vespasian and Titus, the burning of the Temple, and the mass suicide of the remaining Zealots at Masada were all, beyond the understanding of the historian, events that inevitably moved the Jews toward their doom.[9] *Yosippon* in turn engages *Hegesippus* polemically and transforms this belligerent yet elegiac Christian narrative about the figure of Josephus and the fate of Jerusalem into its own diasporic account of Jewish self-destruction and heroic sacrifice within the temporal frame of the Roman Empire. In the process, *Yosippon* also reworks *Hegisippus*'s patristic Neoplatonic theology into a new kind of Jewish spiritualizing rhetoric of resistance that later became particularly influential following the persecutions of 1096 during the First Crusade.

The story of Robert of Cricklade's investigation captures the double history of the Jewish and Christian afterlives of Josephus's works and the collision between these competing narratives in Angevin England. For both Jews and Christians, the many-faceted figure of Josephus as author and authority becomes crucial to the practices of historiography and translation usually associated with the literature of the so-called twelfth-century Renaissance. Under the pressure, moreover, of Salah ad-Din (Saladin)'s capture of Christian Jerusalem in 1187 and the organization of the Third Crusade, both groups laid claim to the final events of the Second Temple in order to articulate a historical relationship between Rome and the medieval European powers and to cast it in eschatological terms. The culminating moment on both sides was the collective suicide of the Jews besieged in York Castle in 1190, with both Christians and Jews reenacting the Roman general Silva's defeat of the last of the Jerusalem "zealots." As will become clear, the Jews apprehended by Prior Robert with their copies of *Yosippon*—and Robert himself—were caught up in a difficult history of translation itself, a series of exchanges between Hebrew and Latin texts that obscured rather than revealed the mutual influences of Judaism and Christianity.

Robert of Cricklade and Gerald of Wales were evidently the first Christian authors to realize that parallel versions of Josephus's *Jewish War* and *Antiquities* were circulating among Christians and Jews. Both clerics were erudite participants in the revival of classical literature and historiography that flourished at the courts of Henry II, and both pursued an especially broad variety of interests.[10] Robert, among other things, dedicated an epitome of Pliny's *Natural History* to Henry II, and he was the likely dedicatee of the earliest Latin translation of Plato's *Phaedo* by his friend Henry Aristippus, the archdeacon of Catania.[11] Robert was in an especially good position to have heard about *Sefer Yosippon* as one of the many Anglo-Norman intellectuals with connections to the multilingual, cosmopolitan courts of Norman Sicily and southern Italy—an area encompassing many long-established and relatively large Jewish communities.[12] He was also the only known fan of the great monastic historian and hagiographer William of Malmesbury, attested by a letter praising his works.[13] Gerald, of course, is best known for the ethnographic imagination he brought to the works about England's colonized neighbors that he presented to the king, his son Richard, Hugh, the bishop of Lincoln, and Stephen Langton, the archbishop of Canterbury: *The Topography of Ireland*, *The Conquest of Ireland*, *The Journey through Wales*, and *The Description of Wales*.[14]

Twelfth-century clerics and monks drew their theory of history, as Beryl Smalley and Bernard Guenée have shown, from Sallust's *Cataline* and *Jugurtha* for his prefaces characterizing the historian as an intellectual who records the merits and faults of others, and for the works' overall moralizing commentary on a corrupt Roman society.[15] These texts complemented the most fundamental medieval historical narrative, Orosius's account within an Augustinian providential and universal framework of the catastrophes during the decline of pagan Rome and the beneficial rise of Christian rule. Josephus, whom Jerome had called a "Greek Livy" and

Cassiodorus "almost a second Livy," was next to Orosius in terms of importance to this Roman-Christian understanding of history.[16] Josephus's stature rested above all on the *Testimonium Flavianum* and Jerome's biography of him in *On Illustrious Men.* Jerome's brief text, derived in part from Eusebius, lists Josephus's works and then asserts that the *Antiquities* "most clearly states that Christ was put to death by the Pharisees because of the greatness of his miracles, that John the Baptist was a true prophet, and that Jerusalem was destroyed because James the apostle had been put to death." A version of the *Testimonium* follows.[17]

Within this classicizing intellectual framework, a remarkable group of Anglo-Norman Latin historians who spanned the century was indebted to Josephus and *Hegesippus* as sources for reconstructing Rome and Jerusalem within a single discourse.[18] The following writers, each with a somewhat different purpose, are just a few related to the topic at hand: the fateful encounter of Christian scholars with a rival Jewish historiography.[19] William of Malmesbury, who declared his commitment to truth and moral example in the prologues in his *History of the English Kings,* had access to an impressive number of classical and patristic texts including Josephus and *Hegesippus* as demonstrated by his celebrated accounts of the kings of England and the church.[20] The very first line of his *History of the English Kings* praising Bede's style echoes the opening of *Hegesippus*: "The History of the English, from their arrival in Britain to his own time, has been told with straightforward charm by Bede."[21] Josephus's works in particular were his source for the geography of the Holy Land with regard to the Crusades.[22] He also showed a deep concern with preserving the classical past in the "Selden Collection," the quasi-continuous historical narrative of "Rome" from Troy to the Byzantine Empire to Charlemagne that he shaped, using Dares the Trojan, Orosius, and the eighth-century historian Paul the Deacon among others in the anthology; this manuscript of patched-together authorities distills the ideal of the *translatio imperii*, the medieval movement westward of the Roman Empire.[23] In a different approach, Geoffrey of Monmouth, chronicler of the Trojan hero Brutus and King Arthur in the Virgilian *History of the Kings of the Britain*, reworks a passage from *Hegesippus* in his invention of the "Britons" who defy Rome. A famous set-piece in which King Agrippa unsuccessfully warns the Jews of the futility of resisting Roman rule by comparing them to the distant subjected Britons becomes the British ruler Cassibellaunus's refusal of subjection to Julius Caesar.[24] The borrowing is a fine example of Geoffrey's literary ingenuity, an observation that structurally at least, the Britons ultimately occupy the same position as the defiant Jews in relation to the armies of the Roman Empire. Geoffrey also initiated one of the great historiographic controversies of twelfth-century England with his genre-defying account of the British-Roman era putatively based on a source written in Welsh. At the end of this extraordinarily influential work, he dismisses William of Malmesbury and Henry of Huntingdon for not having access to his source and by implication to the Welsh language.[25] The true story of pagan Rome becomes a locus of ethnic division. The Augustinian canon William of Newburgh, identified with an unusually critical approach to both historical sources and current events, begins his *History of English Affairs* with a scathing attack on Geoffrey's British "fictions" for, among other things, destabilizing the known history of the Roman Empire.[26] He is also famous for his use of Josephus to interpret the mass suicide of York's Jewish community.[27] In the context of these Christian authors and their readers, well versed in both Josephus and *Hegesippus*, the reception of *Yosippon* among their Jewish counterparts signalled an intervention in the dominant historical culture. *Yosippon*, in the same idiom as the Christian historians' exemplars, also announces an adherence to truth in its narrative. Jews, like Christians, were interpreting the past binding them together with a classical rather than a rabbinic source.

The revival of "secular" classical history emphasized an author's commitment to the truth of his facts, the depth of his learning, and his desire to influence the leaders of his day. Gerald himself, however ironically, quotes Cicero's famous definition in the largely fictional *Description of Wales*: history "is the recording of past events, the testimony of the ages, the light of truth, a living memory, a guide for conduct, and a reminder of what happened long ago."[28] For these leading intellectual figures, Josephus and *Hegesippus* were invaluable sources, providing the words of a Greek-Roman-Jewish historian whose topic was the Holy Land and whose approach reflected their own classical ideals. *Hegesippus* contained these within its patristic context. In the prologue to the *Jewish War*, for example, Josephus stresses his role as an eyewitness who must correct previous historians who have "misrepresented the facts" and record for "subjects of the Roman empire" the narrative in Greek translated from his own language.[29]

The *Jewish War* and *Hegesippus*, while sometimes confused in the manuscript traditions, were recognized as distinct works throughout the Middle Ages, in terms both of content and of readers' ideas about the tasks of the historian himself. In one striking example from the ninth century, Alvaro of Cordoba, a Jewish convert to Christianity, told his disputant Bodo, a Christian convert to Judaism, that he would cite only "your Josephus" as proof, not *Hegesippus*. In the twelfth century, Ralph of Diceto, the dean of St. Paul's and supporter of Henry II, lists in his universal *Epitome of Chronicles* forty-three historians from Trogus Pompeius up to himself as the most "illustrious men": he ignores most of the major Roman pagan historians, but Josephus appears twice, with his two major works listed separately, and later the "histories" of *Hegesippus*.[30] No less a scholar than John of Salisbury names both works in a lengthy list of texts that he had studied.[31] The distinction between the two lies in part with Christian uncertainty about what Josephus really represented for Jews. Unlike the patristic *Hegesippus*, the hybrid Jewish-classical Josephus presented a danger for medieval Christian readers. The text's Roman ideal of authenticity stands in stark contrast to its vulnerability to potential Jewish interpreters. The rest of this chapter argues that the Hebrew *Yosippon*, transmitted to northern Europe, represents a historiographical culture in common with many Latin works of the twelfth century in terms of its classical sources, concern with Rome, and a re-imagined *translatio imperii*. It is *Yosippon*'s noncanonical status within Jewish writing that authorizes the text's most subversive and deadly uses.

## Making Josephus Jewish—Again

In the Christian West, the legacy of interpretation of Josephus's *Jewish War* stems from its extensive descriptions of the city of Jerusalem following Jesus's death. The author of *Hegesippus*, thought by some medieval and modern scholars to be Ambrose of Milan, crucially characterizes Josephus himself as a talented but flawed literary figure: "Would that he were as attentive to religion and truth as he is to reporting events and fine speeches. He showed himself complicit in the Jews' perfidy in his own words . . . he deserted their army but not did not abandon their sacrilege . . . he lamented their distress but did not understand the cause of it."[32] In book 2, *Hegesippus* comments on the *Testimonium Flavianum* in the terms repeated by almost all later readers including Gerald: Josephus, whom the Jews consider so important, reported the truth about Jesus out of a strict classical fidelity to history rather than belief. Book 3 opens with a brief account of the ministry and martyrdom of Peter and Paul in Nero's Rome, marking a narrative shift from Jerusalem to the conversion of the Roman world. Foreshadowing the final act of slaughter, the author transfers the exemplarity of martyrdom from Judaism to Christianity as Jesus returns to tell Peter "I come to be crucified again." Book 4 is devoted to the suffering caused by the rebel leaders John of Gischala and Simon bar Giora. Book 5 opens with an authorial lament, a threnody for the city of Jerusalem that calls upon Moses, Aaron, David, and the Maccabees to witness the end of the Jews who killed not only the priests Ananus and Jesus and the righteous man Zacharias but above all, the other Jesus, the Messiah. Later, as the Romans are about to burn the Temple down, the author comments on Jesus's crucifixion: "This is he whose death is the destruction of the Jews. . . . This is the final destruction after which the Temple cannot be restored."[33] All that remains is the ambiguous suicide or martyrdom of the last Jews at Masada.

Medieval writers elaborated on this text and Orosius's typological account of Vespasian and Titus in their "triumphal chariot . . . bringing back a most glorious victory over those who had offended the Father and the Son" to stress the supersession of the Temple by the Christian church.[34] The extremely popular eighth-century *Vindicta Salvatoris* (*Vengeance of the Savior*), in short, makes Vespasian and Titus into Christians who set out in the name of the "true God and true man" to "take revenge and destroy his enemies from the land of the living and let them know he has no equal on earth." In this wildly ahistorical legend, the emperor Tiberius, Titus (here a king of Aquitaine), and Vespasian all convert to Christianity, the former two having been healed of various leprosies and skin growths by believers. Titus proceeds to attack Jerusalem in order to avenge the Crucifixion, and the Jews finally surrender the city after admitting that they had killed the Messiah; eleven thousand then commit suicide to "escape," while the rest are gruesomely killed or sold into slavery. Before the Romans' final victory, the Jewish leaders admit to them that "this kingdom was no longer ours, but was given you through the Messiah whom you call Christ."[35] Walafrid Strabo, in his ninth-century text *On the Destruction of Jerusalem* cites "Josephus Historiographus" as his source but follows *Hegesippus*'s account aligned with the Gospels: "Jerusalem, Jerusalem: the city that kills the prophets" (Matt. 23:37) is punished by the stabbing, burning, or scattering to the wind of all the Jews who refuse to convert. According to Walafrid's standard exegesis, Jerusalem is both the earthly city Aelia Capitolina rebuilt by Hadrian as well as the spiritual-allegorical church.[36] A series of poets then translated the *Vengeance of the Savior* into vernacular texts associated with the Crusades. The most bizarre of these is the late twelfth-century *chanson de geste* known as *La Venjance Nostre Seigneur*, which includes two characters based on Josephus himself, a warrior and a historian.[37] The *Sefer Yosippon*, among other things, is an answer to the voluminous *Vengeance* literature, a distinctly Jewish account largely derived, like the others, from *Hegesippus*.[38]

*Sefer Yosippon* occupies a unique place in medieval Hebrew literature as a Jewish chronicle modeled on Greek and Roman sources. Yosef Yerushalmi's *Zakhor* points to the text as an exception to his thesis about the absence of historical writing in the Middle Ages, a counterbalance to a rabbinic tradition that for the most part ignored the events of postbiblical Jewish history.[39] Steven Bowman argues that *Yosippon* is also exceptional for its concern with "the relationship between Jerusalem and Rome," a narrative derived from the Hellenistic historian Josephus but transformed by the use of biblical and mishnaic Hebrew and medieval midrashic ideas of language and interpretation to create an "open text" for Jewish readers to understand in dialogue with other works.[40] According to Flusser, *Yosippon* was most likely produced at Naples in the text's internal date of 953.[41] He surmises that the author, a Jew fluent in Latin, had access to the library of Duke John III (928–68); there he could have used an early Italian manuscript containing the first sixteen books of the Latin translation of Josephus's *Jewish Antiquities* followed by *Hegesippus*'s full account of the Jewish war.[42] His other basic Latin sources would also have been at hand, especially the Vulgate (from which he recovered the books of Apocrypha), Orosius's *Seven Books of History*, and the *Aeneid*. In this singular setting for a Jewish author, *Yosippon* was influenced on the one hand by the revival of Hebrew writing that began in Byzantine Italy with the ninth-century liturgical poets (*paytanim*) R. Silano and R. Shefatiah, and on the other by the contemporary rebirth of classical learning and textual production in both the Carolingian-Ottonian and Byzantine Empires.[43] Leo the Archpriest of Naples, in his preface to the *Alexander Romance* that he brought from Constantinople and translated from Greek to Latin for Duke John, praises the depth of his library; in addition to copies of the Old and New Testaments, he had collected works of numerous doctors of the church and classical historians including Josephus and Livy.[44] Possibly his zeal for finding new books—Leo describes his extensive inquiries—brought him into contact with *Yosippon*'s learned multilingual author. Interestingly enough, a slightly later Hebrew version of the *Alexander Romance* translated directly from Greek was interpolated into manuscripts of *Sefer Yosippon* by the mid-twelfth century, immediately following the account taken from Josephus's *Jewish Antiquities* of the conqueror's fictional visit to Jerusalem.[45]

The translator's feat is breathtaking. Admitted to an impressssive aristocratic library, he found a manuscript that he recognized as half of Josephus's *Antiquities*, without Christian rewriting, from the creation of the world up to the reign of Herod the Great; whether or not he was previously aware of *Hegesippus*, he noticed in the second half an abrupt change into a Christian account of the fall of the Second Temple framed as a virulent polemic against the Jews. By excising much of the overtly Christian text and adding other texts from the Apocrypha—a sweeping ideological overhaul—he created a new Josephus, like himself a translator living in exile in Italy. Working around *Hegesippus*'s view of Jesus's prediction of the Temple's destruction and God's rejection of the Jews as the beginning and end of Josephus's narrative, *Yosippon* restores some of Josephus's original interpretation of the fall of Jerusalem as the result of the rebels' innumerable atrocities and abandonment of God. From the beginning of the break in the manuscript from Josephus to *Hegesippus* as his main source, he also engages in an ongoing religious polemic against the latter's patristic theology, punctuating the text with rabbinic references when necessary. For example, *Yosippon*'s final chapter taken from the *Jewish Antiquities*, on Herod's rebuilding of the Second Temple, announces a messianic view of its restoration before he moves into the *Hegesippus* part of the text: the entire people celebrated with all of their instruments at the rebuilding of the Temple, and may it be "built again speedily in our days amen amen" (*"yivneh 'od bimherah be-yameinu 'amen 'amen"*).[46] At this halfway point, the translator looks ahead to the destruction of the current Rome, the Byzantine empire, and rejects the Christian interpretation of the destruction of the Temple that appears at the end of his Latin manuscript.[47]

The translator-author not only represents his own Hebrew text as a copy of Josephus's original work, but also elevates it to an almost sacred status:

> Whoever writes about ancient things must write about them with order and patience so as not to forget any deeds that have been done. And above all, whoever writes such books must write things that are true. This is what Joseph ben Gurion the priest commands, who is the most important writer of those who wrote outside of the twenty-four holy books, the books of wisdom written by King Solomon, and [the books] by the sages of Israel. And I have collected things from the book of Joseph ben Gurion and the books of other authors who wrote about the deeds of our ancestors and assembled them in a single scroll.[48]

*Yosippon* as a whole represents what David Stern has called the "anthological imagination" of Diaspora Judaism, in this case a need to preserve the past by collecting and associating fragments.[49] The first part of this statement about historiography comes from the opening of Josephus's *Antiquities* XIV, a call for truth, accuracy, and inclusiveness that derives from other ancient Greek historians, in particular Polybius.[50] In *Yosippon*, it becomes an account of how to produce history in the medieval Diaspora, discovering or retrieving sources from the world outside of existing Jewish books and reclaiming them as ancient Hebrew sources: in *Yosippon*, the principal new documents other than Josephus and *Hegesippus* are 1 and 2 Maccabees and the Greek versions of Esther and Daniel, all translated from the Vulgate Bible and thoroughly rewritten.

As a detailed account of events from the Second Temple period, *Yosippon* almost immediately became an influential extrabiblical text among medieval authors who accepted it as the work of "Joseph ben Gurion" himself, as he is called instead of Joseph ben Matthias.[51] According to one accepted tradition, the Ashkenazic sage Rabbi Gershom of Mainz (960–1040) copied the text himself, as he had the bible and some books from the Mishnah and Talmud, and used it to provide historical details in his liturgical poems that mourn the Temple and commemorate the fragility of life in the Diaspora.[52] For subsequent northern European sages, *Yosippon* usefully recovered the lost history of both Jerusalem and its conquerors. To cite an example, just as Jerome had used Josephus's works in the fourth century to elucidate the Persian, Greek, and Roman background of the prophecies of Daniel in his commentary on the antichrist and the end of days, Rashi used *Yosippon* in his gloss on Daniel to similar historical and polemical ends. For Rashi, *Yosippon*'s historical narrative, written by a witness of the fall of Jerusalem, supported the very position that Jerome had attributed to the erring *Judaei*: that Daniel 11–12 recounts the destruction of the Second Temple by Vespasian and Titus and so looks ahead in its calculations to the restoration of the Temple and the rule of the Messiah.[53] On a different note, however, Rashi cites *Yosippon* in his commentary on Daniel 11:30 to the effect that the Romans took advantage of the Jews' civil war, the "pointless hatred" (*"sinat hinam"*) of the Second Temple period. Rashi takes the term itself from the Talmudic account that attributes the fall of Jerusalem to this sin as bad as idolatry, and uses the eyewitness Joseph's long narrative of the viciousness of the leaders John and Simon as a vivid reminder of how the Jews inevitably destroyed their own city.[54]

*Sefer Yosippon* also accrued various additions and exists in what Flusser has identified as three distinct recensions, the latest dating to the twelfth century and much influenced by contemporary chivalric literature in its extended battle descriptions.[55] It eventually became incorporated into the twelfth-century Italian anthology that draws heavily on *Yosippon*'s historiographic impulse, *Yerahmeel*. *Yerahmeel*'s aim, like *Yosippon*'s, is to appropriate or reappropriate Latin texts and bind them together with Hebrew texts. Remarkably, he was also aware of Jerome's biography of Josephus from *On Illustrious Men*, which he drastically alters and appends to *Yosippon*. In this addition, the compiler Yerahmeel essentially changes the *Testimonium* into a counter-narrative that he assigns to Joseph ben Gurion, a version of the gospels without a virgin birth or messiah in which Joseph was married to two women named Miriam, the mother of Jacob (James) and the mother of Jesus; the apostles Matthew, Paul, and John are known from the various books they wrote. Transmitted to northern France, where Peter Comestor had access to some version of it through Jewish intermediaries, *Yeraḥmeel* shows the continuing influence of *Yosippon* on midrashic-literary and textual production. For the Jewish anthologists, the process of recovery and translation from Latin as well as other languages was always an incomplete search.

Some manuscripts of *Yosippon*'s later recension also include a much more bitter attack on Christianity than *Yeraḥmeel*'s, related to the early medieval parody of the Gospels known as the *Toledot Yeshu* in its portrayal of Jesus as a fraud and idolater. Like *Yosippon* itself, the story takes an ambivalent approach to the Roman Empire before its Christianization. This interpolation claims that Jesus and his disciples had offered to anoint the emperor Caligula as a God, claiming the authority of an angel sent for the occasion to fulfill prophecies. When the Jews refuse to recognize him as "the son of God," Caligula marches against Jerusalem with an army, but God intervenes and has the emperor's enemies murder him. After Claudius takes the imperial throne, he has Jesus and two of his disciples hanged and hands over the rest to Judas Iscariot and the Sanhedrin for punishment. Presumably, this scurrilous "Jesus" interpolation— or another like it—is what the English Jews wisely erased from their manuscripts before handing them over to Robert of Cricklade.[56]

These examples all show how *Yosippon* over the centuries remained a text that gave medieval Jews the means to interpret and redefine their history in relation to the ruling powers and texts of the Roman-Christian world. In the case of the Angevin sphere, the dynamic is essentially a diasporic *translatio*, a charting of the Roman Empire westward to Jewish territories rather than to new European nations. More specifically, *Yosippon* provides models for two types of medieval literary figure who together negotiate the varying circumstances of the Diaspora after the persecution of Jews during the Crusades: the martyr who dies to sanctify the name of God and the survivor-poet who chronicles the deeds of scattered Jewish communities. This dichotomy ultimately derives from Josephus's own ambivalence, from his position as a Roman citizen, in describing his role as commander of Galilee and the fate of the Zealots at the end of the *Jewish War*. In spite of his hatred for the various factions of Jewish rebels and his ultimate alliance with the Flavian rulers, he gives the leader of the *sicarii* (literally dagger-carriers) Eleazer ben Yair a stirring speech on liberty and the immortality of the soul at Masada.[57] In *Yosippon*, itself radically altered from *Hegesippus*, Josephus becomes the powerful military leader and writer Joseph ben Gurion, and the thuggish Eleazer becomes Eleazer ben 'Anani ha-Kohen, a heroic member of the priestly family who escapes with the just men—*zadikim* and *hasidim*—from the corrupt rebels in Jerusalem led by Simon ben Giora.

*Yosippon*'s Jewish author fashions Joseph ben Gurion into the paradigmatic translator, a cultural mediator who moves back and forth between the Hebrew and Latin worlds; with this emphasis, the medieval author inscribes himself—and his unique cultural role in medieval southern Italy—into the text. Like Josephus himself, he is a Jew with "Roman" Italian patrons; yet his project is to translate—in the most imaginative sense—Latin into Hebrew. In the *Jewish War*, Josephus describes how he surrendered to Vespasian after a futile military stand at Jotapata in 67 CE in which he was nearly killed by his own soldiers, prophesied the general's election as Roman Emperor, and then became his son Titus's spokesman and translator for the duration of the war. In this role, he begs the rebels in "their native tongue" of Aramaic or Hebrew to surrender because God has now abandoned the Jews and subjected the entire world to the Romans.[58] Later, he delivers a precise translation of Titus's words to the rebel leader John of Gischala to stop polluting the Temple with murders, breaking down in tears at the end. *Yosippon*'s patristic source material in *Hegesippus*, leading up to the final assertion that the death of Jesus has destroyed Jerusalem provides Joseph with a much longer speech "in his own language" in which he explains to the Jews that their turn for empire has past and that the Romans now rule the world. From the day when they made Saul their king, the Jews became like other nations: "You had God as a king and you were free, but you wanted to serve other men."[59] In *Hegesippus*, of course, it makes little difference that John refuses Titus's demand to spare the Temple since it had already been lost by the murder of Jesus. Although Titus has honored him, Joseph's translation is pointless: the living Hebrew language is finished along with the Temple.

*Yosippon* in response to its Christian source removes all the references to Jesus but retains Joseph's scathing history lesson: he tells the Jews "in Hebrew words of peace" that, because of their disobedience to God, it is now necessary that they serve the "Kittim" or Romans, who have been good rulers in the past.[60] *Yosippon*'s abbreviated version of *Hegesippus* emphasizes Joseph's role as go-between, and the work becomes a translation in the deepest cultural sense. Joseph tells the Jews how they became a part of world history and how it has played out. From the day they desired to have a king to the present day, they have been subjects of their own accord. *Yosippon* demonstrates this distinctly Jewish idea of a transfer of empire as he lavishly praises Augustus and Vespasian, even beyond his immediate source. The narrative exemplifies the Diaspora perspective since the book itself emerges from the history recorded by *Hegesippus* as a supposedly Jewish account of the Roman position, and also simultaneously refutes *Hegesippus*'s overarching theme of the annihilation of the Jews together with Jerusalem. Both *Yosippon* and his translated character Joseph ben Gurion, author of texts worthy of collecting together with the bible and the Talmud, live in the shadow of emperors as creators of a Diaspora Hebrew. *Yosippon*, then, as a translation of a translator's words back to their supposedly "original" language, offers an illustration of the redemptive sense of translation articulated by Walter Benjamin: translation as a mode of cultural survival, and translation as the potential return of the pure text from exile.[61] The author's messianic Hebrew prayer for the Temple that marks the end of Josephus's *Antiquities* and the beginning of *Hegesippus* in his translation subjects both source-texts to *Yosippon*'s diasporic view of language. The invocation in a pure rabbinic Hebrew, "may it be built again speedily in our days," is a future fulfillment of history in a writing that exists beyond the Latin text's possibilities. It punctuates the middle of the full text that ends with the destruction of Jerusalem, reclaimed from the language of a Roman past and an Italian present. In this place, language itself is re-created, released from "under the spell of another."[62] The author obliquely gestures to the underlying double structure of the Latin manuscript, constructing the exilic—yet grand—Christian library where he is working as itself a kind of diasporic opposite of the Temple.

## The Great Light

There is no way to know precisely who among the English Jews was reading *Yosippon*. It is likely that the prominent scholars like the martyr Elijah of York took an interest in the text, and perhaps even London's rich literate men like Isaac, son of R. Josce, had a copy made. Berekhiah ha-Nakdan, the notable Latin translator, would almost certainly have been familiar not just with the text but also with its author's underlying desire for a purified Hebrew language. The issue of Jewish reception of the text has inevitably focused on its emphasis on martyrdom, a theme that begins with its adaptation of parts of 2 Maccabees and ends at Masada. While *Yosippon*'s shaping of martyrs makes sense in terms of surviving English records, it is also worth considering that the English Jews' relations with Christian rulers and neighbors involved various types of mundane interactions. It is plausible that *Yosippon* was read, if cautiously, for its more positive as well as ultimately negative view of the Christian "Romans" to whom they were subject. The wide readership of *Yosippon* that Gerald of Wales describes, as well as the deeply suspicious way that he describes it, points to the book's larger appeal: in the Latin and Hebrew Josephus-literature and beyond, twelfth-century Jews and Christians shared a culture based on classical ideals and textual recovery that went beyond both groups' exegetical and scriptural traditions.[63] With a few notable exceptions, among them the author of *Yosippon*'s familiarity with Duke John's library, Jewish scholars' reactions to historical works written by Christians are unrecorded or lost. It is likely enough, nonetheless, that in Oxford or London, a few Jews could read Latin beyond business formulas, discussed various matters with Christians even if during religious disputes, and were in some way aware of the Christians' intellectual trends.[64]

In contrast to Joseph's own voice in the text counseling submission to the Romans and his unrelenting condemnation of the wicked rebel leaders—the *bnei belial*—as responsible for the destruction of the city, *Yosippon* also supports a heroic vision of martyrdom as resistance based on an eschatological idea of Rome. *Yosippon*'s greatest departure from its Christian source, *Hegesippus*, is that it positions the end of the Second Temple between the founding of Rome and its eventual destruction. The end of the final empire, still in power, will usher in the messianic age. The book opens with the legend of Ẓefo, the grandson of Esau who becomes, under the name Janus-Saturnus, the king of the "Kittim" and the land of "Italia."[65] It ends, after the martyrdoms of men, women and children and the valiant last stand at the fortress of Masada, with a series of messianic prophecies of the end of Jewish exile that echo the earlier authorial prayer for the rebuilding of the Temple. The prophecies also explicitly call for God's revenge against the Romans, including Ezekiel 25:14: "I will wreak my vengeance on Edom [the most common rabbinic term for Rome and Christiandom] through my people Israel, and they shall take action against Edom in accordance with my blazing anger."[66]

By the eleventh century, the *Sefer Yosippon* supplied a common vocabulary for the sacrifices of Jews who chose to sanctify the name of God by killing themselves and their families rather than convert or die at the hands of Christians. In its translations of 2 Maccabees and the account of Masada from the very end of *Hegesippus*, *Yosippon* reinvents martyrdom itself as a kind of holy war, influenced, as Flusser suggests, by the indulgence granted by the ninth-century popes Leo IV and John VIII to Christians who died fighting the Muslim forces in Europe.[67] Martyrdom becomes a focus of the text, beginning with the events of 2 Maccabees: the murders of the elderly Eleazer and the mother and her seven sons, all of whom refuse to eat pork at King Antiochus's order. The latter story appears in many later rabbinic versions as well.[68] In an astonishing early revelation of *Yosippon*'s hermeneutic concerns, the author identifies Eleazer the martyr with Eleazer the high priest who appears immediately before the account of the Maccabees in a version of the most controversial story about Jewish translation: the production of the Septuagint for Ptolemy II by Eleazer and seventy translator-scribes.[69] *Yosippon*'s story based on Josephus's *Antiquities* addresses the double-edged sword of translation in advance of Joseph ben Gurion's appearance at Titus's side: the scribes, kept apart from each other, produce a perfect translation of the bible for one ruler, but their high priest is soon murdered by another. In the very different talmudic versions of the tale, which the author surely knew, the Jews produce the translation only reluctantly and change the wording between the Hebrew and Greek Bibles to avoid any suggestion of multiple deities, among other things. The rabbinic narrative about transmission and interpretation of the Torah is also perhaps the distant origin of some medieval Christians'—including Gerald of Wales's—rejection of the Hebrew Bible out of fears that mirror the rabbis' own. As *Yosippon* signals with this reading of the Maccabean martyrs, translation from Hebrew to Greek is all too close to the Greek tyrant's demand for Jews to convert to idolatry. Yet the text itself is a translation from Latin. Both the possibly treasonous Joseph ben Gurion, the go-between, and the tenth-century author-compiler perform other acts of translation between Greek, Latin, and Hebrew, all of which have the potential to generate dangers through the ages from Romans, Christians, and other Jews alike.

*Yosippon*'s specifically medieval Jewish construct of noble death develops throughout the text. In its version of the grisly story of the mother and her seven sons, the eldest says that they are ready to die "for God and his Torah"; the youngest says that they will all go to "eternal life" and "eternal light where there is no darkness."[70] At Masada, Eleazer ben 'Anani ha-Kohen tells the Jews that like the heroic King Josiah, they will go to "the great light that is in the Gan Eden" and repeats these terms several times. In the end, the Jews who kill their wives and children at Masada sacrifice them, following Eleazer's exhortations, as a "burnt offering" ("korban 'olah") to God. They will be a "holy offering" that cannot be "defiled with the filth of idolaters."[71]

Much of the language in *Yosippon*, however, while recast in the idiom of biblical Hebrew, comes directly from its patristic source. The author of *Hegesippus*, even though his central polemical idea is the total erasure of the Jews, cannot resist following Josephus by giving them a final burst of magnificent rhetoric. *Hegesippus* simultaneously "Judaizes" and "Christianizes" Josephus's account of Eleazar ben Yair's speech on the immortality of the soul at Masada by adding references to biblical figures, and likewise transforms the basis of Josephus's Greek Platonism into patristic terms.[72] Most strikingly, *Hegesippus*'s author— whoever he was—uses Cain and Abel to illustrate his Platonic and Neoplatonic theme of the body as a "prison of the soul" ("*carcer animae*") in language very close to Ambrose of Milan's explication of Abel as the soul free to fly back to God.[73] In his sermon on *Death as a Good*, Ambrose describes the "kingdom of God" that receives freed souls as a place where "only the brightness of God will shine. For the Lord will be the light of all and 'the true light that enlightens every man' will shine for all."[74] Similarly, *Hegesippus*'s Christian-sounding Eleazar ben Yair, echoing Paul (2 Cor. 5), assures his listeners that after death the soul freed from its bodily fetters "will fly to God, the clear and bright dwelling of the saints and fellowship of the blessed."[75] If *Hegesippus*'s intention is to transform Josephus's scene of "noble death" and contempt for the Romans into primarily a meditation on God and the soul, *Yosippon*'s is to recapture both emphases in a polemic against the "Rome" of the Byzantine Empire and Western Christendom.[76] In *Hegesippus* the Jews have already effectively disappeared even before the mass suicide, converting into patristic subjects. These ethereal Jews reappear in *Yosippon*, a product of the circumstances of the Diaspora in tenth-century Italy. The text's fiction of translation, a "return" to the original Hebrew language, reveals its imagined "authentic" meaning: Abel (in Hebrew *Hevel*) is the emblematic freed soul who escapes from the vanity and misery (*hevel ve-'amal*) of life in an extended pun, and here the soul rejoices to return to the "great light" ("'or gadol") of the Garden of Eden that is the martyr's reward.[77] *Yosippon*'s major change to the Masada narrative itself is that having slaughtered their wives and sons and daughters to protect them from the "uncircumcised" ("'arelim"), the Jews rush out to challenge the Romans to battle and kill many of them before being finished off. Gerald of Wales, when he reports the discovery of *Yosippon* among twelfth-century English Jews, was not entirely off the mark in his suspicions of the subversive material the text might contain; it does literally erase Jesus, yet other signs of its Christian origins remain. *Hegesippus*'s Platonic formulations, drawn from Paul and Ambrose, in turn become a basis for *Yosippon*'s enduring legacy in northern Europe, a call for death in defiance of Christian oppressors.

In a number of evocative articles, Avraham Grossman has argued that *Yosippon*'s favorable portrayal of the Zealots' suicide at Masada was the "principal source" for the Askenazic Jews' ideal of communal suicide during and after the First Crusade.[78] The chronicle of Solomon bar Simson, written ca. 1140–46, describes how in 1096, faced with Count Emicho of Flonheim—"may his bones be ground to dust"—and his army, the Jews of Mainz first took armor and weapons and tried to fight but were finally cornered in the bishop's courtyard. As on the final day at Masada, the men and women, in defiance of "evil Edom" ("*Edom ha-Rasha*") killed their children, and then the men killed their wives and each other. Like Joseph ben Gurion, Solomon describes the killings as Temple sacrifices offered to God and the afterlife that awaits the martyrs as "the Garden of Eden in the presence of the great luminous speculum." For the martyr, "one who is slain or slaughtered and who dies attesting to the Oneness of His Name . . . for such a one a world of darkness is exchanged for a world of light, a world of sorrow for one of joy, a transitory world for an eternal world."[79] Solomon characterizes Isaac, the famous martyr of Mainz who, having been baptized against his will, burned down his father's house—killing his mother—and then sacrificed his children in the synagogue before burning it down, as acting with the wish "to be reunited with my companions and to be admitted to their company in the precincts of the Great Light (*me'or ha-gadol*)."[80] Similarly in Xanten, when the crusaders arrive on Shabbat, the Jews' leader declares "we shall offer ourselves . . . as a sacrifice upon the altar of God. Then we shall enter the world-that-is-all-day, the Garden of Eden, the great luminous speculum."[81] Solomon and the other chroniclers of the 1096 persecutions imagine the afterlife most frequently in terms of the "great light" or its variations, *Yosippon*'s coinage for the paradise of the martyrs.[82]

Grossman, Jeremy Cohen, and others emphasize the importance of aggadic, nonlegal texts in the Ashkenazic communities' justifications of suicide and even murder, acts usually forbidden by halakhah. Grossman treats *Yosippon*, prized for its historical details by Rashi and his students, as a kind of aggadic or midrashic source, albeit noncanonical and nonrabbinic, that allowed Jews to glorify not only suicide but also the murder of each other and their children as *Kiddush ha-Shem* (Sanctification of the Name of God).[83] Solomon's chronicle invokes numerous aggadic sources, including the rabbinic versions of the "mother of seven sons"; versions of the *Midrash of the Ten Martyrs*—an ahistorical account of the executions of R. Akiva, R. Ishmael, and others by the Romans— and the ubiquitous story in the literature of 1096 of an Isaac actually sacrificed by Abraham.[84] Of all these texts, only the noncanonical *Yosippon* with its underlying patristic Neoplatonic imagination explicitly licenses the final scenario in which families slaughter each other together as a sanctification of the name and abandon the prison of worldly life for the Gan Eden. Precisely because it is noncanonical, however, the chroniclers chose not to name Joseph ben Gurion directly. Possibly they sensed its proximity to contemporary Christian ideas of martyrdom. The flexible nature of its authority for carrying out such transgressive acts makes it imaginable yet unspeakable.

### *Yosippon* in the Islands

Gerald of Wales's interest in Josephus as a Jewish-Roman author coincides with the violence against Jews that accompanied preparations for the Third Crusade in 1189–90. Robert Stacey has attributed these attacks, which began with a bloody riot against the Jews of London, to the crusaders' resentment at financing their journey to the Holy Land through wealthy Jewish moneylenders.[85] For Gerald, who "devoutly took the sign of the cross" in 1188 and preached the Crusade in Wales with Baldwin, the archbishop of Canterbury, suspicions of the Jews' textual manipulations of the "authentic" Josephus are also related to the contemporary politics of Jerusalem. If, as Gerald confesses in the opening of *The Journey Through Wales*, God's judgment is "never unjust but sometimes difficult to understand" in Salah ad-Din's capture of Jerusalem, the Christians' ultimate title to the Holy Land—"the patrimony of the Crucified"—is at the center of his interpretation of events.[86] Jeremy Cohen has written about European clerics' hardened views of Jews in the wake of the Crusades, a "Muslim connection" that associated the unbelief (*infidelitas*) of both groups and the concern with the always-dispersed Jews as global Muslim agents. In this regard, the Jews' counternarrative, a version of Josephus or *Hegesippus* that supports neither Christian eschatology nor the immediate aims of the Crusade, is as threatening in its way for Gerald's circle of intellectuals as the Muslim forces.[87]

King Henry II, unlike his son Richard I, famously managed to avoid going on Crusade even as atonement for the murder of Thomas Becket, a crime that had outraged clerics associated with his court. Nowhere is Gerald's imagination of the spiritual association between the recovery of Jerusalem and the expulsion of the Jews more evident than in his strange anecdote about how a knight called Roger of Estreby heard the voices of Peter and the angel Gabriel telling him that he should exhort Henry to fulfill seven commands and then go on Crusade "to recover the cross of Christ from his enemies." Peter and Gabriel also offer to redeem his armor from one "Aaron the Jew." Roger finally reaches Henry and tells him the divine edicts, including to maintain the church and to observe all laws of the realm. The final command is that Henry must expel all the Jews from his dominions without the deeds pledged to them.[88]

Peter of Blois, who accompanied Archbishop Baldwin on the Crusade to Acre in 1190, works with a similar constellation of ideas in his polemical writings.[89] Peter was a prolific humanist letter-writer who, in a passage recalling his own education, mentions reading Josephus and *Hegesippus* along with Livy and Suetonius.[90] In his lengthy tract *Against the Perfidy of the Jews*, Peter devotes an entire chapter to Josephus, quoting, like Gerald, the entire *Testimonium* as the word of a Jew hostile to Jesus who nevertheless recognized the truth. Thereafter he follows the narrative of *Hegesippus* and the *Vengeance of the Savior* in describing the burning of Jerusalem, the grisly slaughters, and the selling of the remaining Jews into slavery: "This was the final destruction of the Temple . . . which Christ clearly foretold in the Gospels."[91] Anna Abulafia argues that Peter transforms Vespasian and Titus into ideal "proto-crusaders" who waste no time in conquering the Holy Land.[92] Earlier, Peter had written two tracts chastising the European rulers—especially Henry II and Richard— for Salah ad-Din's victory. The first is a pseudo-hagiography of the brutal warlord Reginald of Châtillon who died as a martyr at Salah ad-Din's own hand proclaiming his Christian faith. The *Passion of Reginald* also takes the "Western princes" to task: the Holy Land waits for them in vain like "Britons for Arthur or Jews for the Messiah!"[93] In Peter's passionate *Complaint on the Delay of the Crusade*, the entire polemic expresses shock at the fall of Christian Jerusalem in a new threnody: "why unroll the Lament of Jeremiah? All of Jeremiah is insufficient to express such distress!"[94] In Peter's exegesis, the church has taken the place of the synagogue because the Christians have failed to defend the territorial inheritance of their lord: "The blood of Abel cried out from the earth for vengeance and an avenger came; the blood of Christ cries out for help and no help comes."[95]

For Peter, the eschatological certainty of the *Vengeance of the Savior* has collapsed, to the point where even fundamental typologies no longer signify correct meanings. The reinvigorated Josephus tradition, however, produced some of the more fantastic texts of the Third Crusade. The French *Venjance Nostre Seigneur*—outré in so many of its revisions from Josephus, *Hegesippus*, and the earlier *Vengeance* texts—deserves mention here solely for its inclusion of a Josephus divided into two figures. One is Japhel, a soldier who defends a castle from the Romans and then surrenders to Titus to become his advisor; the other is Joseph(us) the clerk, an eyewitness who has written down the story. It goes without saying that both Jews, who represent facets of the historical Josephus, convert in the end. Jerusalem is destroyed except for the Christian holy sites—the Tower of David, the Temple of Solomon, and the Holy Sepulcher.[96] Even the most extreme texts, though, could be answered by a Jewish counternarrative, conditioned in part by the authority of *Yosippon*, that celebrated the victory of Salah ad-Din and the new fall of Jerusalem as a refutation of all of the Christian claims about the Second Temple and supersession. The Hebrew poetry in this vein derides the Holy Sepulcher as much as Christian chronicles of the First Crusade had glorified it as the end of the armed pilgrimage: for these Ashkenazic writers, Jesus's grave is, among any number of insults, a "pit of filth."[97]

The Josephus traditions became even more crucial for the English historians who considered the fate of the actual Jewish community during the Third Crusade, and particularly the explicitly Masada-like episode of self-slaughter by the besieged Jews of York on *Shabbat ha-Gadol*—the Sabbath before Passover—in 1190. For the Christians, it was two days before Palm Sunday. The English historians Roger of Howden and William of Newburgh immediately recorded the grim details of the massacre in Latin; the chronicler and poet Ephraim of Bonn wrote the surviving Hebrew account.[98] Following chaotic attacks on the delegation of prominent Jews who tried to attend the coronation of Richard I in September, a new round of riots erupted in the season of Lent, moving from King's Lynn and Norwich to Stamford, Bury, and other towns. In York, a mob of crusaders burned down the house of Benedict (Baruch), who had been injured in the London riots and then died. Requests from Josce, the leader of the Jewish community, for protection from royal officials were ineffective, and the sheriff of Yorkshire confusingly ordered the Jews removed from York Castle. Ultimately they were besieged there by a mob led by Richard Malebisse, a Yorkshire knight "heavily indebted" to the great Jewish financier Aaron of Lincoln.[99] The York Jews defended themselves at the castle for a few days until the situation became hopeless; finally on Shabbat, Rabbi Yom Tov of Joigny, an eminent Tosafist scholar and poet then residing in England, urged them to a mass suicide like those of 1096.[100]

This catastrophic moment became the point where the Latin and Hebrew Josephus-translations intersected, the violent ends of *Hegesippus* and *Yosippon* revivified and intensified by the events of the Crusades. The dean of St Paul's, Ralph of Diceto, a reader of Josephus among other classical historians, assesses the situation at York with greater accuracy than any of his contemporaries—"[the Jews] preferred to be killed by their own people rather than to die at the hands of the uncircumcised"—and strongly condemns the crusaders who carried out the attacks.[101] He immediately follows these comments in his *Ymagines Historiarum*, curiously, with a list of all the times Jerusalem has been overthrown, beginning with the Pharaoh Nechao and Necbuchadnezzar and ending with Titus, the city's conversion to Christianity, and finally, the Saracens, the Frankish crusaders, and Salah ad-Din. The effect of Ralph's juxtaposition is to recall the Jews' suicide at Masada in Titus's era as part of a litany that ties it to the defeat of the crusaders, a history of miserable failures.

William of Newburgh's famous version of the events at York relies more directly on the Latin version of Josephus's *Jewish War*, although with the supersessionist logic of *Hegesippus*. He characterizes Yom Tov as a "most famous teacher of the law" whom the others "obeyed like one of the prophets."[102] William transports the scene to Jerusalem to the point where he imagines him exhorting the Jews in language that echoes Eleazar ben Yair's speech: "God, to whom we should not say 'why have you done this?' orders us now to die for his law. . . . We should prefer a glorious death to a most foul life. . . . For many of our people in various tribulations have been known to act laudably, preparing the way for us to make the proper choice."[103] Yom Tov's reasoning, however, echoes the voices of those who carried out the suicide/murders during earlier Crusades: the Jews must adhere to the law and not become apostates. This speech is not a direct quotation, but rather a set piece William apparently remembers in snippets.[104] He then describes the mass suicide in detail, beginning with Josce cutting "his dearest wife" Anna's and his children's throats and then Yom Tov cutting his throat. He concludes the pathos-laden scene with the comment: "whoever reads Josephus's *Jewish War* will understand that whenever they were oppressed by harsh misfortune, [the Jews did this] out of their ancient superstition."[105] While William refers to Yom Tov as "a crazy old man" ("*senior insanissimus*") as well as a great scholar, he recognizes in him a mirror image of his own practice of interpretation through exemplarity. In William's text, the Jewish leader inspires his followers to martyrdom by citing Josephus's narrative of Masada, just as

William himself understands the concept of imitating a "noble death" through the lens of his own readings about the early Christian martyrs from Eusebius to the recent accounts of the Crusades.[106] For both William and Yom Tov, York—rather than the crusaders' Holy Land—is Jerusalem. He also recognizes that Josephus's Roman ending of the Masada narrative has replaced the Christian historical trajectory of *Hegesippus* here. The Jews who reject Yom Tov's call to Jewish martyrdom and emerge from the castle willing to become Christians are murdered by "Richard, rightly called Mala-Bestia" and his followers.[107] Despite the reenactment of the fall of Jerusalem, these Jews who truly desired baptism become Christian martyrs in spite of the crusaders, baptized in their own blood. This type of textual insight also informs William's political stance. Taking a considerably less positive view of the crusade than Gerald of Wales or Peter of Blois, he reaffirms the idea that Vespasian and Titus were "ministers of divine vengeance" to the Jews but focuses primarily on the sinful behavior of the Christians in Palestine that has led to their own cleansing punishment by the Muslims.[108]

Both the Latin and Hebrew versions of *The Jewish War* inform the events of 1190: the outset of the first of the Crusades in which Englishmen—led by Richard the Lionheart—played an important role, and the reenactment by English Jews of the last days of Jerusalem. The Christian and Jewish afterlives of Josephus had first come into direct conflict following the crusaders' attack on Rhineland Jews in 1096 and continued to reverberate in subsequent Crusade literature. In a decisive shift, Jerusalem, previously spiritual and metaphorical in the writings of medieval monks and clerics, acquired new significance as historical and political territory for Western Christians. For Diaspora Jews in Europe, however, the holy city of Josephus's era remained largely a spiritual idea.[109] *Hegesippus* gave eleventh- and twelfth-century Christian writers a sense of Jerusalem as a literal "inheritance" from Christ. The various accounts of Pope Urban II's speech calling for the First Crusade underline precisely this idea: in the words of Baldric of Dol (Baudric of Bourgueil), Jerusalem is "this land we have deservedly called holy in which there is not even a footstep that the body or spirit of the Savior did not render glorious and blessed . . . and [that] drank up the blood of the martyrs shed there."[110] According to Robert of Rheims, Urban concluded his speech by asserting that "Anyone who has a mind to undertake this holy pilgrimage and enters into that bargain with God, and devotes himself as a living sacrifice, holy and acceptable, shall wear the sign of the Cross on his forehead or his chest."[111] Every crusader was a potential martyr—an idea exploited most fully by *The Song of Roland*.

William of Malmesbury, the best-read of medieval English historians, takes the occasion of Urban's speech one step further and actually has him take the place of Eleazer ben Yair in *Hegesippus*, encouraging the martyrs at Masada with the idea of "Death as a Good": "While [souls] are bound fast in the meshes of the body, they draw the contagion of earth . . . and are dead, for the earthly does not unite properly with the heavenly." The passage ends, "Those whose lot it is to die will enter the halls of heaven, and those who live will see the Holy Sepulchre."[112] With Fulcher of Chartres's *Chronicle* as his source for the First Crusade, William transforms the crusader ideal of martyrdom in war into a meditation on the escape of the soul; those still trapped within the prison of a body will only get to see Jesus's empty tomb, even if that is the greatest earthly happiness. The "Jews" not only have vanished into Christianity as they do at the end of *Hegesippus*, but have reappeared as rhetorically perfect martyrs—much as they do for the Jews in *Yosippon*. William affirms that his language has preserved the "truth" of Urban's words, a fiction that reveals his own ambivalence to his historical source. He clearly prefers an imaginary city to the current Jerusalem.

For twelfth-century Christian writers, Josephus was essentially the figure created by *Hegesippus* and the interpolated *Testimonium Flavianum*, a Jew who was nevertheless a master of classical historiography, and a nonbeliever who reported the truth about Jesus. These same classicizing churchmen were also the first to speculate about what Josephus might mean to Diaspora Jews. For Christians, Josephus provided the link that connected them with both imperial Rome and Jerusalem and cast their European rulers as the inheritors of Vespasian and Titus as they set out for the Holy Land. For contemporary Jews, the *Sefer Yosippon*, a Jewish-Roman-Christian hybrid, made the same connection with different consequences. Shmuel Shepkaru, following Flusser's and Grossman's readings, has traced the transmission and impact of *Yosippon*'s language of martyrdom and salvation from Byzantine Italy to the eleventh-century French rabbis and then the liturgical poets and chroniclers of the First Crusade.[113] A number of other recent critics have emphasized the degree to which the Jewish chronicles of the First Crusade assimilate and respond to aspects of Christian culture, beginning with the concept of a "Holy War" itself.[114] In the case of England, just as the Christians ultimately drew their view of the earthly "Roman" Jerusalem from *Hegesippus* and subsequent Christian adaptations of Josephus, so the Jews conceived of a spiritual "anti-Roman" Jerusalem from *Yosippon*'s Hebrew translations of the same *Hegesippus*.[115]

In *Yosippon*, *Hegesippus*'s long threnody for Jerusalem becomes the lament of the text's supposed author Joseph ben Gurion; it follows the Latin original closely, except, naturally, for attributing the destruction of the city to the murder of Jesus. The effect of this shift is to align *Yosippon*'s Jerusalem with rabbinic interpretation; as in *Midrash Lamentations Rabbah*, the city fell to God's "blazing wrath" because the Jews abandoned Torah and shed the blood of priests and prophets in the Temple.[116] Eleazar's speech at Masada becomes an eschatological statement, an idea of sacrifice that, while not a full atonement for the sins of Jerusalem, rejects the Romans' idolatry and assures the martyrs—souls freed from the fetters of flesh—a heavenly dwelling-place in the Gan Eden. *Yosippon*'s final description of the Jews' self-slaughter and attack on the Romans also transforms *Hegesippus*'s death knell for the Temple into the first heroic and even chivalric act of the Diaspora. With its sharp focus on the relationship between Jews and Romans, subjects and imperial rulers, and the imagined reversal of roles that will come in the days of the Messiah, *Yosippon*, as Flusser remarks, resembles in a sense the "chivalric" historical fantasy of Geoffrey of Monmouth's *History of the Kings of Britain* in which King Arthur defeats a Roman army as a marker of distinct British identity.[117] By the time of the twelfth-century recension with additions lauding Joseph's military prowess against the Romans, the resemblance between narratives shows the Jewish fantasy of a Rome/Edom aligned with a European present. In *Yosippon*, needless to say, the Romans win at least in this world, establishing a diasporic rather than national and territorial identity for Jews. Masada has little in common here with its central role in modern Zionist symbolism as the site of a military defeat never to be repeated. A site of Neoplatonic transcendence, the fortress emerges rather as something closer to a spectral Avalon, a place that can never really be visited.[118] Influential as its story is in the Middle Ages, it is never mentioned in rabbinic literature and never named in medieval chronicles. As a territorial loss, Masada is recalled only in this most diasporic of texts and then as a place for martyrs who will enter the other place of the Gan Eden.

The few medieval Hebrew poets who wrote about the events at York capture the sense of *Yosippon*'s complicated dialogue with Christianity. Susan Einbinder's readings of earlier French liturgical poems (*piyyutim*) show that their representations of medieval martyrs exceed both *Yosippon*'s defiance and its eschatological claims. According to Ephraim of Bonn's narrative of the York massacre in the *Sefer Zekhirah* (*Book of Remembrance*), Yom Tov of Joigny himself kills around sixty people, a heroic act in keeping with his stature as a scholar.[119] The martyrs themselves Ephraim calls "holy bodies" ("*gufim kedoshim*"), an originally Christian use of "holy" to describe people and things adopted by *Yosippon*.[120] Yom Tov had written a defiant lamentation for the thirty-two martyrs burned at the stake in Blois in 1171 following a Christian's accusation of a child's murder by Jews. Einbinder argues that he transmitted the French "martyrological ideal" of his poetry to England, where he also put it into action. In "Yah Tispokh Ḥamatkha" ("Lord Pour Out Your Wrath"), Yom Tov idealizes the murdered scholars as warriors: "Among your pious ones, remember Yeḥiel who fought with brandished arm."[121] Both the young scholar and the poet here reenact crucial aspects of *Yosippon*; Yeḥiel by figuratively emulating the Jews at Masada whose last act is to attack the Roman army, and Yom Tov by imitating "Joseph ben Gurion" himself in recording the ongoing relationship with Rome/Edom in the Diaspora.

Joseph of Chartres, who composed a long lament for the Jews of York soon after their death, links the martyrs, figured as a Temple sacrifice, to the fate of Rome: "in place of their herds, they offered their children." Having described these ritual sacrifices (*korbanot*), Joseph adds "let [God's] Land atone for his people."[122] The body of the poem is a memorial for the notable Jewish leaders of York murdered together with Yom Tov and evoked by name: Elijah, Joseph (Josce), Jacob (Jurnet), and Moses.[123] These were the ideal readers of *Yosippon*, sensitive to its nuances in regard to both the Romans in the text and their European descendants. Joseph curses Richard I's England, "May there be no dew nor rain on the Land of the Isle; from the day your king was crowned, woe to you O Land!" The "Land of the Island" ("*ereẓ ha-ii*"), however, is also the Jews' land, capable, like Jerusalem, of playing a role in the eschatological drama of atonement and redemption. For Joseph, the crusader "King of the Islands" ("melekh ha-i'im") and his people are synonymous with the Romans, whom he calls "Kittim," the biblical name that *Yosippon* and later authors had reserved for them: "May God avenge the slain of the daughter of my people on the bands of Kittim, whose portion in life is of this world." As in *Yosippon*, the Romans—or Christians—exist only in the world of flesh rather than spirit. The legacy of Josephus—and especially *Hegesippus*—for twelfth-century Christians was above all a rallying cry for a new Crusade to win back "the patrimony of Christ," the land forfeited by the Jews to Rome. For twelfth-century Jews, Josephus, via *Hegesippus* via *Yosippon*, strangely enough shaped the image of a spiritual Jerusalem that could exist anywhere the "Romans" were—and of Rome as a European world that would soon fall just as Jerusalem had fallen.

# Diaspora without End and the Renewal of Epic

The *Etz Ḥayyim*, Yaakov ben Yehuda of London's late thirteenth-century compendium of Jewish law and ritual, includes a penitential poem that concerns relations between the Jews and Edom, the Christians of late thirteenth-century England, framed in geographical terms.[1] His poem "'agdalah shemkha ẓur misgabi" ("I will exalt your name my rock, my haven") implores God, "If forever there will be no boundary to my exile (*gevul 'im 'ein le-galuti le-'olam*), please remember your compassion and lessen my pains."[2] Yaakov goes on to ask, "Kill the seed of Edom my adversary, my enemy; / Curse them all in your wrath, send them all into desolation and captivity (*le-shimemot sim u-va shvi*)." While much of the territorial language in these lines comes from Malachi 1:1–5, where God declares Edom a "border of wickedness" and assures the prophet that "The Lord will be magnified beyond the border of Israel," Yaakov here imagines the Jews' current exile from Jerusalem as an inversion of empire, a powerless realm without end or limit. Ignoring strict logic in favor of a prophetic idiom, he also desires an exile for Edom even after its annihilation.[3]

Writing appropriately enough in 1286, shortly before the expulsion of the Jews from England by King Edward I in 1290, Yaakov vents his fury at the oppressions of this period. A witness to multiple executions of Jews for financial crimes as well as ever-greater economic restrictions, the poet identifies England with the larger empire of "Edom," a name for the Christian world in rabbinic literature. In his biblical geography, there is a suggestion of Edward's own ambitions as a new crusader who aspired, however unrealistically, to reconquer the Holy Land.[4] Above all, the poem reveals how the imagination of a Roman-Christian Empire figures in the geography of Jewish Diaspora. Edom, whose rule extends from Rome over a land without boundaries, must be exiled—driven to newly conceived borders—rather than utterly destroyed. The poet realizes that the Jews' longed-for reversal of power with Edom, when Israel is finally restored to a Jerusalem, "the city of your Temple," rebuilt from its destruction by Titus and the crusaders alike, is a matter of empire. Indeed, he considers the idea of an "empire without end." According to his initial plea, Edom should be nonexistent after God takes vengeance; finally for Yaakov ben Yehuda, however, it must continue to exist as a rhetorical and theoretical anti-Rome, powerless, captive, and at last incapable of imperial expansion.[5]

The first chapter focused on the best-known part of the *Sefer Yosippon*, ultimately taken from Josephus, about the Jews' revolt against imperial Rome, the ambiguous role of the author and go-between "Joseph ben Gurion," and the destruction of the Second Temple. With its medieval transmission to Rashi and his circle and to the martyrs of Northern Europe, *Yosippon* defined a historical Edom or Rome that had defeated a sinful Jerusalem. The anthology of Latin translations begins, however, with a novel and subversive approach to Rome, a work at the center of developments in secular European literature but entirely new to Hebrew: a version of the *Aeneid*. Only 145 lines long and deliberately garbled from Virgil's epic, the text addresses Rome and Latinity in a way that engages a completely different set of temporal and territorial ideas than *Yosippon*'s later account of Jewish decline and defeat, "after which we were subjugated [to Rome]" in Joseph ben Gurion's words.[6] *Yosippon*'s author prefaces the bulk of his work that he designates as "history," therefore, with a tenth-century fiction of Diaspora, a late midrashic response to the Latin Middle Ages' many uses of the great imperial poem in which Jupiter announces that for the Romans he has "set no bounds in space or time but has given empire without end."[7]

*Yosippon*'s Hebrew "Aeneid" is set as a sequel to a talmudic story that represents another foundation narrative, with the two ingeniously combined in Joseph, the emblematic Jewish figure who succeeds in bridging two competing cultures.[8] In the aggadah, Esau prevents Joseph and his brothers from burying Jacob by quarreling over the ownership of the tomb of the patriarchs in Hebron. Hushim, the son of Dan, clubs him to death, Jacob briefly revives to laugh at the situation, and so the twins' burials take place on the same day.[9] The future animosity between Jacob's and Esau's sons is determined. *Yosippon*'s "Aeneid" opens with Zefo ben Elifaz son of Esau escaping from Egypt after the death of his cousin Joseph, who had captured him following the confrontation in Hebron. Zefo arrives in Carthage where "Agneus" is the "King of Africa" and becomes the leader of his army; Agneus, accompanied by his brother Lukas (Evander) and nephew Pallas, goes off to fight with Turnus, the "King of Benevento," for the hand of the "very beautiful and wise Yania" (Lavinia) who has inherited Italy and its main city "Pozimagna."[10] Having killed Turnus, Agneus returns to Carthage with Yania. Rome and Carthage remain culturally distinct: when Yania falls ill, Agneus has to bring earth and special water from Italy for her. Zefo, meanwhile, leads raids with the Gondoli (Vandals) against the Kittim, finally invading Italy with his African armies. After more adventures, Zefo changes sides and becomes Janus-Saturnus who rules over all of Italy. His grandson Latinus, the codifier of the Latin language and alphabet, attacks and defeats Agneus's son Ashdruval (Hasdrubal) in order to win his beautiful, aptly named daughter Especiosa.[11] A long list of Latinus's descendants follows, kings who resume the genealogy of the *Aeneid*: Aeneas, Ascanius, Silvius, and finally down to Romulus, the ruler at the time of King David, who by this time had already defeated Aram and Edom. Fearful of David's power, Romulus surrounds all the buildings, temples, and hills of his kingdom with a wall and founds the city of Rome. What Flusser calls *Yosippon*'s "Italian Antiquities" ends with Tarkinios's rape of a Roman woman (Lucretia), her suicide, the end of the Roman kings, and the beginning of the Roman republic. Under the senate, the Romans "conquered all of the West."[12] Clearly, this short if eventful narrative bears little resemblance to Virgil's poem about the journey of the Trojan Aeneas to Carthage and then to Latium, his war with Turnus and his allies, and his marriage to Lavinia. The most significant absence is Troy itself, replaced with the tomb of the patriarchs; instead of the Trojan War, the plot begins with the simultaneous deaths of Jacob and Esau, the twin founders of Israel and Edom—the Jews and the Romans.

Like the explicitly prophetic and vengeful language about Edom that *piyyutim* like Yaakov's articulate, the opening of *Yosippon* became another part of the medieval Jewish fantasy of Rome, a text used to interrogate Europe's borders and Rome's foundation myths. The question is what it means to translate—in any way—perhaps the most famous classical text and the foundation of so much of the medieval political imagination from Latin into Hebrew. To that end, this chapter traces *Yosippon*'s "Aeneid" from its original tenth-century location within a European revival of the Roman imperial ideal up to the Angevin twelfth century and its own celebration of empire. In this reconstruction, the cultural contexts reveal the stakes of an act of translation that inscribes the Jews into new paradigms of both imperial power and epic literature. In these migrations, Virgil's imperial poem becomes an "epic" text of the Jewish Diaspora, written in the holy language. The Hebrew text counters the linear narrative of the *Aeneid* with its multiple doublings and dislocations; it represents a reversal of power on Edom's own terms. My larger argument about how medieval Hebrew texts challenge Rome through ideas of translation encompasses another heroic tale, the *Midrash Va-Yissau*, also known as *The Wars of the Sons of Jacob*. Thematically related to the midrashic background of *Yosippon*'s "Aeneid," this text from Byzantine Italy about a military showdown between the offspring of Israel and Edom subordinates Rome yet also participates in a contemporary desire for epic character and history.

I have described earlier how the texts bound together in *Yosippon* are translations from Latin, the work of an author who made the most of his time with Duke John's collection in Naples and with other southern Italian manuscripts to familiarize himself with the texts that—together with the *Aeneid* and Servius's commentary (late 4th–early 5th century)—provide a narrative of Rome's origins. These include Orosius's *Seven Books of History*, Jerome's *Chronicle*, and probably Eutropius's *Abridgment of Roman History* and its continuation, the *Historia Romana* by the Montecassino monk Paul the Deacon.[13] *Yosippon*'s methodological statement characterizes the entire anthology as a collection of "books that deal with the deeds of our ancestors (*ma'aseh 'avotenu*)"; this clearly includes Josephus's historical works and the Apocrypha reclaimed from the Vulgate Bible. There is a role as well, if limited, for texts that narrate the deeds of the Romans' ancestors rather than the Jews'. The challenge is to understand why and how the author frames the two "non-Jewish" texts in the anthology—the Pseudo-*Aeneid* and a short account of the Second Punic War—as essential to a larger diasporic idea of translation as cultural appropriation.[14]

*Yosippon* begins, after a very brief summary of Noah's three sons Shem, Ham, and Japhet and God's destruction of the tower of Babel and scattering of languages, with a list of nations that in its geographical specificity and concern with the present owes more to Orosius's interpretation of Genesis 10 than to its Jewish counterparts.[15] It also situates *Yosippon*'s author as one of many early medieval historians who preface their works with geography as a central element of identity, including Paul the Deacon, Bede, and Gildas.[16] *Yosippon*, as opposed to both Orosius and the Jewish accounts of Noah's descendants from Josephus's *Jewish Antiquities* to *Midrash Genesis Rabbah*, is concerned solely with Europe rather than the tripartite division with Africa and Asia: "the sons of Japhet and the lands where they were scattered, by tongues and by places and by peoples."[17] Although the author's "geopolitical map" is disordered and drawn from various sources, he reasonably enough opens with the Franks (*Frankos*) who live on the river Seine, followed by the Bretons, who live on the Loire.[18] With this, he essentially describes the current territories of post-Carolingian *Francia*, and by naming the Frankish realm first reveals an awareness of the political and cultural dominance of the descendants of Charlemagne during most of the ninth century.[19] His knowledge of Italy is, as one would expect, much better, including the "Germanic" Lombards in the north and the Romans in "Campania," whom here he calls the "Kittim"; only later in the text does he mention his own city of Naples in passing. He only vaguely enumerates the "Turkic" Pechings, Alans, Ugars, Bulgars, and others. At the northern borders of Europe, he includes an intrguing passage about some mysterious "Danes"—biblical *Dodanim* "who are the *Danishki*"—who fled from their own island to the ocean to escape the Romans but failed because Roman rule extended "even to the islands of the sea (*'ii ha-yam*, Britain)."[20]

For Orosius, geography leads into a discussion of *translatio imperii*, the sequence of four empires from Babylon to Macedon to Carthage to Rome, and the universal history of misery and disaster under pagan rulers. *Yosippon*'s choice to focus primarily on the Latin West rather than the Byzantine East and Jerusalem is itself the impulse for an exploration of empire and dispersion; the lands of Japhet naturally produce a Jewish *Aeneid*. The work's outline of Europe also announces *Yosippon*'s central concern with language and translation. If this is a map of a potential Jewish Diaspora rather than, as for Orosius, a potential Christian "fifth" empire that follows pagan Rome, it is also the site where the newly reborn literary Hebrew of Italy challenges a universal Latin in subversive hybrid texts. Gerson D. Cohen pointed out that the Jews and the Romans—seen "most notably in the works of Virgil and Livy"—had much in common: "Each considered itself divinely chosen and destined for a unique history. Each was obsessed with its glorious antiquity. Each was convinced that heaven had selected it to rule the world."[21] *Yosippon* narrates the high points of this contest, culminating in the failed Jewish revolt against Rome. On the level of language, both the holy tongue, Hebrew, and imperial Latin represent ideologies of territorial unity and legibility against a Europe of fragmented "barbarian" vernaculars. Some scholars have interpreted the Hebrew *Aeneid*'s narrative structure as a way to reconcile two Jewish ethnographic ideas of the Romans, one in which they descend from the Kittim and in the other from Edom back to Esau himself.[22] The entire text beyond this is also marked by doublings. In the wandering heroic character of Ẓefo ben Elifaz, modeled in part on Aeneas, the two origins join when he rules the Kittim in the land that will become Rome. Ẓefo, appropriately, also acquires the name Janus, evoking the Roman double-faced god. Through Latinus, the land of the Kittim is also the origin of the written Latin language that reflects the Jewish author's dual linguistic identity and the imperative of Hebrew-Latin translation in Europe.

With this scheme, the text also invokes the long tradition of Christian polemics that identifies the elder brother Esau with Jews, and Christians with the younger Jacob. From its ultimate source in Paul's Letter to the Romans 9:6–18, and through the exegeses of Ambrose, Jerome, and

Augustine among others, the typology of a Jewish Esau and a Christian Jacob—the "True Israel or "New Israel"—defined the church's theology of supersession.[23] By writing Esau himself into Virgil's epic, *Yosippon* shifts the discourse from biblical exegesis to the pagan source of European national myths. Like the *Aeneid* itself, the narrative encompasses the geography of Asia and Africa as well as Europe. The author subverts Roman origins from the opening of his text; Troy has disappeared altogether, and Zefo is forced to flee instead from Joseph in his double role as Israelite cousin and Pharaonic ruler. Later under the new identity of Janus, Zefo himself becomes the two-faced cultural mediator between Italy and Carthage—a figure who anticipates Joseph ben Gurion, Jew and Roman, and indeed the author himself, in Cohen's words "a South-Italian who was much enamored of his country" in the Diaspora.[24] His Italian Jewish audience, who began to circulate *Yosippon*, evidently had an affinity for his negotiations of dual identity.

## The Specter of Hannibal

Carthage, with Dido glaringly absent, is in *Yosippon* Agneus's home together with his Italian queen Yania and their son Hasdrubal; this second incarnation of Virgil's hero is not a refugee, but rather a native African. Zefo too is connected to Carthage, as the leader of the Vandals at first and then as their conqueror. Carthage is, as in the *Aeneid*, the empire that across the centuries competes with and damages Rome, but crucially it stems from neither Esau nor Jacob. In the course of this short narrative Zefo subdues Carthage, but in the narrative of *Yosippon* as a whole it remains Rome's historical African enemy, from the Punic Wars and the "avenger" Hannibal threatened by Dido at her death at the end of book 4 of the *Aeneid*, to the Vandals under Geiseric who sacked the city of Rome in 455.[25] By *Yosippon*'s own day, what was left of Carthage was under the rule of the Fatimid Caliphate, new kings of *Ifriqya* from the third great biblical ethnic group together with Israel and Edom, the Ishmaelites.[26]

Carthage soon reappears in another text drawn from a non-Jewish source, inserted into *Yosippon*'s version of 1–2 Maccabees. Following Judah Maccabee and his brothers' defeat of Antiochus Eupator's army, the author explains the *translatio imperii* that led to the Jews' fateful treaty with the Romans: "in those days, God raised the Fourth Kingdom [Rome] over the Third Kingdom [Greece]," according to the scheme from Daniel 7:7.[27] Then the Romans "devoured and crushed" all other kingdoms including Antiochus's, and also Carthage, the "southern" empire from Orosius's scheme conspicuously left out of Maccabees 1:8, which only describes the Romans' victories over Gaul, Spain, and the Greek Empire in Asia.[28] Hannibal, in *Yosippon*'s interpolation, is, like Agneus, "the proud King of Africa" ("Gaon Hannibal Melekh Ifrikya"), and in the course of his march to Italy via Spain, he conquers—like the Romans—the Franks and the Saxons and also, out in the sea, the British. The highly idiosyncratic narrative then describes Hannibal's stunning victory against the Romans at Cannae, his advance on Rome "up to the gates of the city," and the ongoing war for eight years. Rather than let the Romans make a treaty with Hannibal, Scipio takes his army to Africa to fight the Carthaginians there; he kills Hannibal's brother Hasdrubal in battle and, in one of the author's most dramatic exaggerations, personally takes his head back to Rome and waves it from the city walls while taunting Hannibal into defending his own land. Finally Hannibal returns to Carthage to be defeated by Scipio at the Battle of Zama. In another invention, the author claims that Hannibal fled to Egypt, was returned to Carthage by "Ptolemy the king," and killed himself. The point of this "history" of the Second Punic War, such as it is, is that "the Romans grew in power over all the other nations" and in a fateful moment made a friendly treaty with the Jews.[29]

In *The Interpretation of Dreams*, Sigmund Freud famously analyzes his admiration of Hannibal as a heroic Semite, an avenger who wreaked havoc on the Romans on the orders of his father Hamilcar; the Carthaginians in his "fantasies" are exemplars of classical military virtues who represent a "warrior ideal" as opposed to what he perceived as his own father's eastern European Jewish timidity when attacked by a Christian anti-Semite.[30] At the same time, "*Hannibal* and *Rome* symbolized the contrast between the toughness of Jewry and the organization of the Catholic Church."[31] Freud describes his longing and frustration in traveling by train "in the footsteps of Hannibal" to Campania, "past Lake Trasimeno" but stopping short of "the eternal city." In what he called his "*meshugeneh* (crazy) letter" to Wilhelm Fliess, Freud similarly describes a "neurotic" longing for Rome connected to Hannibal: "I did not reach Rome any more than he did from Lake Trasimeno."[32] While distant from Freud's "neurotic" desire to see—and not see—an "eternal" Rome at once classical and Christian and in both cases menaced by the specter of a heroic "Jewish" Hannibal, *Yosippon*'s Italian-Diaspora author invests Carthage and its heroes with a similarly fantastic role. Hannibal, and before him the non-Trojan "African" Agneus/Aeneas, serve as epic foils to a historically continuous Rome. If Troy is the origin of Rome and of the European Christian translations of empire after Rome's fall, then Carthage becomes, for the medieval Jewish author, the origin of an unassimilated foreignness. This "anti-Rome" is also marked by an always-incomplete geographical narrative not entirely unlike the allegorical train voyage that Freud describes.[33] Medieval fictions of Troy or "Virgilian" histories have been studied extensively as the conceptual origin of the European nation, legitimizing territories and reigns in opposition to Orosius's patristic transcendence. The Jewish fiction of Carthage, another lost city, challenges this Western narrative, yet its figures are enigmatic, located between Rome and Jerusalem like *Yosippon* itself.

In *Yosippon*, Hannibal's war on Rome is the story of a missing empire situated between Greece and Rome, an incomplete *translatio*. Hannibal's fictional empire, moreover, at one point includes much of the Western Roman world, including *Francia et Saxonia*, the declared kingdom of Otto I in the author's own day.[34] Part of the account of the wars of the Macabees with the Seleucid "Greeks," the Second Punic War is both a demonstration of Roman strength and—in retrospect—a warning to the Jews. Rome makes no treaty with Hannibal, and Scipio destroys him. Even as Judah makes the Jews' first treaty with the Romans, however, the conquest of Jerusalem by Rome slowly begins—a narrative that culminates in the actual conquests by first Pompey and then Titus. In some rabbinic accounts, the Carthaginians also occupy a privileged place as the one nation that agreed to leave the Promised Land when the Israelites arrived; as a reward, God gives the "Girgashites" Africa, "a land as good as your [former] land."[35] Something of the curiously positive view of these ancient Phoenecians carries over into *Yosippon*'s fantasy of Carthage, which in this sense is similar to Freud's. Removed from its subsequent history as part of the Muslim world, Carthage functions as an imperial double for Diaspora Jews, an empire that mirrors their own former land before the fall of the Second Temple. In historical memory and imagination, Carthage is, albeit briefly, as powerful as the contemporary Christian Edom of the Carolingian-Ottonian Empire.

*Yosippon*'s author, in his productive encounter with the *Aeneid*, joins the many Christian poets of the *renovatio*, the renewal of the Roman Empire that begins in the West with the reign of Charlemagne, crowned emperor in 800.[36] Like them, he evinces an interest in creating a new type of epic, however formally removed from its classical models. *Yosippon*'s project is to "recover" from Virgil's Latin text a Hebrew work on the epic theme of heroic journeys, wars, and fateful marriages; the Hebrew narrative, however, counters the fictions of the Romans from the beginning with the truth of the Torah and the holy language. However problematic the concept, this epic or anti-epic is the tale of Esau's line, told in the language of Jacob. The arms and the man that are *Yosippon*'s subject could likewise refer both to Ẓefo and to Agneus, the epic voice doubled and distorted between Rome and Carthage. The Jewish author's approach to Virgil, is not entirely unprecedented; the *Aeneid*'s historical value was undermined by the influential sixth-century "eyewitness" account of "Dares the Trojan" who describes Aeneas's treason before and during the fall of Troy, and by Orosius's anti-imperial rhetoric that describes Aeneas as a "fugitive" from Troy who caused wars that afflicted the land with hatred and destruction.[37]

Some of *Sefer Yosippon*'s medieval Jewish readers recognized in the text's version of the *Aeneid* an affinity with epic ideas that sparked further Hebrew translations and anthologies. These projects were aligned with developments in contemporary Latin literature. At the behest of Duke John, as the previous chapter notes, Leo the Archpriest in the mid-tenth century acquired a manuscript of the Pseudo-Callisthenes *Alexander Romance* in Constantinople and translated it from Greek to Latin at the same library that *Yosippon*'s author used. Leo's translation, the basis of three versions of the *Historia de Proeliis* (*History of the Battles of Alexander*), became, according to Richard Stoneman, "the foundation stone of the whole medieval European tradition."[38] The interpolation of a late eleventh-century Hebrew version of the immensely popular Pseudo-Callisthenes into manuscripts of *Yosippon* shows its continuing cultural influence as a text exemplifying the migration of empires and literary texts from East to West. This Byzantine version of the *Alexander Romance* translated directly from Greek recounts in part Alexander's battles following the death of his father, his conquests of Persia and India, and his encounters with some of the innumerable marvels of the East including the specifically Jewish "land of darkness" where the ascetic biblical Rechavites live.[39] The text ends with a short Byzantine chronicle "from Alexander to Augustus" of the transition from the third to the fourth of Daniel's empires; "Ioulious" is the first king of the Romans, followed by "Augostos Kaisar" under whose rule Herod rebuilt the Temple "twofold in its beauty."[40] A second interpolation from an earlier part of the *Alexander Romance*, translated from the Latin *De Proeliis*, was added to *Yosippon* in the twelfth century, and both were disseminated throughout Europe; the two Hebrew texts taken together became sources for several later medieval Hebrew Alexander romances.[41] As a narrative associated with the long tradition of Alexander's friendly relations with the Jews, the interpolated text evokes nostalgia for the heroic Greek emperor who preceded all of the disasters recounted by Joseph ben Gurion up to the destruction of the Temple, adding even more ambiguity about the powerful Caesars who follow, the *renovatio* of Rome, and the uses of epic literature.[42]

The so-called Carolingian Reniassance of the late eighth and ninth centuries refers in part to the literary aspect of imperial *renovatio* or renewal, the vast project of Latin textual collection and dissemination by scholars and scribes at the court of Charlemagne and in the monasteries and cathedrals of his territories, including northern Italy.[43] The revival of Latin literature, as exemplified by the court libraries of Charlemagne and his son Louis the Pious, included the preservation of classical as well as patristic writers, including Virgil, Livy, and the Latin Josephus among others—all authors central to the formation of Frankish identity.[44] The new Latin poetry of this period, especially the works produced at the courts of Charlemagne and his sons, was not only deeply indebted to Virgil's formal models, or in Peter Godman's words "the omnipresence of Virgil," but to the ideological formation of a "New Rome."[45] Matthew Innes observes that at the end of the ninth century, Notker of Saint-Gall reconfigured the Carolingian kingdom itself as the Frankish Trojan "fourth empire" in the traditional sequence; not just an extension of Rome, it was now "God's chosen successor to the Roman Empire."[46]

The new European powers in these propagandistic works are therefore not only a continuation or geographical shift of the Roman-Christian imperium but an improvement on its piety, effectiveness, and beauty.[47] The most celebrated of the Carolingian poems is the so-called *Paderborn Epic*—usually attributed to Charlemagne's biographer Einhard—which describes the emperor as "Pius Karolus," both a new Aeneas and a new King David who "illumines the earth" from a "second Rome" (*Roma secunda*). While overseeing the building of his city Aachen, "the high walls of a future Rome" (*Roma ventura*), Charlemagne is called upon to rescue Pope Leo III from a bloodthirsty group of his enemies in the corrupt old Rome.[48] Einhard's later imitator, Ermoldus Nigellus, similarly addresses Louis the Pious as "O best Caesar" in an epic about his defense of his empire's frontiers from Spain to Denmark. He also begins the poem, *In Honor of Louis*, with a Virgilian acrostic: "Ermoldus sings of the arms of Louis Caesar."[49] This epic opens with the victory of King Louis and Duke Guillaume of Toulouse over the "Moors" at Barcelona in 801 and progresses to Louis's crowning by his father "with Christ Himself conferring it"; Charlemagne also refers to his title of Caesar as a name associated with Romulus, a curiously dissonant element within the rest of his speech on ideal Christian governance.[50] Francine Mora-Lebrun argues convincingly that this epic is the ideological precursor of the *chansons de gestes* concerning the "Carolingian myth," especially the *Coronation of Louis* from the Guillaume d'Orange cycle and *The Song of Roland*. The Latin epic, like the later *chansons*, ignores the complex political realities of the campaign in favor of a religious triumphalism characterized by Duke Guillaume's railing against the Saracens before the battle.[51] The *Aeneid* links all of these works together in their "tension between *pietas* and *furor*," as the epic rage of the battlefield, subordinated to Christian peace and order in the Carolingian poems, reappears with a vengeance in heroes of the *chansons*.[52]

The library that Duke John of Naples assembled was doubtlessly inspired by the Carolingians' textual work: the preservation of Latinity and the translation of classical works from Greek to Latin, East to West; yet it was also indebted to the Byzantine libraries and the tenth-century literary revival in Constantinople.[53] The ideal of the "New Rome" or "Second Rome" would have reached the author of the *Yosippon* in semi-autonomous Naples as a cultural and political struggle between the Byzantine Empire and the Saxon Ottonian Empire, both of which controlled parts of Italy.[54] Writing in the geographical zone between the two new

Caesars, Otto I and Constantine VII Porphyrogenitus, the author was in a good position to think about an abstract Rome in a new way, distinct from his sources in both Josephus and the rabbis. William Hammer writes of the idea of a New Rome, "for both the admirer of past pagan culture and the Christian, the prediction of the future greatness of Rome which Anchises had made to Aeneas . . . retained its practical and ideal significance."[55] The pretensions of the new emperors, in whatever form he may have heard about them, clearly convinced the Jewish author that the first thing to say about the relationship between Jews and Romans was that the *Aeneid* itself is a thoroughly inaccurate poem; his own Hebrew literary intervention into the discourse of "empire" from the position of Diaspora strikes at its historical root.

## Twinned Narratives: Rome and Hebron

Ermoldus Nigellus's *In Honor of Louis* provides a meditation on empire and epic in a Virgilian ekphrasis describing paintings that line the walls of the church of the imperial palace at Ingelheim: the passage includes an account of Orosius's version of the *translatio imperii* from Persia to Carthage to Greece to Rome, although not strictly in order. Among these classical themes:

> [They depict] how Romulus and Remus laid the foundations of Rome
> and how the wicked man struck down his brother;
> how Hannibal after a lifetime spent
> in endless wicked wars lost an eye;
> how Alexander claimed to conquer the world for himself
> and how the might of Rome grew up to the very skies.

And elsewhere, "To the imperial conquests of the excellent city of Rome / Are linked the Franks and their marvelous achievements."[56] For Ermoldus, an exiled court poet trying to win back the favor of King Louis, the connection between Romulus, Rome, and the Franks is not without irony. Rome's fratricidal origins—although ignored by both *Yosippon* and rabbinic texts about the twins—are a sure way to attack the entire idea of a Roman Empire and its translations westward.[57] Not all medieval Jewish texts, however, entirely avoided the violent story of Romulus and Remus. The *Midrash Va-Yissau* or *Wars of the Sons of Jacob* addresses the fratricidal moment, but in an oblique fashion that conflates the twin nations of Jacob and Esau with the twin founders of Rome.

Most likely composed around the same time as *Yosippon*, this text about relations between Jacob and Esau demonstrates another instance of a medieval Jewish appropriation of Rome and a type of epic literature. Although apparently translated and adapted from a Greek source, it circulated only in the West. Martha Himmelfarb has suggested a route from Byzantine southern Italy to a northern Italian community in Lucca or Rome and then to Provence.[58] It first appears in *Bereshit Rabbati*, a lengthy eleventh-century compilation by R. Moshe ha-Darshan of Narbonne, unique in Europe for including pseudepigraphic texts and fragments from the Second Temple period, as well as citations of virtually all known earlier rabbinic texts.[59] The midrash is found next in the twelfth-century northern Italian *Yeraḥmeel* together with a version of *Yosippon*; from there it traveled to northern France and the Rhineland. *The Wars of the Sons of Jacob* is an anomaly of medieval Hebrew literature, an interpretation of a few passages of Genesis having to do with the fate of the Amorites and Esau that becomes a series of drawn-out battle scenes between Jacob's sons' and their enemies' armies involving—among other deadly weapons—lances, iron coats of mail, and catapults.[60] The text's emphasis on these plausibly contemporary aspects of medieval warfare has led the few scholars who have written about its transmission and popularity, including Eli Yassif and Joseph Dan, to consider it an early Jewish version of a *chanson de geste*, a tale of chivalry set within an expanded narrative of the Hebrew Bible.[61] While the midrash itself predates the chansons, it stands to reason, as these scholars contend, that its triumphalist military narrative would have increased its circulation in Northern Europe in the twelfth century as a story to emulate and rival the Crusade-era vernacular poems about knights and war. It was popular from the time it arrived in Europe, however, in the way *Yosippon*'s early texts were, for its allegorical negotiation of the relationship between Jews—Jacob and his sons—and their European Christian neighbors and rulers—Esau and his sons—who were at the time in the process of reclaiming "Rome" as their founding identity.

The original *Wars of the Sons of Jacob* consists of two parts: in the first, the kings of the Amorites attack Jacob's family seven years after they have destroyed the city of Shechem and settled in its place; Judah leads his brothers into battle, and they not only defeat the besiegers but also capture a number of other cities. In the second, which is the focus of this argument, Esau, his sons, and an army attack Jacob as he and his sons are in mourning for his wife Leah—evidently at Hebron, here imagined as a "fortress" (birah).[62] Jacob unsuccessfully tries to make peace with his twin brother, but Judah finally insists that these negotiations are futile; Jacob then shoots Adoram the Amorite from the wall, and with another shot hits Esau in the right shoulder (or in other versions his right buttock); his sons carry him away, and he dies. The text adds in all versions—in an ambiguous midrashic fashion—that some say that Esau didn't die. A bloody battle follows in which Judah, Gad, and Naphtali in particular kill Edomites right and left.

The *Wars* is actually a radical revision of part of the *Book of Jubilees*, a second-century BCE retelling of Genesis as revealed by God and an "angel of the presence" to Moses on Mount Sinai.[63] There are elements of the battle that also evidently derive from some version of *The Testament of Judah*, part of *The Testaments of the Twelve Patriarchs*.[64] In *Jubilees*, Esau gathers together an army from Edom, Moab, Philistia, and the Kittim and goes to the city of Hebron, where he recites metaphorical poetry about his enduring hatred to Jacob, who is standing on the battlement. Finally, at Judah's urging, Jacob first shoots Esau in his right side, killing him unambiguously, and then shoots Adoram in his left side. The rest of the story is essentially the same: Jacob's sons win the ensuing battle, chasing Esau's sons back to their land of Seir, where they live under a permanent "yoke of servitude." The striking difference from *Jubilees* is that the medieval version adds two details that point to moral ambiguities in the twins' histories: Elifaz the son of Esau—the father of Ẓefo in *Yosippon*—refuses to take part in the attack "because Jacob was his teacher," and more obviously, Joseph is absent from Hebron because "he had already been sold" by his brothers.[65] The sons of Jacob—other than Joseph and Benjamin—are a compromised and extremely violent band of warriors, and one of Esau's sons has studied Torah with Jacob himself. From the outset, the two families, origins of the Jews and the Romans, contain elements of the other.

The *Wars* circulated widely, and the text is preserved in a number of later manuscripts as well as in the great thirteenth-century Ashekenazic midrash collection *Yalqut Shimoni*. The earlier anthologies *Bereshit Rabbati* and *Yeraḥmeel* exemplify two related trends in the Jewish culture of southern Europe in common with *Yosippon*. The revival of Hebrew as a literary-liturgical language began in the eighth and ninth centuries in Byzantine Italy, occasioned by greater contact between European Jews and the communities in Palestine following the Arab conquests; at the same time there was a desire to recover and, if necessary, translate works from Greek and Roman Palestine, the period of the Second Temple.[66] The actual route of these texts' transmission to Europe remains uncertain, but Himmelfarb and John Reeves have both argued that an itinerary from Palestine to Byzantine Italy is likely.[67] Whatever the case, Moshe ha-Darshan had access to Jewish pseudepigrapha in Hebrew in eleventh-century Provence, including parts of *The Testaments of the Twelve Patriarchs* and the *Life of Adam and Eve* as well as *Jubilees*, none of which survives today in a full Hebrew version.[68] In the context of late antique Palestine, the preservation or recovery of a work like *Jubilees* that emphasizes the theme of the triumph of Israel over Edom, and by metaphorical extension the later Jews over the Byzantine Romans, would have been most welcome.[69] Cohen traces the first identification of Esau and Edom with Rome back to Rabbi Akiva and the defeat of the "messianic king" Bar Kokhva by the emperor Hadrian.[70] Esau, the embodiment of the Roman Empire, often appears in rabbinic literature with the simple epithet "wicked"—*Esav ha-Rasha*.[71] Like the prophets Obadiah's and Malachi's prophecies of the downfall of the kingdom of Edom, *Jubilees*'s treatment of Esau throughout the narrative of Genesis as entirely malevolent could by the early Middle Ages be read solely with reference to Christianity.

*The Wars of the Sons of Jacob* in all likelihood originates from an Italian Jewish culture similar to *Sefer Yosippon*'s in its revival of biblical Hebrew. It also bears some remarkable resemblances to its treatment of Rome's foundations. The midrash that *Yosippon*'s author invokes as a preface to his *Aeneid*, which explains why Ẓefo needed to escape from Joseph, and the *Wars* are both set at funerals in Hebron and both concern the day of Esau's death. In *Yosippon*, Esau's demise at the hand of Jacob's grandson and then his own grandson's escape from Egypt provide the occasion for a quasi-epic narrative that includes the enigmatic Elifaz, the father of Ẓefo who, like Joseph, is also strongly present through his absence as a positive figure in the *Wars*. As Jacob's reverent student, he represents yet another figure mediating between Edom and Israel. The *Wars* became a popular medieval text in part because it echoes not only its ancient Hebrew source on "the wicked Esau" but also the similarly ancient narrative of Rome's foundation, the murder of Remus by his twin brother Romulus at the half-built city walls. What scant evidence there is suggests that the author of the text may have been familiar with both Greek and Latin sources.[72] In any case, the narrative of the other famous set of twins, Romulus and Remus, is a fortuitous intertext, and the midrash, like *Yosippon*, speaks to an anti-Trojan account of Rome's origins.[73] Both are Hebrew narratives— one direct and one indirect—that obscure the European myths of origin based on the *Aeneid*. Above all, both the *Wars* and *Yosippon* articulate their audience's desire for a Hebrew epic, and both could be considered works of the medieval *renovatio* that in their early contexts reveal ambivalence rather than absolute hostility toward the new Rome.

*The Wars of the Sons of Jacob* in its medieval Hebrew form is perhaps best understood within a tradition of rabbinic accounts of the founders of Rome, descendants of Esau. Mireille Hadas-Lebel, most recently, has discussed several of these midrashic versions; in the best-known, which dates to the third century, the founding of Rome and the Roman Empire is a divine punishment of Israel for idolatrous acts: "The day when Jeroboam erected two golden calves, Remus and Romulus came to build two great huts in Rome. The day when Elijah departed, a king was established in Rome for so it says 'There was no king in Edom but a prefect of the king' (Kings I, 22:48)."[74] In another similarly ancient version in *Midrash Esther Rabbah*, the twins are left for Esau himself to raise: "You have been the orphans' help (Ps. 10:14): two orphans were left to [Esau], namely Remus and Romulus and You gave permission to a she-wolf to suckle them, and afterwards they arose and built two great tents in Rome."[75] Like Esau himself, the twins had their role in the rabbinic imagination of Rome—the city as well as the people. Louis Feldman considers a later midrash about the founding of Rome: According to R. Levi, two huts were built in Rome but kept falling down until an old man named Abba Kolon advised the Romans to mix their mortar with water from the Euphrates. Although interpretations abound, Feldman dates the text to ca. 1000 and tentatively suggests that the two huts, in earlier versions the Capitoline and Palatine

Hills of Romulus and Remus, now represent the competing capitals of Rome and Constantinople, the Eastern "Second Rome."[76] As these texts show, Rome, its renewal, and the politics of empire were a medieval Jewish concern in terms of different versions of Esau or Edom.

*The Wars of the Sons of Jacob*, written in the trilingual zone of southern Italy, reflects an awareness of some version of the fratricide, unlike the rabbinic accounts of the twins. Certainly, some of its readers would have known the story. It is tempting to imagine that the scholars who first encountered it had some knowledge of Orosius's *Seven Books of History*, or even, given the wide circulation of Virgil manuscripts in Italy, Servius commenting on the twin sons of Mars in book 1 of the *Aeneid*. In the latter narrative, Remus sees six vultures in an augury and Romulus sees twelve, causing the war in which Remus is killed.[77] In the context of the Roman-European world of the text's reception, one set of twins uneasily maps onto the other, and while Hebron—the ancient city of the patriarchs—doubles for both Rome *and* Jerusalem, Jacob stands on the wall and kills Esau, or perhaps he just wounds him. After the epic battle scenes, the midrash once again questions whether Esau was buried near Hebron or taken by his sons to Seir; whatever the case they make peace with Jacob's sons, and as in *Jubilees* "since then they have paid tribute" to Israel.[78] Israel has taken revenge on Edom, yet the curious detail of Elifaz remains—a trace of a Roman's love for Israel or, conversely, of a Jew's new love for Rome.

As it intersects with the Roman foundation narrative, the midrash performs a kind of cultural work not unlike *Yosippon*'s own rewriting of Rome. Remus is, by all accounts, little more than a victim—even in Livy's dramatic version, where he makes fun of his brother Romulus by jumping over the wall of Rome—whereas Esau is generally the personification of imperial oppression. Jacob, likewise, is not the power-hungry Romulus even as he reenacts his violent role at the walls of Rome. An ambiguous figure in Latin literature, Romulus, like Aeneas, appears in a much more negative light in patristic texts in which he consolidates power through "a succession of acts of cruelty" including murdering Remus.[79] *The Wars of the Sons of Jacob* is a response, like *Yosippon*, to the linear idea of *translatio imperii*. Like the Hebrew *Aeneid*, the *Wars*, in its travels to Northern Europe, can be read as a counternarrative on the topic of Rome—a brief medieval Hebrew "epic" from a corner of the Latin world. Jacob himself is a reluctant Romulus who nevertheless shoots his brother from the walled city, initiating an account of arms and conquest; Esau is a Remus who only actually dies in some versions of the story, which, beyond its "midrashic" formula, is itself a comment on the alignment of these two legends and their productive instabilities. The descriptions of actual warfare are much more detailed in the medieval text than in *Jubilees*; the battles are gruesome and prolonged. Judah, the ultimate "founder" of European Jews, fulfills the role of the epic warrior-hero. Like Aeneas, he is aflame with *furor*: literally, "his wrath was ignited" ("bi'er ḥamato") before killing dozens of Edomite enemies.[80]

With its evident reversal of roles, in which Jacob and his sons found an imperium with its center at Hebron or Jerusalem and make the Romans their tributaries, *The Wars of the Sons of Jacob* functions as a European-Jewish diasporic version of the ideas of *renovatio* and *translatio imperii*, however distantly related to Charlemagne's and his successors'. Just as western Europeans could claim that Rome had been reborn in another city like Aachen—and *not* in Constantinople for example—this Italian-Hebrew text undermines such claims to Roman power with an assertion of Jacob's definitive founding victory at the walled city of Hebron, including a sacrifice of Esau that mirrors the sacrifice of Remus for imperial unity. *The Wars of the Sons of Jacob* is a work of historical imagination, needless to say, produced for readers with no military or political power; what gives it its force is that it, like *Yosippon*, recognizes the epic narrative itself as the basis for imperial legitimacy. With the death of Esau, Rome becomes the city of the hapless Remus rather than his powerful twin brother, and Israel becomes more Roman in its authority.

## Migration to Angevin Edom

By the time that Yaakov ben Yehuda wrote his poem cursing Edom, "I will exalt your name my rock, my haven," Edward I had determined the fate of Jews in England.[81] The best that Yaakov could imagine for the English king under these dire circumstances was an eternal exile, a geographical erasure or even total annihilation, that would make Jews the world-rulers, "beyond the borders of Israel" from Jerusalem. In Edward, crusader to Acre and conqueror of Wales, Yaakov sees a ruler of the Western Christian empire, Edom in Britain. At the time when the *Sefer Yosippon* was recorded among the more popular books of English Jews a century earlier, this work offered its readers a different, if ultimately no less hostile, approach to Edom. The literary world of Angevin England is known for at least two developments that are related to *Yosippon*'s account of Rome's origins: a deep interest in both the *Aeneid* and the Trojan counternarratives of Dares and Dictys in the service of courtly ideals, and a new theory and practice of translation from Latin into the French or Anglo-Norman vernacular. With the defiantly anti-Trojan epic of *Yosippon*'s Pseudo-*Aeneid* and the reversed narrative of Romulus and Remus echoed in *The Wars of the Sons of Jacob*—a text likely known by the twelfth century in the Angevin territories—twelfth-century Jews could use their migrating midrashim to frame a parallel culture of antiquity, epic, and even the new vernacular genre of "romance." Just as at some point certain widely read Jews realized the central importance to Christians of the *Testimonium Flavianum* in Josephus and began adding parodic versions of Jesus's life to *Yosippon*, Jewish scholars and book owners living in England surely recognized the *Aeneid* and the pagan Trojan myth as a main current of the Anglo-Norman culture around them. Indeed, if a scholar had sufficient interest in the Hebrew version of the *Aeneid* in *Yosippon* and could read Latin, he could have sought out a copy of Geoffrey of Monmouth's foundational text on Trojan origins, the extensively copied and circulated *History of the Kings of Britain*.[82] In Geoffrey's Virgilian account of Britain's origins, Aeneas's grandson Brutus travels from Troy to Albion, receiving on the way a vision of the goddess Diana in which she directs him: "To the west, beyond the kingdoms of Gaul, / lies an island of the ocean" and "It will furnish your children with a new Troy. / From your descendants will arise kings, who / will be masters of the whole world."[83] This is the prophecy that foretells King Arthur's imperial conquests and his defeat of the Roman armies before his betrayal by his nephew Mordred.

The combined realm of Henry II and Eleanor of Aquitaine included England, Normandy, Anjou, a large part of southern France, and the colonized parts of Wales and Ireland; whether or not this constituted a true "Angevin Empire" in political terms or rather just an "Angevin Zone," the literary production at Henry's courts demonstrates the imperial ambitions of his rule.[84] Jean-Yves Tilliette, canvassing Norman Latin and Anglo-Latin epics from the *Song of the Battle of Hastings* (ca. 1067–68), a poem influenced by Ermoldus Nigellus's *In Honor of Louis*, to Joseph of Exeter's *Ylias* (ca. 1188), based mostly on the account of Dares the Trojan, sees these texts' Virgilian references and metaphors as marks of authenticity and "mechanisms of exchange." Any author's use of Virgil, whether in imitation or subversion, enhanced his own prestige with learned readers.[85] Christopher Baswell's study of insular Virgil manuscripts and Virgil's influence on twelfth-century English literature interprets all texts about Troy, whether the *Aeneid* or the rival traditions of Dares and Dictys, as propaganda for "a new European empire in the reign of Henry II, explicitly connected by genealogy and emulation to the people of the *Aeneid*." Furthermore, "the later literary patronage associated with Henry's court . . . would center around the classical literature of empire and *translatio imperii*."[86] For Baswell and other scholars, this trend culminates in the masterpiece of the *Roman d'Enéas*, a *roman antique* that reworks the *Aeneid* into a French courtly idiom. Baswell reveals a striking foretaste of Henry II's later Virgilian ideology, however, in an obscure 124-line poem by his tutor Pierre de Saintes that quickly traces the fall of Troy through Helen and the rise of Rome through Aeneas's battles and marriage: in the final line, "Romulus's race rises up from Hector's." Henry Plantagenet himself is clearly still in some sense a Roman king, a descendant of both Aeneas and Romulus.[87]

The Angevin Empire's intellectuals for the most part read Virgil as literary glossators and mythographers, practicing a Latinity that connected them closely to the ancients and put them in the line of the early commentators Servius and Macrobius.[88] At the same time, the Plantagenet court was a center for writers who theorized about translation. Wace, Thomas of Kent, and the authors of the *romans antiques* all invoked a discourse of *translatio studii* linked to the new *translatio imperii* from Rome to the Angevin courts: their poems would now articulate the classical culture transmitted from Greece and Rome in the vernacular language of the geographical and historical present.[89] In *Le roman de toute chevalrie*, written for the court of Henry II, Thomas of Kent situates his discussion of translation between cataloging Alexander the Great's conquests from Rome to Arabia to Persia and naming himself as the author ("Thomas ai non de Kent"). Using Jerome's model of translation for sense, he asserts that he has translated his text from Latin to French not word for word but for its meaning and beauty, enhanced with courtly ornaments. The historical truth about Alexander's Greek Empire is unchanged, but the language is elegant and current.[90] Wace, the author of a history of the Norman dukes commissioned by Henry II, the *Roman de Rou*, and an Anglo-Norman free translation of Geoffrey of Monmouth's *History*, the *Roman de Brut*, also puts historical change at the core of his idea of translation. In the *Roman de Rou*, he implies that the knowledge of empires necessary for *translatio imperii* may depend on translation. Thebes, Babylon, and Nineveh have disappeared, and Alexander the Great and Julius Caesar were both murdered; they can live on only in histories and epics, but Wace complains that though he may "write and translate books and compose romances and *serventeis*," he has no compensation from patrons other than praise.[91] He begins this work by comparing himself to Virgil and others, contending that the poet writing for great figures like Henry and Eleanor shapes the historical narrative of an empire but also depends on the would-be emperor for support. In this view, translation is literally a transaction that can either produce or erase historical continuity.

The English and Norman Jewish communities of the late twelfth century had little to do directly with contemporary courtly literature. Those English Jews regularly involved in business with Christians were nonetheless well versed in the multilingual Latin, Hebrew, French, and English aspects of their regular transactions and knew the respective roles of Hebrew and Latin—as opposed to the vernacular languages—as biblical, official, literary, and international.[92] I earlier considered the insular Jewish reception of *Yosippon* as a work of classical history aligned in many ways with the Latin chronicles of the twelfth century. *Yosippon*, which provided Jews with a nonrabbinic history of the Second Temple and war with the Romans, became, once Christians eventually discovered it, a source of controversy precisely over its original language. *Yosippon*'s author assured Jewish readers, in emulation of Josephus's own classically formulated truth-claims, that he had collected the Hebrew works of Joseph ben Gurion, military leader and eyewitness to the Jewish War. Robert of Cricklade, the learned reader and "translator" of *Yosippon*, found that the text exemplified all the traditional dangers of the Hebrew language, constantly used by Jews to alter or misrepresent the bible itself and, as he correctly imagined, Josephus's unique "historical source" about Jesus. *Yosippon*'s Hebrew is, however, a mask for an anthology of originally Latin texts, and the deception that Robert identified was in fact part of the author's strategy of loose translation of *Josephus* and *Hegesippus* from patristic Latin to biblical and mishnaic Hebrew. Both the Jews and Christians involved in this episode, two centuries apart, construct the Hebrew of the Second Temple as the language of origins. Ultimately accompanying that claim in both cases, however, is an understanding of Latin as the language of both authority and recovery. For Robert, who was familiar with the scholars translating Greek philosophy and science in Sicily, the role of Latin is unquestionably to reclaim Greek learning as well as Hebrew, while for *Yosippon* the cultural weight and historical continuity of a Latin library is the first necessary means to reclaim Josephus from a succession of European Christian empires.

Beyond the interactions of the various language communities of the Angevin Empire, however, is simply the question of how Jews might have received the first part of *Yosippon*'s anthology, the deeds of the Romans and Carthaginians apart from the histories of the Jewish civil war, the fall of Jerusalem, and the Masada martyrs. Abraham Ibn Ezra, the Spanish biblical exegete and polymath who lived in Angevin Normandy and England in the mid-twelfth century, used the early chapters of *Yosippon* to discuss geography. In his interpretation of "Woe is me that I live with Meshech" (Ps. 120:5), Ibn Ezra cites the authority of "Joseph ben Gurion" to identify Meshech, a son of Japhet, with "the people of Tuscany" and therefore the Jews' exile in Christian Europe.[93] Presented with a Hebrew version of the *Aeneid* written in response to the ideology of a new Eastern Roman Empire and the corresponding *translatio imperii* from Rome to the Carolingian and Ottonian kings, Jewish readers could easily enough translate the text itself across the centuries to their own current versions of Christian and imperial Edom. In its way, this short and remote derivative of Virgil's epic offered a point of contact with the local Angevin culture's Virgilian fictions. Despite its convoluted plot and references, the text nevertheless functions precisely as Tilliette's "mechanism of exchange"; even in Hebrew, a literary challenge to Virgil signifies the author's Latin and European authenticity. *Yosippon*'s "Aeneid," with its distortions, could give its Angevin Jewish readers a vocabulary with which to re-create its new Edom from its own mythic and misdrashic discourses. The Hebrew *Aeneid*, *The Wars of the Sons of Jacob*, and the early versions of the Hebrew *Alexander Romance* are all Jewish fissures in the Angevin epic or romance tradition, texts that emerge from a diasporic context yet address issues associated with the new vernacular literature.

A Hebrew *Aeneid* that erases all signs of Troy is an intervention into the theory of history at the heart of Anglo-Norman translation. *Translatio studii*, the celebration of transferring texts from one language to another in the service of imperial power, generates the contradictions and anxieties that animate Angevin literature. *Yosippon*, while following a path of transmission through the European Diaspora, positions itself, like its Latin pagan, Jewish, and patristic textual models, outside of the historical change marked by translation.[94] This collection of texts put together by a master translator and largely about another translator—Joseph—on the surface admits no trace of a transfer from Latin. The texts of Joseph ben Gurion are among the most important besides the books of the bible itself, according to *Yosippon*'s author; the crucial fiction is that his work is not actually translatable at all because it is written in the Holy Language. By extension, the "Aeneid" bound together with Joseph's histories is a similarly untranslatable midrash that defines the Romans before they became Roman. The author's actual transfer from imperial Latin to biblical Hebrew in the ducal library nonetheless captures the authority of both, the language of power and the language of sacred writing.

In late twelfth-century Anglo-Norman vernacular texts like *Le roman de toute chevalrie* and *Le roman de Rou* the author's decision to translate from Latin raises inevitable anxieties about the texts' impermanence and by extension the instability of empires. Thomas of Kent consciously translates the *Alexander Romance* out of the authoritative Latin into the "courtly" vernacular specific to his historical moment and audience, no longer within a "Roman" empire. Wace, writing to the king, warns that empires and their languages come and go, but poets at least keep their memory alive in the language of the subsequent empire, in this case Henry II's own. The three so-called *romans antiques*, however, are the most remarkable Angevin literary works to translate ancient sources freely into "romances," self-reflexive vernacular courtly poems. The *Roman de Thebes* (ca. 1150), *Roman d'Enéas* (ca. 1155), and Benoit de Saint-Maure's *Roman de Troie* (ca. 1160) are ideal expressions of *translatio studii*, the Latin poetry of Statius, Virgil, and Dares renewed and thoroughly reconceived for the amusement and edification of twelfth-century patrons.[95]

The *Roman d'Enéas* is the Angevin text that most clearly intersects with *Yosippon*'s interests. A sweeping retelling of the *Aeneid* in a chivalric idiom, the *Enéas* bridges the epic and the *roman de geste*. The poem draws out the battle between Enéas and his vassals, encamped in their medieval castle of "Montauban," and the "Marquis" Turnus and his Italian vassals; it culminates with the crowning of Enéas and Lavine. Most often, the *Enéas* has been characterized as a poem intended to legitimate empire and to erase the disruptions of Norman history, emphasizing the importance of lineage and peace as personified by the then-happily married royal couple Henry and Eleanor. Most critical interest in the poem has focused on new Ovidian material that the author worked into the Virgilian narrative to create erotic tension between the lovers Enéas and Lavine, who within the new terms of the romance genre have become a consenting couple. *Enéas* remains nevertheless, like the *Aeneid*, a poem about territory and empire. Baswell in particular argues that the text emerged from a political culture already found in an early twelfth-century commentary attributed to Anselm of Laon and in pedagogical marginalia in twelfth-century *Aeneid* manuscripts. Following Servius, the commentators recapture Trojan history, Italian geography, and the "imperial destiny" of Augustus's reign. The "romance" of Enéas based on these texts is a French announcement of imperial renewal.[96] As in Virgil's poem, Anchises shows Enéas all of the "barons" who will descend from him, and he sees that his line will "rule without end."[97]

The *Roman d'Enéas* represents the pinnacle of Angevin Virgilian literature, or, if translated into the less happy language of contemporary Jewish poetry, the literature of Anglo-Norman Edom. *Yosippon*'s Josephus texts on the Romans' destruction of Jerusalem ultimately became one of the strongest expressions of resistance to crusader violence for the Hebrew chroniclers and martyrological poets of the twelfth century; the much shorter "Aeneid" had its place as well, as a Virgilian counternarrative about the nature of the "fourth empire" and the new Romans who claim that they will rule until the end of history. Like the *Aeneid* itself, this text performs its own fiction of *translatio*, migrating westward in the Diaspora from Italy to northern France to the farthest kingdom of England. When taken in isolation from the rest of *Yosippon*, the text appears strangely familiar within the Angevin literary scene: a text about the foundation of Rome, with various new epic diversions and bride exchanges

like Especiosa's involving Europe and Africa. *Yosippon*'s "Aeneid" epic
narrative, however, moves not from Troy to Carthage to Latium, but from
Joseph's Egypt to a geographical scheme that produces two Aeneases, two
Lavinias, and finally the two "Romes" of Agneus's Carthage and Ẓefo
ben Elifaz ben Esau's Kittim. Each of these doublings reflects the cultural
exchanges that characterize *Yosippon*'s Italian author and his hero Joseph
ben Gurion: the translation of Latin to Hebrew, the inclusion of a different version of Carthage as a failed foil to an ascendant Rome, and
the substitution of a rabbinic legend that recalls Esau's violent death in
Hebron for the legend of Western origins in Troy. As Cohen argues, the
text speaks more of ambivalence than hatred toward Rome; nevertheless it severs Rome from Troy and the "heroic" Aeneas in such a way as
to present a continual challenge to the linear Virgilian plots of Europe.
*Yosippon*'s renewal throughout the European Diaspora functions as a
Jewish counterpart of *translatio studii*. A text that positions both Hebrew
and Latin as universal languages, it circulates outside the competing forces
of cultural continuity and discontinuity that mark vernacular translations.
The author's affinity for the Latin of empire, as well as the Hebrew of
scripture, enabled him to create an "Aeneid" that perpetually destabilizes
the epic voice and recalls a dialogue between the two languages that will
define the Roman Empire until the messianic age.

# A Fox among Fish?

## *Berekhiah ha-Nakdan's Translations*

Sometime in the mid-twelfth century, Berekhiah ha-Nakdan, a prolific Anglo-Norman rabbinic scholar, poet, and philosopher, obtained an early manuscript of Adelard of Bath's scientific and medical treatise *Natural Questions* (ca. 1120) and translated it into his own idiosyncratic Hebrew version. Decades later, in the 1190s, he produced a collection of Aesopic fables from a variety of sources, also mostly translating from Latin. These two works, *Dodi ve-Nekhdi* (*Uncle and Nephew*) and *Mishle Shu'alim* (*Fox Fables*), are the first literary translations of their kind and similar in scope to the anthology of texts in *Yosippon*. The *Fox Fables*, like *Yosippon*'s versions of Josephus and Virgil, is an adaptation of classical texts into a midrashic style, from one genre to another. The circumstances of these cultural transfers are intriguing in terms of the author's intentions as well as his access to manuscripts. He asserts one of his reasons for translating, however, with perfect clarity: he must rescue knowledge written in Latin for a higher expression in Hebrew. In *Uncle and Nephew*, he refers to his version of the *Natural Questions* as a cleansing: "When I saw such splendid wisdom restored to you in an ugly setting, I purified [the text] from the hand of strangers and wrote it out in the Holy Language, which is the most elevated language."[1] This chapter argues that Berekhiah's singular idea of cultural contest is at the heart of his two translations, and it situates these works in the reigns of Henry II and Richard I, a period that saw the beginning of a drastic decline for the Jewish community. Berekhiah is a truly avant-garde trilingual author who engaged with some of the most prominent aspects of the contemporary Angevin Latin and French literary world. His third known translation is a now-lost version of an Anglo-Norman lapidary; an extant Hebrew lapidary called *Ko'ah ha-'Avanim* (*The Power of Stones*) evidently derives from the earlier text.[2] This work like the others shows Berekhiah's interest in the philosophical and scientific ideas of the late twelfth century across Europe and beyond.

In addition to his translations, Berekhiah wrote two treatises, the *Sefer ha-Hibbur* (*Compendium*) and the *Sefer ha-Mazref* (*Book of the Crucible*), anthologies based on the ethical thought of Saadiah Gaon, Solomon Ibn Gabriol, Bahya Ibn Pakuda, and other philosophers; evidently he also composed several lost works of biblical exegesis.[3] His title "ha-Nakdan," means a "pointer," a scribe who adds vowel marks and the Masorah to a biblical text, but in a larger sense a grammarian who knows all the intricacies of the Hebrew language. His immense learning is apparent, for example, in the puns based on the roots of Hebrew words that structure almost every rhymed prose line of the *Fox Fables*. Berekhiah's two major adaptations taken together are a tour de force of translation from a dominant Latin cultural model into a diasporic Hebrew idiom; yet beyond his celebration of the holy language, like *Yosippon* he preserves a dialogue between the two. The fiction of *Uncle and Nephew* is that it reclaims "Arab" natural science for Jews via Latin intermediaries, and the *Fox Fables* deals harshly with both the Jews and the Christians of England, "the islands of the sea (*'ii ha-yam*)."[4]

There are, unfortunately, only three documents outside of his philosophical, literary, and scientific works that mention Berekhiah and can be firmly attached to him. A codex written in Rouen by his son Elijah in 1233 celebrates him as a biblical commentator and Talmud scholar as well as a collector of proverbs; a badly damaged second codex expands on the first, mentioning Berekhiah's commentaries on all of the bible and his rabbinic responsa, calling him a "prophet" (*nabi*), and comparing him to Solomon in his wisdom and abundant parables.[5] The third, which locates him in Oxford under the French equivalent of his name, "Benedict le Puinteur," records his contribution of £1 6s. 8d. to the 1194 *Northhampton Donum*—the heavy tallage levied when Richard I returned from captivity in Germany. The evidence that Berekhiah, at least later in his life, resided in Oxford is significant for his literary productions. Oxford was a center of Jewish learning and certainly one of the easiest places in England for a Jewish scholar to obtain Latin books like the Aesopic collections or Adelard's *Natural Questions*.[6] Since it appears that he lived there on and off throughout his long career, he would have most likely borrowed these works from monastic or university scholars, or perhaps Christian fellow scribes.[7] There is even a good chance that Berekhiah was personally acquainted with his fellow fabulist and exact contemporary in Oxford, Alexander Nequam, an eminent lecturer in theology; both wrote poetry in the Latin fable tradition as well as works indebted to Adelard of Bath's scientific ideas.[8] Nequam, moreover, was highly unusual among scholars of his time for including a Talmudic parable about resurrection and the unity of body and soul in one of his Oxford sermons, a passage that Berekhiah also cites in his *Compendium*, copied from Saadia Gaon's *Book of Beliefs and Opinions*.[9] Nequam also refers to "Gamaliel," a Christian term used for rabbinic texts in general, several times in his writings along with a few telling references to his cordial conversations with Jews.[10] Berekhiah was perhaps one of the "litteratores Hebraei" or grammarians whom he consulted.[11]

### Uncle and Nephew: The Soul of Translation

Berekhiah's *Uncle and Nephew* is, Gad Freudenthal has observed, the first medieval Hebrew translation of a scientific work written by a non-Jew.[12] Given the early insular manuscript transmission of Adelard's *Natural Questions*, Berekhiah almost certainly wrote the work in England.[13] Having composed this text no later than the 1160s, he next appears in Provence in the famous circle of R. Meshullam of Lunel, sometime before this patron's death in 1170. In the *Compendium*, he already refers to *Uncle and Nephew* as "the scientific work that I have rendered into Hebrew

from a non-Jewish source."[14] Having explained the difficulties of distill-
ing Saadia Gaon's and others' ideas in a preface, he dedicates the *Compendium* to "R. Meshullam, a shining light of the world, one clothed with
righteousness as with a garment."[15] Although the *Compendium* itself is
not a translation, in Lunel Berekhiah was part of the same community and
Jewish cultural moment within Christian Europe as Judah Ibn Tibbon, the
"father of translators" originally from Grenada. At Meshullam's request,
Judah translated from Arabic to Hebrew Baḥya Ibn Pakuda's *Duties of
the Heart*, the grammatical works of Jonah Ibn Janaḥ, and Judah Hal-
evi's religious dialogue, the *Kuzari*.[16] At this time, in Isidore Twersky's
words, "Provençal Jewish learning changed from Torah-based study to
the cultivation of philosophy and other extra-Talmudic disciplines."[17] The
basis for later Jewish religious philosophy, these studies were considered
*ḥokhmot ḥizioniyyot*, nonrabbinic "alien science." By the twelfth-century
standards for innovation in the lands of Christian "Edom," as opposed
to in the more cultivated Islamic world, Berekhiah's adaptations of Latin
non-Jewish works were versions of barely acceptable literature, "alien"
far beyond anything previously translated in Provence.[18]

During his time in Lunel, Berekhiah no doubt became familiar with
Judah Ibn Tibbon's theories of translation, which in some ways mir-
rored his own. In the preface to his translation of Baḥya's *Duties of
the Heart*, Judah describes their common patron R. Meshullam as "a
lamp of the Torah and the commandment," who "craved for books of
wisdom and according to his ability assembled, disseminated, and had
them translated."[19] Judah characterizes the need for such translations as
a consequence of the Jews' exile and dispersion throughout the Islamic
world: "most of the *geonim* [heads of academies] lived in the Diaspora
of the Muslim Empire, Iraq, Ereẓ Israel and Iran, and spoke Arabic,
and all the Jewish communities in those areas spoke that tongue." Even
though Arabic, he admits, is a superior language in terms of vocabulary and rhetorical possibility even for rabbinic commentaries, biblical
Hebrew is nevertheless the holy tongue (*lashon ha-kodesh*) and, above
all, understood by readers in his new home in Christian Provence.[20]
Berekhiah places a similar emphasis on Hebrew as the holy language
but takes up the further challenge of translating works written by non-
Jewish authors. The Diaspora has left Jews without crucial "gentile"
texts that must be reclaimed, but Berekhiah expresses little regard in his

works for the wonders of the Latin language. For Berekhiah, Adelard's *Natural Questions*—in Charles Burnett's estimation a scientific "literary masterpiece"—was material to be recovered and purified from a polluted source.

In one of his final works, a treatise on the astrolabe (*De opere astrolapsus*), Adelard of Bath praises the future King Henry II for wanting to know not just "the writings of the Latins" but also "the opinions of the Arabs" concerning astronomy. For this philosopher king-to-be, knowledge of what Adelard calls the "wonderful beauty" of the world will emerge from the East and, needless to say, from the work of the translators of the East to the West.[21] During roughly the same period, Abraham Ibn Ezra—grammarian, philosopher, and poet—was traveling around Christian Europe, including England, where he produced a series of astronomical and astrological works that translated the main ideas of Arab scientists from the previous centuries in Baghdad and Spain into a uniquely Hebrew idiom.[22] In his translation from Latin, Berekhiah ha-Nakdan participates in a related contest over the possession and articulation of a certain type of "Arab" learning in the Angevin Empire.

Adelard of Bath has been called "the first English scientist," an early exponent of rationalism over revelation, and a philosopher who, together with a small group of other early twelfth-century English scholars including Walcher, the prior of Malvern, and Robert Losinga, the bishop of Hereford, brought Arabic and Greek learning to the West. His best-known work, the *Natural Questions*, is a dialogue between Adelard and his ignorant and increasingly combative nephew on a list of problems on natural philosophy ranging from the growth of plants to the functions of the human body to the celestial realms. Later in life he "translated"— with collaborators who were possibly Arabic-speaking Jews—Euclid's *Elements*, Al-Khwarizmi's *Astronomical Tables* (*Zij*), Abu Ma'shar's *Abbreviation to the Introduction to Astrology*, and various other Arabic scientific texts.[23]

The *Natural Questions* takes the form of earlier works on medicine, lists of questions from the school of Salerno in particular (such as: Why do men go bald from the front part of their head? Because the fumes rising from the stomach exit through wider pores). In the manuscript tradition, the work was quickly linked with Seneca's *Natural Questions*, which focuses on meteorology. Adelard distinguishes his approach to the genre, however, with an elaborate account of his personal circumstances and experiences. Having left his nephew to study in the cathedral school at Laon, he had journeyed far away to study with his "Arab masters" for seven years. He returned to the England of Henry I, where he found his fellow courtiers and clerics to be corrupt, barbarous drunks. At this point his nephew shows up demanding to hear about the knowledge of the Arabs, whom he calls "Saracens." Adelard hesitates because of the Western bias against "the discoveries of the moderns" but proceeds into the main work.[24] The *Questions* prepares the reader for a dialogue between the epistemologies of France and a fictional Arab philosophical world: formal logic and revelation as opposed to scientific discovery and the mathematical arts. This line of enquiry would inevitably lead to heresy at some point, and in fact the nephew never mentions scripture at all and simply either rejects or grudgingly accepts most of the elements of natural philosophy that Adelard sets out. The conflict, Adelard explains, is between his own reason and judgment and his nephew's beast-like adherence to the "name[s] of ancient authorit[ies]."[25] Adelard's "nature," moreover, is predominantly a Neoplatonic universe derived from Calcidius's version of Plato's *Timaeus*, Cicero's *Nature of the Gods*, and Macrobius's *Commentary on the Dream of Scipio*. The Arab studies, that is, turn out to be entirely Latin with virtually no trace of Arabic language or culture. The rhetorical function of the Arabs, as Adelard himself claims, is that he "shall defend [their] cause, not my own"; these non-Christians will absolve him of any blame for his ideas, especially about Platonic aspects of the cosmos like the souls of stars—and also what the stars eat.[26]

The most original aspect of Adelard's self-definition is an account of the geography of his travels. He calls himself a "man of Bath" at various places in his works. In his allegorical account of the seven liberal arts, *On the Same and the Different*, he mentions having traveled to Norman Salerno and in the *Natural Questions* alludes to having visited the Norman principality of Antioch at the height of its power. In Mamistra, he is caught on a bridge during an earthquake, which was caused by air trapped in the earth rushing out to meet the outer air; and in Tarsus an old man tells him about the webs of nerves and blood vessels in a human body.[27] His experiences of the "natural," then, follow the path of the Norman conquest of the Muslim Middle East up to the aftermath of the First Crusade in which Tancred, Bohemond of Antioch's nephew, ruled over a territory that stretched from the modern Syrian coast up to eastern Turkey. And then he returns to Bath. In the "Microcosmos" of his *Cosmographia*, Adelard's contemporary Neoplatonist Bernardus Silvestris claimed that through a redeemed mastery of nature humans could ascend to their true place in the heavens. Adelard's conquest of nature, however, clearly depends neither solely on his Arab teachers' abstract "reason" nor even his experience of the exotic world beyond Europe, but rather directly on the crusaders' military occupation of specific cities of the East: a conquest of territory, texts, and language.[28]

Adelard's *Natural Questions*, as Burnett notes, "had an immediate success," judging from the number of manuscripts produced in England and France; Berekhiah evidently learned about it not long after it appeared.[29] He translated the work because, as he explains in his *Compendium*, it adds to what the Jewish philosophers Saadia Gaon and Abraham Ibn Ezra have to say about the tripartite soul: "Now, according to the statements of these authorities of ours, combined with that which I, Berekhiah, have learned from the scientific work which I have rendered into Hebrew from a non-Jewish source, I have come to the conclusion that the *neshama* (soul) is in the brain . . . and that for this reason man has been created erect in stature, so that the *neshama* should point to heaven, and thus have before its view, and ever present to its gaze, the place from whence it derived its origin."[30] Berekhiah uses this extended conceit taken from Cicero's *Nature of the Gods* by way of Adelard about why people, as opposed to animals, stand up, in order to support Ibn Ezra's use of the word *neshama* for the human soul. *Neshama*, for the Neoplatonic Ibn Ezra, contrasts with the two lower souls, *ruah* (animal) and *nefesh* (vegetable).[31] Berekhiah's appropriation also shows his eager desire to participate in the literary culture of Angevin England, and indeed by citing the text as "non-Jewish" to present himself as a mediator between the two discourses of Latin and Hebrew philosophy. By means of Adelard's formulations, Berekhiah recovers a lost Latinity for Hebrew; the language of the Jews' traditional enemies serves the contemporary Jews of the Diaspora. As he frames it here, the production of European Jewish knowledge can result from the unintended affirmation of Jewish authorities by a Latin thinker.

For Berekhiah, however, Hebrew translation itself is also a challenge to Adelard's assumptions about reason and science as transparently conveyed in the Latin language. He characterizes his project in *Uncle and*

*Nephew* in these terms: "I Berekhiah, son of Natronai, was anxious in thought until I girded my loins, and translated these subjects into Hebrew. I found them in writings of the Gentiles, copied as they were from the Arabs. In them were concealed matters coming from the wise men of our age, and this splendid knowledge of the expert was not even looked at by the eye of the untutored."[32] And elsewhere, in the *Compendium*: "I have culled all this information from the learning of the Greeks, which had been translated into their own languages by certain non-Jews; I have redeemed it from the hand of the stranger, and have given it a purer turn of my own."[33] To translate into Hebrew is to redeem, to sanctify, and to cleanse from Adelard's impure Latin, itself a translation from the Arab or Greek masters of natural science. The whole enterprise, however, is, as he claims, spurred by his anxiety. This speaks to a diasporic sense of cultural loss, a need to recover the inaccessible texts of Christian Europe in order to address an incomplete, fragmented knowledge among Jews. The fact that Berekhiah had a copy of Adelard's *Natural Questions* at all nonetheless suggests that he was on quite friendly terms with, at the very least, a Christian scribe or librarian, and that he was therefore more interested in the potential for Jewish–Christian collaboration than his disdainful language suggests.

*Uncle and Nephew* is neither about Adelard and his nephew nor Berekhiah and his nephew; instead he stresses that the dialogue is between "two [Arab] scientists (or *wise men*) of our age" arguing about natural history. Berekhiah emphasizes that his own Hebrew book was ultimately "translated from the Arabs," not from an English scholar.[34] This distinction about the scientists' origins allows him to reconfigure Adelard's evocation of the crusader Middle East, a geography that subordinates the phenomena of the natural world to a catastrophic post-Crusade history. Berekhiah's challenge begins, pointedly, with the old Roman town of Bath itself. Adelard, in his chapter on the workings of springs, alludes to the baths of Minerva in a passage about a familiar example of how the earth exhales its moisture. In an untranslatable pun he writes: "So that we consider it with plainer Minerva (wisdom), let the matter be dealt with through examples."[35] The town was widely known for its medicinal waters: as the *Deeds of [King] Stephen* (1148) explains for example: "little springs through hidden conduits send up waters heated without human skill or ingenuity from deep in the bowels of the earth."[36] Berekhiah's polemic has the nephew inquire: "For when I was in Tiberias, I bathed in the hot water of the great river and I could not understand the cause and reason of its temperature," which his uncle attributes to underground mines of brimstone.[37] For Berekhiah, as he constructs an authorial voice to counter Adelard's, Tiberias is in many ways the ideal anti-Bath, a site marked by the same natural wonder at the lowest stratum of the earth below, but also known as a place of learning that embodied a form of resistance. For medieval Jews, Tiberias was associated with the sages of the Palestinian rabbinic academy in the centuries following the fall of Jerusalem to the Romans and—significantly for Berekhiah's occupation as a "nakdan" or scribe—with the "Tiberian" copiers of the bible who sought to establish a correct Hebrew text.[38] Earth or nature is here the foundation of the universal Roman Empire that once included both England and Palestine and has since become the foundation of the fragmented regions of the twelfth century. In Berekhiah's own day, Tiberias also had a relatively flourishing Jewish community of fifty compared to the handful of Jews left in crusader Jerusalem. Berekhiah's contemporary, the traveler Benjamin of Tudela, mentions the "hot waters" and the tomb of R. Yoḥanan ben Zakkai, the sage who according to rabbinic accounts had escaped from Jerusalem before the fall of the Second Temple to reestablish the Sanhedrin at Yavneh.[39] For the Diaspora Jewish scholar of *Uncle and Nephew* this is a worthy fictional "home" in the Holy Land, a town of exile and erudition after Jerusalem had yet again fallen to a new Western power.

Again, the "Arab" uncle recapitulates Adelard's earthquake experience from Antioch, but in this version he describes crossing a bridge "in the land of Cush" or Ethiopia; in contemporary Hebrew literature Cush sometimes signifies a land beyond either Christian or Muslim rule, the distant territory of the ten lost tribes of Jews—an empire of its own.[40] In a chapter on the question of "why does a man weep in an hour of joy?" Adelard has just "come from the Orient" to his tearful nephew, whereas Berekhiah's uncle has specifically been in Tyre and Sidon and touring "Philistia" (the coast of Palestine)—crusader strongholds but also significant Jewish communities.[41] Berekhiah's Middle East, although like Adelard's in the hands of crusaders, is his site of translation as a cultural challenge. While the scientific "answer" to the question—joy causes the soul to diffuse heat through the body to the brain, where it causes moisture to flow—is much the same, the translation follows Berekhiah's principles. He has purified the text from "the hand of the stranger" not only by replacing Latin with Hebrew but also by erasing Europe, Adelard's native England and France, from the text's geography. The two protagonists are exponents of "Arab study"—or thinly veiled Jews—but it is never clear where they reside except for a perpetual Diaspora. Berekhiah here also alludes to Ibn Ezra's assertion of natural philosophy that the Holy Land, the center of the earth, is the most perfect climate for acquiring knowledge; England, in this geography, is naturally the end of the earth. Nevertheless, Ibn Ezra wrote his major work on the *mizvot* (commandments), *The Foundation of Awe*, in England, and Berekhiah himself worked at least some of the time in England.[42] The holy language of the translation necessarily produces a radically different map of the Holy Land from the Norman crusader empire. If the *Natural Questions* posits a universal "natural" human body in terms of brain moisture, for example, Berekhiah's *Uncle and Nephew* makes translation a matter of ridding the "natural" from the universalizing and colonizing "hand" of the western Europeans' Latin.

Berekhiah, in formulating an idea of Hebrew translation as purification, takes his lead from one of his favorite thinkers, Ibn Ezra, who presented theories about the Hebrew language in numerous works of grammar and in biblical commentaries. Shlomo Sela has noted, however, that curiously it is only in his treatise on the astrolabe, *The Bronze Instrument*, that he discusses translation at length. Diaspora has made Hebrew a "forgotten" language that resists the expression of new ideas, since Jews have been "left only with the books of the prophets." It is nevertheless still the most perfect language, even for describing an object from outside Jewish culture.[43] Hence, Ibn Ezra mined biblical Hebrew for an idiosyncratic set of scientific terms mostly unrelated to the standard Arabic or Greek vocabulary. Sela cites the striking example that Ibn Ezra uses the word "gevul" (boundary) to approximate the Ptolemaic "climate" instead of the Arabic word "iqlim"—going far out of his way to reclaim a "holy language" with which to describe the natural world.[44] Berekhiah incorporates not only this radical concept of Hebrew into his translation along with many scriptural passages that support Adelard's "reason," but on a few occasions he cites Ibn Ezra's "scientific" *Commentary on Ecclesiastes* as a way of aligning the Hebrew language with Adelard in his dialectical tension with his nephew.

The point at which both Adelard's and Berekhiah's considerations of natural science reach a kind of impasse is the thorny Neoplatonic question of whether or not "brute animals" have souls (*animae*). For both writers the issue becomes central to establishing an authoritative voice. The question is, as Adelard's nephew puts it, "uncertain, at least to men of our time."[45] The debate focuses on philosophical definitions of the various faculties—sensation, opinion, and judgment or discernment— and whether they reside in the body or the soul. Adelard maintains the somewhat unorthodox and conveniently "Saracen" position that animals have both sensation and judgment and that their souls are eternal, whereas his nephew sticks with the "popular view" that animals have sensation, which is just part of the body; the most he concedes is that animals could have a soul that dies with them. The question touches on many of Adelard's interests in his work, for example the nature of reason that sets humans apart from animals and the relationship of body and soul, but it is at the same time a satire about authority, with a dog as the central character. Arguing that dogs have discernment and can understand language, Adelard explains that if a dog picks up two scents of wild animals, "mindful of his master's (*magister*'s) command he spurns the one and follows the other. For he has somehow pictured in his mind that 'this is the one I must follow, but that is another scent, different from this.'" The dog is the perfect subject of the French schools, a student like his nephew, whom elsewhere Adelard accuses of being an "animal . . . led wherever one pleases by a halter . . . the authority of written words."[46] The dog's master in the schools (*magister*) gives him orders, and he obeys. The nephew, in other words, has discernment but doesn't fully use the reason that is uniquely human and the basis of "Arab Study." When the nephew insists that the animal soul perishes, Adelard fires back that "rather you perish, when you so wrongly define an essence!"[47] In this particular passage, the fully "human" rational subject is Adelard himself at the time when he was preparing to make his actual Arabic translations; the fiction he establishes in the non-Arabic *Questions* is that by following in the path of the crusaders, he had abandoned France for the Middle East and returned with new authorities that would displace the old ones.

For Berekhiah as well, this is a central passage. While the dog is still the central figure, the animal whose soul displays discernment and intelligence because "otherwise you would find no animal to come at your bidding," the humor about the dog-like French students appears to be lost in translation.[48] Rather in Berekhiah's account, the word for soul (*neshama*) that he initially applies to both human and animal souls proves insufficient to translate the Latin *anima*, itself already supposedly translated from Arabic. When the nephew reaches the point at which he asserts that the animal soul disappears like smoke after death whereas the human soul ascends to heaven, Berekhiah interrupts with his authorial voice: "I Berekhiah can arrive at this conclusion by way of scripture for the word 'soul' (*neshama*) is only applied to man, and the most convincing proof is found in the verse 'He gave soul (*neshama*) to the people upon it, and spirit (*ruaḥ*) to those who walk therein' [Isa. 42:5]."[49] He goes on to assign another word for soul—*nefesh*—to animals: "This is also the explanation given by Ibn Ezra . . . that the *nefesh* is the 'growing power' resident in the liver, in which all living things share."[50] The solution essentially derives from Ibn Ezra's terms for the tripartite soul mentioned above—*neshama* (brain-study), *ruaḥ* (heart-anger), and *nefesh* (liver-desire)—from his Neoplatonic biblical commentaries on Lamentations and Exodus. Although both he and Ibn Ezra vehemently disagree with Adelard about the immortality of animals' souls, Berekhiah's concern here is really with the authority of translation.[51] In his view, biblical Hebrew rather than Latin has the vocabulary for different kinds of souls and is therefore the language best equipped to understand the workings of nature. He uses the dialogue between the uncle and his nephew to enact this very problem of word-to-word equivalence in his text. Although the word *neshama* may never refer to an animal in the bible, the two "scientists" themselves apply it to animals throughout their discussion as the equivalent of *anima*. It is only when Berekhiah in his own voice reveals himself as the translator that he abandons the Latin original and its Hebrew approximation, the "ugly setting" of natural science for the more nuanced Hebrew of his favorite sage. Like Ibn Ezra, Berekhiah identifies Hebrew with loss through Diaspora, the Jews scattered from England to the land of Cush; yet, while limited in vocabulary, the language is pushed by the new Arab and Greek sciences to come up with new usages. The vocabularies of medieval astronomy and Neoplatonic philosophical texts, among other specialized discourses, reinvent and are in turn reinvented by Hebrew. In his polemical engagement with Adelard, Berekhiah rightly claims to take the best from the wisdom of the non-Jews about nature, but he makes it clear that the hot springs of Tiberias are clearer and healthier than their counterpart in Bath.

## A Prophetic Aesop

The literary scene of late twelfth-century England is known for, among other things, the popularity of Aesopic beast-fable collections. The most famous of these works is justifiably Marie de France's *Fables*. In addition, the theologian and scientist Alexander Nequam wrote both a *Novus Aesopus* and *Novus Avianus* in elegiac verse as rhetorical exercises, and an otherwise unknown "Walter the Englishman" composed by far the most popular metric fable collection, which became a standard Latin school text.[52] In this multilingual culture, Berekhiah ha-Nakdan produced his own collection, the *Fox Fables*—a stunning feat of adaptation and translation from secular Latin in the service of biblical prophecy.[53] Berekhiah, like the others, for the most part translated his tales from the medieval prose versions of the first-century Latin poet Phaedrus known in various medieval forms as *Romulus*.[54] It is possible, given his Anglo-Norman literary milieu, that he was acquainted with Marie's Old French *Fables* as well.[55] He also drew on fables written by the late antique poet Avianus (ca. 400), and on three occasions he used extra sources, specifically from the Hebrew version of the Arabic frame-narrative *Kalila wa-Dimna*, Petrus Alfonsi's *Disciplina clericalis*, and, to great dramatic effect, the Babylonian Talmud.[56] He emphasizes from the opening of his work that he is drawing on fables by "people of every language," a universal genre ideally suited to his larger project of reclaiming texts from the Diaspora.[57]

While it leaves him with three decades between his surviving Latin translations, Berekhiah seems to have written the *Fox Fables* during the reign of Richard I, at the beginning of a century's reversal in fortune for English Jews. He takes on his society precisely at this moment of crisis. Before 1189, the Jews in London and elsewhere in the country had become fabulously wealthy through dealing in precious metals, pawnbroking, and moneylending.[58] In one notable case, the abbot of Peterborough pawned his church's relics, "including . . . the arm of St. Oswald."[59] Through moneylending to the gentry, Jews frequently acquired the land of their debtors, which they would usually sublet or sell at a profit.[60] The Jews' legal status defined them and their possessions as the crown's property, and therefore their great fortunes were always available to the Angevin kings. Henry II in particular exploited the Jews' wealth for short-term credit and then later increased Jewish taxes.[61] The kings' enemies, who often borrowed from Jewish lenders to pay the crown, viewed these quasi-foreigners as royal agents.[62] Nevertheless, they lived in relatively secure luxury within Christian England. Unlike the Jewish communities in France and Germany, they were spared the large-scale violence that finally erupted at the beginning of Richard's reign. A fury fueled by both crusading zeal and the gentry's widespread resentment of the Jews led to the 1190 massacre at York where Jewish bonds were also destroyed by erstwhile debtors.

In direct response to the disastrous events of 1189–90, as Susan Einbinder and others have argued, the prevalent cultural ideal in England became deeply connected to the martyrological verse and chronicles written by the Northern French Tosafist poets in the wake of the pogroms of the First and Second Crusades.[63] The first chapter discusses how these texts exalt their subjects' sanctification of the Name, a heroic act that revivifies previous sacrificial ideas. Among its models, this martyrdom takes both the intimate experience of Abraham's sacrifice of Isaac (the *Akedah*) to account for parents killing their children, and by way of *Yosippon* the epic reenactment of the mass suicide at Masada. These poems stress an absolute refusal to convert to the oppressors' religion and an urgent appeal to what Israel Yuval has pointedly called a "vengeful messiah."[64] The commemorations of the York martyrs by the continental poets Joseph of Chartres and Menachem ben Jacob exalt those who sacrificed themselves and their families and call for revenge on "Edom."

Together with many other French and German examples, these texts express a common literary voice in the face of Christian violence: a defiance through the cultivation of memory and lamentation in liturgical texts, a glorification of martyrs past and present who have atoned for their community's sins, and a call for divine salvation and the destruction of the Christians. Against this Jewish ideological background to the era of

King Richard the Lionheart, Berekhiah's voice in his introduction to the *Fox Fables* is shocking. Far from offering any kind of praise or immediate comfort to his fellow English Jews, he excoriates them in the manner of the biblical prophets for their "radical corruption."[65] The most inherently strange aspect of his work is not even that Berekhiah chooses to apply the prophets' responses to the imminent fall of the First Temple to the crisis of the 1190s, but rather that he does so in a work almost entirely translated from Latin that also links him to the larger intellectual trends of the Anglo-Norman twelfth century. These dichotomies in the *Fox Fables* make Berekhiah's text generically unstable and culturally transformative. For the most part, a translation of Latin prose into Hebrew rhyme, it necessarily questions contemporary literary ideas that celebrated the renewal of classical texts. At the same time, it is a work meant to be read only by Jews that never quite abandons a love for the culture of Edom, the "Roman" oppressors who destroyed the Second Temple and the Christians who destroyed the York Jewry alike.

Ancient and medieval European fable collections crucially define translation itself as their project, since their origins are always with a distant and mythical author "Aesop" who serves the works' ideological claims. The most influential *Romulus* collections begin with a prologue by the fictional Roman emperor "Romulus" explaining to his son "Tiberinus" that he has translated Aesop's fables from Greek to Latin for his edification in all moral matters.[66] Berekhiah's contemporary Marie de France, in her opening dedication to "a flower of chivalry," traces her fables to Aesop, who in this version translated them from Greek to Latin for his master Romulus and his son in another articulation of *translatio studii*, the transfer of learning from East to West. Her epilogue then reveals her own noble patron as "Count William" and inscribes her name as "Marie." She has translated the text into "Romanz" from the "Engleis" of King Alfred who had long before translated it from Latin.[67] Marie's elaborate *translatio imperii et studii*, from a Roman Empire rooted in Greek culture to Alfred the Great's ninth-century kingdom to an ideally unified polyglot Angevin Empire, exemplifies how the popular fables support a linear model of transmission that, in Rita Copeland's terms, underlines historical difference.[68] Marie's fiction of the displacement of the Latin text by two subsequent vernacular versions—Old English and French—in different historical eras emphasizes the long-established authority of an insular vernacular culture. It emphasizes as well her own affinity with "Aesop" the wise translator.

Berekhiah's *Fox Fables*, while influenced like Marie's or Nequam's projects by concerns with textual recovery, Latinity, and transmission, turns to a different model of translation and history. His introductory poem creates one of the text's many dualities between Hebrew and Latin: the genre, he explains, is a collection of instructive "fables of foxes and beasts (*mishle shu'alim ve-ḥai'ot*)."[69] With the term "Fox Fable" itself, he invokes a specific type of Talmudic parable, many of which were in turn derived from Aesopic fables and associated with figures of great erudition, in particular Rabbi Meir who was said to have known three hundred. The rabbinic genre also alludes to the gradual loss of the great sages' wisdom and culture—including fables—after the destruction of the Second Temple.[70] Berekhiah makes it clear, nonetheless, that if his work recovers an ancient Jewish past it is intercultural as well, and that he is actually translating texts from other traditions, written down by "people of every language." Since his "faith is different from their faith," he has added much material and versified the fables so that they are now "overlaid with sapphires" (Song of Songs 5:14); that is, they are endowed with a value possible only in the Hebrew language.[71] In a sense this is a Jewish version of *translatio studii,* with a different historical trajectory; the common medieval language—the unspoken "imperial" Latin of the "Romulus" texts or Avianus—is made holy through a translation into a prior language that infuses it with biblical meaning and metaphor. Berekhiah's dialectic of rejection of and desire for Latinity is an expression of the multifaceted medieval Jewish response to the Roman conquest of Jerusalem exemplified by *Yosippon.* In the central rabbinic text devoted to this theme, *Midrash Lamentations Rabbah,* the Jews and their Roman rulers alike bear responsibility for the *ḥurban,* the destruction of the Temple. In *Yosippon,* the Jewish rebels, as in Josephus's *Jewish War,* are to blame along with Vespasian and Titus. In the subsequent European Diaspora, the Jewish and Roman cultures become necessarily intertwined more than ever.

The locale of Berekhiah's work, like the other fable collections, is Angevin England, but his Hebrew is an exilic idiom. In this diasporic rather than linear model, the fables come from "various tongues" rather than the distant Greek "Aesop" whose name is never mentioned, and

Latin becomes one of many languages to convert into a different religion, transfer to a true rather than an illusory eternity, and in the end ideally erase. Berekhiah here repeats his idea of translation as a form of purification from "the hands of strangers" that he had set out in *Uncle and Nephew*: even a work as thoroughly produced by the Latin tradition as Adelard's can be recuperated and improved with Hebrew. By this account, the *translatio* or transfer geographically follows the scattered communities of Jews rather than the intellectual centers of a new European empire. A. M. Haberman, the most recent editor of the *Fox Fables*, suggests that "Rabbi Berekhiah ben Natronai ha-Nakdan" saw himself as a peripatetic translator, deliberately following in the footsteps of the Talmudic sage Bar Kappara, who in a famous midrash recounts hundreds of fox fables for both entertainment and criticism of his peers. Berekhiah's text is in this sense a recovery of the fables themselves, stories told by scholars in ancient Palestine but not written down. His son's exaggerated claim that he wrote three thousand proverbs would at least support an identification with Bar Kappara.[72]

Berekhiah's initial meditation on literary practice gives no warning about the scathing polemics that immediately follow. In his prologue, he confronts the plight of late twelfth-century Jews not as a result of oppression from their external enemies but as a communal internal catastrophe. His opinion of his fellow Jews is low at best: "the congregation of England is bereft of intelligence / and crowned with shame."[73] His inspiration in tone is the Hebrew prophets, whom he quotes throughout the text, and his message is theirs: the injustice, pride, and idolatry of the Jews will lead to utter ruin unless they heed his warning. He begins by characterizing his text as divine, a "scroll" that refers to Malachi 3:16: "A scroll of remembrance has been written at His behest concerning those who revere the Lord and remember his name." The authority he claims for his "pen," however, is not only for his prophetic message but also for the translated fables that follow.

The governing image of Berekhiah's prologue is a malevolent wheel of fortune "that turns in England, for the one to die and the other to live." "I will direct my pen to a parable (*mashal*) about the falsehood that rules (*mashal*)," Berekhiah announces. The same wheel (*'ofan*) has also upended the community's own moral status, overturning truth for falsehood: "righteousness has become abomination, honesty treachery, prayer vanity, sacrifice injustice, discretion whoredom."[74] The rich live in their "palaces" and "covet silver and love gold," but hoard their wealth and "will not bend their necks to worship their Creator." Berekhiah saves a special disgust for those who have profited the most from financing the king, although he couches much of his invective in biblical quotations: "They have become fat and sleek (Jer. 5:28) from guile, and they profit from fraudulent dealings and hypocritical flattery." As for their delusions about their London mansions and their place in English society, he characterizes them with one of the gloomiest psalms: "They call lands by their own names, they who are like cattle" (Ps. 49:12). Worst of all, "there is rejoicing in the community of hypocrites . . . but in the camp of the upright a voice is heard wailing."[75] His message is clear enough, and disturbing: the recent misfortunes of the English Jews have been brought on by their own relentless acquisition of money from Christians and Jews alike without regard for righteousness. As any of the prophets might say, they deserve punishment for their terrible injustices to their own congregation. The passage from Jeremiah above, for example, continues: "Shall I not punish for these things? says the Lord; shall My soul not be avenged on a nation such as this?" (Jer. 5:29). More specifically, Berekhiah's message is that Henry II and now Richard have kept the Jews as their subjects for mutual benefit; but regardless of how much property they have, the king's boot will always be on their necks. Berekhiah warns of this again at the end of the famous Aesopic fable of the frogs who demand a king and end up with a devouring snake: "when you get close to him, he'll burn you."[76] Even a horrifying incident like the massacre of Jews at Richard's coronation—when the eminent Tosafist Jacob of Orleans, among other scholars, was killed—could be said to have happened because of the London magnates' own arrogance, insincere flattery, and impiety. In his own prophetic terms, "Berekhiah curses and abjures the times."[77]

Berekhiah concludes of his community's fall from good to evil: "the wheel that joins all this together constantly runs over us."[78] The wheel of change is a common ancient image.[79] Given his translation project, Berekhiah here specifically evokes the Boethian wheel of Fortuna ubiquitous among Christian scholars in an opening display of Latin learning. His central frame of reference, however, is ultimately not to a wheel that represents the changeable nature of the world within a Neoplatonic frame. Rather, he refers to the wheels in the book of Ezekiel, the great postexilic prophet. In his prologue, Berekhiah describes his metaphoric wheel as part of a "chariot" (*merkavah*), choosing a term that immediately evokes the celestial chariot in Ezekiel's visions of the throne of the Divine Presence.[80] Rashi explicates Ezekiel 1:4, "A tempest was coming from the north": "That is the chariot (*merkavah*) of the throne of the glory of the *shekhinah* [God's presence]. Since it came with fury to destroy Israel, it is therefore likened to a tempest and a cloud."[81] In the prophet's elaborately detailed visions of the chariot, the spinning wheels, their rims lined with eyes, support the fiery heavenly beings or cherubs who attend first to God's call to Ezekiel in book 1 and then to the doom of the Temple and Jerusalem in book 10. These wheels are the opposite of the Boethian wheel of fortune destroying the English Jews from a human perspective; they represent a divine perspective that now foresees the destruction of a Diaspora city rather than Jerusalem. He cites Boethius only to dismiss this most culturally important of Latin authors in favor of the Hebrew Bible. The imagery becomes clear with Berekhiah's even more explicit and bizarre reference to Ezekiel. He describes himself as filled with a kind of prophetic "secret" discourse and then tells his readers—as God tells Ezekiel—to "eat this scroll, for out of the eater shall come forth meat, and sense shall enter from the sensible."[82] The "scroll," however, is not Ezekiel's message of lamentation but rather the collection of translated Aesopic beast fables, which Berekhiah explains are intended "to strengthen hands that are weak."[83] Berekhiah's readers would have been steeped in the prophets from Shabbat and festival haftarah readings as well as liturgical poetry both ancient and recent, yet the prophetic language with which Berekhiah blasts his immediate community is destabilized and reinvigorated by its new context. Berekhiah interprets the prophets beyond the realm of traditional rabbinic commentary and poetry in a work that is "external" ("hiẓoni"), outside any kind of Hebrew canon, and almost entirely derived from other languages. His fables, given this dizzying combination of interests, are cryptic, polyvalent, and self-reflexive.

Berekhiah shows his identification with Ezekiel in another particularly clever pun in Fable 66, remarkable because of its relation to another sometime "Anglo-Norman" author, Petrus Alfonsi. He borrows a short parable from the Jewish convert Petrus's *Disciplina clericalis* about a mule who, when asked by a curious fox about his parents, responds with shame over his ass father by talking instead about his uncle, a powerful horse. In

Petrus's frame-narrative, the occasion for this fable is an Arab poet insulting another poet with a "noble mother" and a "lowborn father" who glories in his famous poet uncle instead.[84] Berekhiah, with some subtlety but not too much, savages the author by means of his own Latin text. For Berekhiah, Petrus, who had converted in name and faith from "Moses" to one of the most vehement Christian opponents of his erstwhile religion in his *Dialogue against the Jews*, deserves a special kind of translation from his "new" literary Latin back into his "original language" of Hebrew. Not only is Berekhiah's fable unusually heavily laden with biblical and Talmudic phrases, but it also ridicules the very idea of conversion. Petrus Alfonsi, celebrated by the Christians for his attacks on rabbinic literature in the widely circulated *Dialogue*, is an ugly mule, an ignorant poet, and worse. In the end, he declares: "I Berekhiah said rashly," woe to the one who will be called "from the family of *Buzi* (shame) / All who fall from their father's merits [that is, Petrus] would be better off as stillborn fetuses." The punning wordplay here is on "Ezekiel son of Buzi" (Ezek. 1:3). On the one hand, the name literally refers to the disgraceful essence of the convert's actions; on the other, Berekhiah himself has spoken rashly because he has recalled his literary connection to the exilic prophet and by extension his father, Buzi. He perhaps even refers here to a midrashic tradition that the prophet Jeremiah, despised (*nibzeh*) by the people of Israel and so called "Buzi," was actually Ezekiel's father.[85] Jeremiah's prophecies, as might be expected, are among his favorite biblical sources. Berekhiah ben Natronai, even if despised like the prophets, announces his own authority in this fable as a Hebrew scholar and poet who, unlike the Latin author Petrus, claims an immutable Jewish identity.

If the collections of "Romulus," Marie, and "Walter the Englishman" intend to impart wisdom to the reader, so too does the *Fox Fables*. Berekhiah elevates this pedagogical function, however, to potential salvation for his corrupt community, and he carries over his prophetic voice into the unit of the fable. As in the other collections, each fable has an epimythium, which he calls a "mashal," explaining its meaning; frequently, Berekhiah, writing in first person and sometimes inscribing his name, adds a second epimythium in verse, gesturing toward a very cranky frame-narrative. Berekhiah's authentic work consists of around 110 fables taken from various sources but predominantly the familiar

Latin texts.[86] Three fables from different sources demonstrate his theory of translation, ambivalence toward his source material, and adaptation of the genre into his style of fiery social criticism. For Berekhiah, the *Fox Fables*'s palimpsest of Hebrew texts produced from Latin and other languages is a means of presenting a polyvocal account of a fragile England ca. 1200. Just as Marie de France's *Fables* occasionally offer an overt critique of the Angevin courts that she seems to have known first-hand, Berekhiah's prophetic scroll unravels the woes of a Jewry that eventually would be ruined by the very same powers.[87]

Berekhiah's Fable 7, "The Dog, the Ewe, the Eagle and the Wolf," is a classic Aesopic tale of harsh injustice and pathos that appears in both the *Romulus Nilanti* and Marie's *Fables*: A dog accuses a ewe of stealing bread and has two false witnesses, a wolf and an eagle (a kite in the other versions), back him up.[88] The judges are duly bribed and sentence the ewe to pay back the weight of the bread she had stolen. The ewe has nothing other than her fleece, which she has shorn off and uses to pay the false debt. Without her fleece, she is subject to the torments of summer and winter, and she sorrows for her children as well. When she finally dies, the wolf and the eagle reappear and devour her carcass. Berekhiah's epimythium explains that the fable is for a generation that commits violence and deceit, and "the ruler listens to falsehood."[89] While this "mashal" likely sums up the opinion of most English Jews following the persecutions of Blois, London, and York, Berekhiah's geater innovations to the text are of an exegetical nature. The meaning of his fable hinges on a pun based on the word for ewe (*rekhelah*) and the matriarch Rachel: the ewe (Rachel) weeps for her children (Jer. 31:15), and then in the snow, the ewe (Rachel) "died by the way" (Gen. 35:19).[90] These intertexts, besides underlining Berekhiah's originality and addition of lambs to the fable, demonstrate how translation from Latin to the holy language of Hebrew—*ovis* to *rekhelah*—reveals the text as an allegory of Jewish identity and exile.

Berekhiah's text represents one strand of medieval exegesis on these two texts derived from midrash. One of the glosses of *Genesis Rabbah* to "And Rachel died and was buried" reads "R. Simeon b. Gamaliel taught. . . . We find Israel [the nation] called after Rachel as it says: *Rachel weeping for her children* (Jer. 31:15)."A further gloss explains: "What was Jacob's reason for burying Rachel in the way to Ephrath? Jacob foresaw that the exiles would pass on from thence, therefore he buried her there so that she might pray for mercy for them. *Thus it is written, 'A voice is heard in Ramah . . . Rachel weeping for her children.' . . . Thus says the Lord: refrain your voice from weeping . . . and there is hope for your future.*"[91] The ewe of the fable may be the victim of a predatory Christian "Roman" society that is a condition of exile—hence the imperial symbol of the eagle—but the focus of Berekhiah's text shifts to the figure of Rachel as both the Israelite nation and intercessor for the nation's sins. With this, the allegory returns to the prophetic idea of the prologue in which the drama of Jewish Diaspora and return has little to do with Rome or Christendom.

Given that the fable does, however, consider the oppression of Jews by Christians, the well-known Christian interpretations of the same biblical passages also underlie Berekhiah's text. Jerome, notably, reads Jeremiah 31:15 as a major point of controversy between Jewish and Christian exegesis, citing the "literal" Jewish exegesis about a return from exile in order to discredit it.[92] The Christian tradition derives from Matthew 2:16–18; for the apostle, the passage refers to Herod's futile attempt to murder Jesus in the "massacre of the innocents" after Mary and Joseph flee to Egypt: "Then was fulfilled what had been spoken through the prophet Jeremiah." Berekhiah incidentally refutes the Christian interpretation through his linguistic certainty about the meaning produced by Hebrew itself, as opposed to a Latin translation of Hebrew and Greek like the Vulgate. His view of the gospel, nonetheless, is ultimately the same as his view of Jewish scripture: its leading believers have become deeply corrupt, violent, Herod-like rulers who have abandoned their own texts.

In Fable 6 Berekhiah is at his most subversive, reinventing the most famous "Fox Fable" in the Talmud, "The Fox and the Fishes." This story is not precisely a translation; rather, it shows Berekhiah's impulse to rewrite a rabbinic text within a set of translations, and to make the familiar unfamiliar in order to illustrate his view of a world in which the Jews have become as corrupt as their Christian-Roman rulers. In B. Berakhot 61b, Rabbi Akiva tells the parable to Pappas ben Judah in order to explain his own willingness to die for the Torah by publicly teaching against the edict of the Roman government. The text as a whole is one of the most frequently invoked passages of the Talmud to address the nature of martyrdom itself, and as such is vital to Berekhiah's polemics against his contemporaries. In the fable, a fox sees swarms of fish swimming around frantically and asks them what they're fleeing; they reply that they're trying to escape from fishermen's nets. The fox tries to trick them into coming up onto land by offering them the memory of a distant peace that they used to have with his ancestors. The fish, however, answer that since they live badly enough in their own element of water, it would be much worse on land where they would die. The conclusion that R. Akiva provides is: "So it is with us. If such is our condition when we sit and study the Torah, of which it is written, 'for that is thy life and the length of thy days' (Deut. 30:20), if we go and neglect it how much worse off we shall be!" R. Akiva, having affirmed his own element as Torah itself, is martyred with the exemplary death of suffering his body to be raked with iron combs while reciting the *Shema*. After his death, "a *bat kol* went forth and proclaimed, happy are you, R. Akiva, that you are destined for the life of the world to come."[93]

In Berekhiah's essentially parodic version of the fable, the fox observes that in the water the fish are ruining each other with dissension, with the big ones chasing and attacking the small. The fox gives a political speech much lengthier than the original in his effort to capture them; he first asks them whether the law of their community (*kahal*) is to destroy each other: "Each one fights his brother and every man his neighbor."[94] The fox then rather persuasively cites a number of messianic passages from the bible as part of a vision for his kingship, including "Nation shall not lift sword against nation" (Isa. 2:4) and "Nothing evil or vile shall be done" (Isa. 65:25). One of the fish finally replies more or less exactly like R. Akiva's fish: their situation is precarious because, even when they are living in peaceful waters, external forces like fishermen and hunters assail them. The fish then warns the fox that even if he were king he could never be secure, and finally offers as a kind of excuse for the vicious fish-hierarchy the ironic comment that "even humans quarrel with each other out of jealousy / But one high official is protected by a higher one, and both of them by still higher ones" (Eccles. 5:7).[95] The fish are still united against the would-be fox king but persecute each other in a community far removed from Isaiah's vision of peace in the messianic era.

Having twisted Rabbi Akiva's fox fable from a parable of martyrdom into a tale of hypocrisy, Berekhiah proceeds to deliver a damning epimythium followed by a second, in which he repeats the same rabbinic condemnation : "The face of this generation is the face of a dog," that is, shameless.[96] In its context in the Mishnah, this expression is a dire pronouncement about the state of things after the fall of the Second Temple but before the advent of the Messiah. In the current era, when the Roman Empire has become Christian, the Jews will abandon all values of scholarship and family—"insolence will increase and honor dwindle." Berekhiah's further biblical curses include, "When there is rebellion in the land, hypocrites multiply (Prov. 28:2, with "kings" replaced by "hypocrites"); and, in the second epimythium, "they are spies but there is no Joshua or Caleb among them."[97] In this display of creative commentary on rabbinic exegesis, Berekhiah's point is nonetheless focused: he undermines his own English community's claim to R. Akiva's and other martyrs' exemplarity to define their current situation, despite the literary precedents of the Crusade chronicles and liturgical laments. Against the grain as it is, Berekhiah's acid tone actually leaves open the possibility that he rejects the authority of twelfth-century martyrological writing altogther. His epimythium, with its multiplying hypocrites, can be taken in particular as an attack on his contemporaries' celebration of well-known rabbinic legends like the *Midrash of the Ten Martyrs*, which describes the Romans' grisly executions of ten of the great sages including R. Akiva, R. Ishmael, and R. Ḥaninah ben Teradion. The possibility of the Jews' finding a pure source of imitation in such a text, or in the Talmudic "Fox Fable" about R. Akiva, is foreclosed by their rampant hypocrisy: Berekhiah's fish destroy *each other*, but then claim the idiom of martyrdom. No longer Torah scholars, the fish have become foxes. His era, Berekhiah finally declares, is like that of the disobedient spies whom God punishes in Numbers 13–14; just as there are no righteous men like Joshua and Caleb, there are also none to follow the rabbinic sages. Jews may still die at the hands of oppressive rulers, but almost none of them have the merit to be martyrs.

Fable 95, "Statue and Man," the most self-reflexive and therefore trickiest of Berekhiah's parables, features a talkative idol as both protagonist and antagonist. The fable is one of several that Berekhiah takes from the late Latin poet Avianus, a source used neither by the *Romulus* collections nor by Marie de France. In the original text, a craftsman puts a marble statue of Bacchus up for sale, and the potential buyers are a man who wants to put it on his future tomb and a man who wants to put the god in his temple. The statue pipes up and attempts to persuade the crafts-man that consigning him to his "death sentence" will reflect badly on his work. The outcome is unresolved, and Avianus simply concludes that it applies to those who have the power to do good or bad.[98] The idol, Haim Schwarzbaum notes, is a satirical powerless figure, reduced to begging for his life.[99]

Berekhiah's version is counterintuitive since the idol—by definition the worst possible object in Judaism—retains some of its charming if pathetic character. Berekhiah immediately establishes that the statue is absolutely an idol, a "no-god" (*lo elohim*) in the vocabulary of the prophets. A rich man nonetheless wants to make it his god because of its beauty, "drawn and painted in vermilion" (Jer. 22:14; Ezek. 23:14), another derogatory description of idols by the prophets; and, as in Avianus, a second man wants it to adorn a tomb. At this, the idol starts to cry and begs the crafts-man to sell him to the man who will "fear" and "worship" him, and perversely he uses phrases to seduce the craftsman that in the bible apply to God's relationship with His people: "[I am] the clay, and you are the potter" (Isa. 64:7) and "Do not subject me to the will of my foes" (Ps. 27:12). His final plea is that if his maker sells him to the idol-worshipper, "everyone in the Isles ('iim) will agree and bow down to the work of your hands."[100] Finally, the craftsman gives in and sells him to the Englishman who will turn him from a no-god into a god.

The fable appears to be yet another condemnation of the English for their idolatry, Christians and Jews alike. Possibly Berekhiah even literally means to suggest idols common to Christians and Jews like the aforemen-tioned arm of St. Osbert and other religious articles pawned to Jews, or Christian religious items produced by Jewish metalworkers.[101] The epimy-thium, however, vindicates the idol's obsequious personality by approving of flattering the powerful. Quoting passages from the Talmud, Berekhiah affirms that a "great sage" said, discussing Jacob's flattery of Esau, that "it is permissible to flatter the evil in this world." Another sage, referring to Joseph's brothers bowing to him, recommended the "popular saying": "bow down to the fox in his day of power!"[102]

In this extraordinary conclusion, Berekhiah refers to the unvoiced underlying theme of the precarious relations between Jacob, the meta-phor for the Jews, and his brother Esau, the metaphor for the Romans and then the Christians. In doing so, however, he projects an ambiguous

Jewish identity back onto the abject idol who flatters his powerful seller. Although it lacks a certain coherence as a Jewish "Fox Fable," the tale operates on an allegorical level that shows Berekhiah's consideration of his own relationship to the work of "Esau," his Latin sources, and by extension the suppressed, even if absurd, idol of Bacchus from Avianus's original text. For Berekhiah, this is the moment to assess his practice of translating the words of the Roman "idolators" into the "holy language." While the transformation from the Latin works to the full Hebrew text is in a sense thoroughgoing, filled with biblical and rabbinic material and characterized as a prophetic message, the genre of the fables and even the epimythia in many cases remain much the same. Berekhiah's Bacchus is, then, in addition to the no-god of the prophets, the allegorized no-god or *integumentum* of the Latin medieval poets, a symbol of drunkenness and transgression distantly derived from Ovid's havoc-wreaking trickster. Berekhiah's English contemporary, the so-called "Third Vatican Mythographer," attributes a wide range of meanings to Bacchus, most having to do with wine; he also, however, draws a connection between Bacchus and poetry, both because "poems merit eternity" like the ivy consecrated to the pagan god and because "like the Bacchae, poets are insane."[103] Bacchus's trace in Berekhiah's fable is the sign of his own transgressive literary practices within his Hebrew poem: while he has recuperated for Jacob the multiplicity of lost Talmudic "Fox Fables" recited by Bar Kappara or R. Meir, he has also flattered Esau for his Latin poetic art.

Berekhiah ha-Nakdan is a unique medieval Jewish author both in his fury toward his peers together with their oppressors, and in his attraction to and transformative rejection of Latin in his Hebrew poetic adaptations. He should be considered, despite his situation within a marginalized community, a writer of the Angevin historical moment. Berekhiah's choice of genres, including his lapidary text, are those on the cutting edge of Anglo-Latin and Anglo-French literature revived from ancient sources. His translation of beast fables from the popular prose *Romulus* into moral and pedagogical poetry aligns his authorship with his contemporaries Marie de France and Alexander Nequam. By shaping Adelard's *Natural Questions* into his own discourse of natural science, he joins another celebrated intellectual figure, Henry II's tutor William of Conches, who likewise uses the earlier text to claim a new authority in his *Dragmaticon*. Berekhiah's voices resound from his brilliant and damning reinvention, the *Fox Fables*, as the "prophet" that his son Elijah called him, enraged by the entire society around him, but also as a master of cultural adaptation and appropriation. For Berekhiah the fox, Latin was always there to be stolen.

# PLEASURES AND DANGERS
# OF CONVERSION

*Joseph and Aseneth*

The previous three chapters consider primarily how medieval Jewish readers and writers reconceived ancient texts in order to negotiate the place of Jews within a Christian European society. In the cases of *Sefer Yosippon*'s reception of Josephus's *Jewish War* and Virgil's *Aeneid* and Berekhiah ha-Nakdan's adaptation of the Aesopic fables of Phaedrus and Avianus, the medieval Hebrew text represents an intervention in the original classical texts' transmission and translation within the Christian tradition. By reappropriating the Greek Jewish Josephus from the patristic *Hegesippus* or subverting the Greek Aesopic corpus from Latin medieval models, the Jewish translators claimed these uncanonical texts for a medieval Hebrew tradition that used them to engage their Latin counterparts over some of the crucial ideas of their time. Whether through the understanding of martyrdom in Josephus, the emergence of empire in Virgil, or more prosaically, the scientific paradigms derived from Cicero and Macrobius in Adelard of Bath's work, the Hebrew texts argue for a superiority of language and a Jewish narrative of authenticity that asserts the priority of the translation over the translated "original."

The study returns at this point to the responses of Christians to texts like the Hebrew *Yosippon* that they believed were newly discovered witnesses to the Second Temple era. While the cultural and intellectual focus so far has been on the twelfth-century Angevin sphere, it moves now to mid-thirteenth-century England and translation from "originally" Greek texts to Latin. Each of the next two chapters deals with a well-known text from the Old Testament pseudepigrapha: a body of ancient Jewish writings written in Hebrew or Greek, many of which survived only for Christians. The "romance" *Joseph and Aseneth*, about the marriage of the patriarch to his Egyptian wife, was probably composed in the mid-first century in Egypt. *The Testaments of the Twelve Patriarchs* may have been completed around the same time, although the latter text's dating varies by many centuries. Modern scholars link these two texts written by Hellenic Jews as part of a larger late antique tradition of moral narratives about Joseph, and medieval scholars linked them as well in their manuscripts. The celebrated theologian and scientist Robert Grosseteste made the first translation of the *Testaments* from Greek to Latin in 1242, and a member of his circle translated *Joseph and Aseneth*. Soon after, the encyclopedist Vincent of Beauvais presented versions of the two texts together in the *Speculum Historiale*. The circumstances of these thirteenth-century Latin translations reflect contemporary Christian–Jewish relations during the reign of Henry III. An ever-worsening time for the English Jewish community economically and politically, the period also saw a renewed interest in Hebrew learning among Christian scholars, including Grosseteste himself. The remarkable group of Hebrew Bible manuscripts with interlinear translations and glosses in Latin witnesses this trend. Associated in part with Grosseteste and his circle, these copies made by Jewish scribes for Christian students attest to a history of collaboration as well as antagonism that came to an end soon after.[1] At around the same time, the English recovery of two Greek Jewish texts long lost to European Jewish readers ironically reconfigured them within a Christian discourse about contemporary Jews. Two of the major themes of *Joseph and Aseneth*—conversion and female agency— provided its readers with an immediate connection to relations between Christians and Jews.

The Jewish story of *Joseph and Aseneth* is a text of the Diaspora in Egypt that imagines the circumstances of the marriage of Joseph, then second in command to Pharaoh, to the Egyptian beauty Aseneth. The daughter of the Egyptian priest of Heliopolis Pentephres. she begins an immediate, radical, and erotic conversion from the moment she sees Joseph, a man desired by all. After throwing away her idols and then praying and mortifying her body for seven days, she is visited by a heavenly messenger who affirms her mystical transformation at length; Joseph then returns, and they are married by their lord Pharaoh. Scholars differ widely as to the purpose of this text, although most reject the notion that it was originally intended to persuade non-Jews to convert; some suggest that the text advocates full inclusion of proselytes and of intermarriages with gentiles who convert within Jewish communities.[2] In the Middle Ages, it becomes a narrative of its heroine's conversion to Christianity. In the era following the Crusades, however, Jewish conversion was a deadly topic.

## Violent Resistance

According to the chroniclers of the 1096 persecutions, the Jews who were faced with a choice between survival and conversion rejected Christianity with a perfectly Jewish death. The martyrs gave voice to a certainty that they would enter the "realm of the saints—Rabbi Akiva and his companions, pillars of the universe, who were killed in witness to his Name."[3] The writers vilified every aspect of what they characterized as forcible conversions: at Regensburg, in the words of Solomon bar Simson, "the people of the city forced them into the river and then the enemy made an evil sign over the water, vertical and horizontal [a cross]." The so-called converts in these cases continued to observe Rabbinic Law, only going to church with "coercion." Solomon adds that "the Gentiles themselves knew they had not converted out of conviction but rather in fear of the errant ones, and that the Jews did not believe in the object of their reverence but remained steadfast in their reverence for the Lord."[4] Conversion in the chronicles is strictly a performance with no interior religious dimension: the Jews go through the motions of being Christian with so little display of fervor that the Christians themselves understand that nothing has changed. The crusaders, in effect, can conquer territory including Jerusalem—the "holy city"—but not Jewish believers.

The chronicles emphasize heroic resistance to Christianity by women as spectacularly as men. Perhaps the best-known martyr of 1096 is Rachel of Mainz, who sacrifices her four children rather than let "the uncircumcised ones come and seize them alive and raise them in their ways of error."[5] While her two sons offer some resistance, Rachel's daughters sharpen the ritual knife themselves and offer their throats to her in rejection of an involuntary conversion. As she mourns over her children, Rachel is killed by the crusaders in a scene that recalls the martyrdom of "that other righteous woman and her seven sons," all victims of a pagan ruler, who die rather than bow to an idol.[6] Solomon also includes this account of women martyrs being led to a church for forced baptism: "When they arrived at the temple of their pagan cult, the women refused to enter the edifice of idolatry. . . . When the errant ones saw that the women stood firm . . . they fell upon them with their axes and smote them. Thus the saintly women were slain in sanctification of God's name."[7] Ephraim of Bonn writes in the Second Crusade chronicle *Sefer Zekhirah* that "Gutalda, of blessed memory, was seized . . . but she refused to be profaned with the bitter, accursed water. She sanctified the Holy Name and drowned herself. . . . May God remember her for good, as he recalls the matriarchs Rachel and Leah."[8] The instrument of conversion itself becomes her weapon.

The Crusade literature also generated some striking if obscure legends about both martyrdom and conversion by sons of prominent sages. These stories are sometimes revealing in terms of gender among other things. One such account describes an incident that evidently took place in thirteenth-century England, the tragic story of the son of R. Moses "the Mighty of the World" of London.[9] The young man, R. Yom Tov, hangs himself with a belt. The evening before the burial, R. Moses sees his son in a vision: he is a type of martyr now living in a "Great Light" that recalls *Yosippon*'s heroic ending and the chronicles of the First Crusade. He had killed himself because a demon had appeared waving a cross in front of him, pressuring him to convert. An even more baroque tale appears in a commentary on a *piyyut* composed by R. Gershom Me'or ha-Golah, whose son apparently did convert. One Yom Kippur, the legend recounts, R. Gershom's son threw the book in his hand to the ground and went off to become a Christian; he subsequently becomes pope. R. Gershom's wife then reveals that she had once been raped by a knight and had bitten off part of his ear, an encounter that produced this highly successful Christian. Having seen the preserved piece of ear, R. Gershom is reassured that such an evil man could not be his son.[10] This narrative, like the first, reveals a primary anxiety about the vulnerability of young Torah scholars to conversion; yet it also features a woman who, although fiercely defiant toward Christianity, is fated to play an ambiguous role.[11] In an account that emphasizes her sexuality as well as martial skills, she is the vessel of a convert.

The work of recent scholars has tended to assess this kind of literature as primarily reflecting the survivors' desires and fears, conversion foremost among them as something that demanded complete repression.[12] There were among them, nevertheless, willing converts. Most of the sources about conversion are difficult to interpret, from rabbinic responsa to the tosafists' comments on the Talmud. The picture that emerges is that the rabbinic authorities of Ashkenaz tried to be as lenient as possible to both coerced and voluntary converts since their goal was to avoid any restriction that could prevent an apostate's speedy reversion. R. Gershom and Rashi to this end emphasize the principle that an apostate is a "sinning Jew" who nevertheless keeps a "Jewish identity."[13] David Malkiel notes that Rashi and others "accept the traditional Jewish assumption that women who chose to apostatize do so for romantic or erotic reasons," an aspect of the connection between sexual desire and idolatry.[14] While the surviving documents suggest that few medieval Jewish women actually ran off with Christian lovers, this "assumption" in its negative way plays into a larger set of medieval European cultural ideas about women's religious conversions. Steven Kruger, within a larger discussion of Jewish corporeality, considers the early thirteenth-century Cistercian writer Caesarius of Heisterbach's narratives of "sexually attractive" Jewish women who seduce clerks but in the end receive baptism; in one story the clerk and his newly converted wife join the Cistercian Order. Here as with the rabbis, an erotic current runs through the process of conversion.[15] For Christian vernacular poets, the fantasy of religious conversion reached full expression in crusader romances. *Joseph and Aseneth*, likewise, retells the same story of an erotic change of faith for its new audience.

The issue of conversion from another religion to Judaism went through vast conceptual changes between the writing of *Joseph and Aseneth* and the Middle Ages. Rami Reiner and Shaye Cohen have both charted the medieval rabbinic controversies over the status of proselytes, from the negative view of Rashi, who saw them as a potential danger to the community, to the later positive approach of Rabbi Isaac of Dampierre and his disciples in favor of full acceptance of any Christian so ideologically committed to a more difficult life.[16] One commentary in the Tosafot from the latter school goes so far as to cite a Talmudic claim that the Jews were dispersed among other peoples for the purpose of encouraging conversion.[17] Whatever else French and English Jewish readers of the twelfth and thirteenth centuries thought about converts to Judaism, however, the figure of Aseneth no longer provided an ideal case for thinking about the issue. While some midrashic texts cite her as a virtuous convert, the Jewish Aseneth tradition, as opposed to the lost Hellenic fiction, tends to imagine Joseph's wife as already a Hebrew and a close relative in no need of conversion. Here she the unfortunate daughter of Dinah and Shechem, whom Jacob himself saves from his sons when they massacre her father and his family; through various means, she is brought to Egypt where she eventually meets her uncle/husband.[18] This narrative of purity would presumably appeal to medieval communities concerned with condemning or rescuing apostates more than celebrating proselytes.

## Monastic Readings

If the Jews reacted to the problem of apostasy with new narratives of martyrdom that stressed a continuity from the fall of the Second Temple to Rabbi Akiva to the current day, Christians too needed to account for the Jews' inexplicable behavior. From the Christian perspective, the problem of Jewish conversion in the era of the Crusades and after—successful or not—demanded a new look at some old texts. The cultural world of one English manuscript from the Benedictine monastery of Christ's Church Canterbury addresses some of these issues. Written and compiled in the decades preceding the expulsion of the Jews in 1290, it includes a wide-ranging collection of Old and New Testament apocryphal texts and apocalyptic material.[19] The works, all in Latin versions, besides *Joseph and Aseneth* (called *Liber de Aseneth*) include the ever-popular *Vindicta Salvatoris* (*Vengeance of the Savior*), the early medieval reimagining of the fall of Jerusalem; the even more popular Pseudo-Augustine sermon on the Jews, the *Life of Adam and Eve*; and the so-called *Infancy Gospels of Matthew* and *Thomas*. These texts are followed in the manuscript by the *Revelations of the Pseudo-Methodius on the Beginning and End of the World* and a series of letters, also compiled in Matthew Paris's *Chronica Majora*, to and from various European princes and clerics about the apocalyptic significance of the Mongol invasion of 1241.

Pseudo-Augustine's sermon on the Jews begins with an enduring challenge: "I call upon you, O Jews, who even today still deny the son of God. Was it not your voice, when you saw the miracles he performed, which said "How long will you keep us in suspense? If you are the Christ tell us plainly."[20] So asks one of the most popular and forceful statements throughout the Middle Ages on the Jews' refusal to accept "their own" prophecies concerning Jesus as the long-awaited Messiah. A restatement of the evidence from the prophets, beginning with Isaiah and Jeremiah, interspersed with direct rebukes to the Jews, the text's importance lies in its historical scope. Whatever its specific context, it emphasizes the absolute continuity of the Jews of Jesus's day with current-day Jews as eternal misreaders of their own scripture who stubbornly resist conversion—and who will continue to do so until the end of days. Later, before turning to various "gentile" prophecies, the sermon warns: "Is this not sufficient, O Jews? Are not so many witnesses and testimonies of your law and your people enough? But perhaps you will have the impudence to dare to say that another people or nation should bear witness to Christ? To this he himself answers you, 'I was sent only for the sheep who have strayed from the house of Israel.'"[21] The manuscript represents a monastic anthologist's attempt to use these disparate legendary narratives to respond to the challenge posed by the Pseudo-Augustine sermon on the refusal of Jews to convert. If the "spectral" Jews—to use Kruger's term— that this text both invents and calls upon necessarily remain silent faced with the true sense of Hebrew prophecies, the compiler speaks for the "lost" Jews of his own time by supplying other possible narratives of conversion from traditions outside the authority of canonical scripture. In the case of *Joseph and Aseneth* (hereafter *Aseneth*), translated from Greek to Latin in the late twelfth century, most likely at Canterbury itself, the compiler engages with the post-Crusade "romance" representations of religious conversion found in contemporary Anglo-Norman *chansons de geste* and Latin monastic histories alike. In *Aseneth*, as in a *chanson de geste* like *Fierabras*, the desirable heroine's overwhelming passion for a physically beautiful man is a sign of the inner perfection of her spiritual ascent.

## Jewish Textual Culture

In the century following the First Crusade, Brigitte Bedos-Rezak has argued, monastic writers had become increasingly aware of postbiblical Jewish writings and reacted with hostility to the perceived threat of Jewish textuality to their own hermeneutic and "scribal monopoly."[22] In response to this more sophisticated understanding of Jewish culture and to a crusader ideology that emphasized an eschatological interpretation of the Christian conquest of the Holy Land, monks were forced to confront the inadequacy of the traditional Augustinian view of Jews as living ruins of Old Testament practice, continuing in their ancient errors more or less benignly until the end of days. Evidence of the Jews' dynamic textual culture, epitomized by the Talmud, as well as more generically familiar works of biblical commentary, argued instead that their refusal to convert was based not on a blind lack of eschatological understanding but rather on an alternate, implicitly anti-Christian narrative. In England, the enthusiastic twelfth-century reception of Petrus Alfonsi's *Dialogue against the Jews* introduced clerical thinkers to the concept of the Talmud and other rabbinic literature as the source of Jewish error and malevolence.[23] This work, by a Jewish convert to Christianity, reinvigorated a formal genre of polemics against English Jews. Such pieces were penned by, among others, Bartholomew of Exeter, Peter of Cornwall, and, with the most vehemence, Peter of Blois.[24] Moreover, the *Dialogue* gained an even wider circulation later in the thirteenth century when Vincent of Beauvais included a much-abridged version in his *Speculum Historiale*.[25]

Alfonsi's *Dialogue* takes the form of a debate between the Christian author "Peter" and his former Jewish self "Moses"; in his mockery of the Jews' "doctores," the rabbinic sages, Peter reveals a previously little-known range of Jewish postbiblical texts and hermeneutic strategies to his Christian audience. He is at pains to charge the Jews not only with

replacing the Torah with the falsehoods of the Talmud and reading biblical prophecies according to the letter rather than the spirit, but with stubbornly resisting the implications of their own historical narrative. Over
the Jew's weak objections, Peter lectures Moses that the Second Temple
was destroyed and the Jews dispersed among the nations because of the
Jewish leaders' depraved killing of Jesus, whom they knew to be the Son
of God, forty years earlier; ever since, the rabbis have distorted textual
sources in order to conceal or justify the murder. In the second chapter
of the *Dialogue* Peter systematically forecloses any alternate Jewish interpretations of exile from Jerusalem and indeed subordinates all Jewish legends to the demands of Christian eschatology; perhaps the most striking
example of Peter's rewriting of a Jewish text is his claim that the ten rabbinic martyrs of the famous medieval midrash were killed as repayment
for Jesus's death rather than, as the legend claims, as atonement for the
kidnapping of Joseph by his ten brothers.[26] The only possibility for Jewish
redemption from exile lies not in a future messianic age, but in conversion
to Christianity. The *Dialogue* concludes with Moses admitting defeat and
Peter anticipating his opponent-self's baptism.

The accusations that Petrus levels at the Talmud reappear not only in
subsequent polemics, but in the later accusations brought by the convert
Nicholas Donin in Paris in 1239, which Pope Gregory IX included in
apostolic letters sent to the archbishops and kings of France, England, and
Spain ordering them to seize all Jewish books on the first Shabbat during
Lent.[27] Two years after Donin's "disputation" with four rabbis on the
meaning of various Talmudic passages together with Rashi's commentaries in 1240, copies of the Talmud were publicly burned in Paris. In England, these ideas echo in the peculiar order given by Henry III upon the
death of the prominent Jewish financier David of Oxford in 1244 that his
large personal library be examined for any book found to be "against the
law of the Christians or the Jews."[28] In this formulation, Jewish postbiblical texts become a violation not only of the Christian narrative that they
actively deny, but also of the authentically "Jewish" role within Christianity, limited solely to the Hebrew Bible.

This new hostility to Jewish textual culture coincided in mid-thirteenth-
century England with King Henry III's unusually keen interest in Jewish conversion. Robert Stacey, in his exploration of the "social reality"
of conversion, adheres to Jeremy Cohen's thesis of an intellectual shift

brought about by the Franciscan and Dominican friars' theological justifications of converting Jews and Muslims, yet also stresses the driving role of the crown in the English context.[29] In 1232 Henry III founded the London *Domus Conversorum* to house, finance, and reeducate converts, and later in his reign provided Jews with a strong incentive to convert in the form of disastrously high taxation.[30] Nevertheless, as Stacey points out, King Henry's brutal financial policies and personal investment in new Christians, including sponsoring converts in the royal household, did not succeed in producing his desired rates of conversion. While Stacey's figures allow for a possible peak of three hundred converts out of a Jewish community of three thousand during the 1240s–50s, this number falls short of the universal response demanded by a missionizing theological vision that, influenced by the friars, imagined conversion as the sign of an imminent messianic age.[31] Among English Jews, however, the king's policies principally had the effect of fracturing traditional communal and familial structures, pitting the newly baptized Richards, Johns, and Julianas against those who embodied the errors that they had rejected. Joan Greatrex has documented that by 1255, Henry III had sponsored the housing of some 150 converts, often torn away from their families, at around 125 different monasteries and convents of all orders. Since both Henry's and his son Edward I's payments of corrodies to these institutions were irregular, the converts were also frequently shuttled around from abbey to abbey.[32]

## Conversion/Madness

Robert Grosseteste's exegetical writings are exemplary of the limits that Christian discourse about Jews and conversion had reached by the thirteenth century. In *De cessatione legalium* (*On the Cessation of the Ritual Torah*), Grosseteste sets out to prove that the practice of Jewish law after the Incarnation is both mortal sin and heresy. Running through the standard prooftexts from earlier polemics to show that Jesus had fulfilled all of the Jewish messianic prophecies, Grosseteste argues that the *legalia* of the Torah are merely "signs and shadows" of Christ's future passion.[33] Although the recent editors of *De cessatione legalium* argue forcefully that Grosseteste produced this work entirely within an "academic context" and not in order to engage in debate with English Jews or lend support to the king's *Domus Conversorum*, the author himself gestures toward contemporary "infideles Judei" who do in fact continue to observe the laws and condemns their belief in a future messiah.[34] Moreover, Grosseteste's "academic" concerns clearly resonate with his political actions, especially, as Richard Southern has suggested, exhorting Simon de Montfort to expel the Jews from Leicester in 1231 while he was archdeacon.[35] In his well-known letter of the same year, Grosseteste further urges Montfort's great-aunt, the Countess of Winchester, to force the displaced Jews from her property in the eastern suburbs of the town unless they stopped oppressing Christians with usury and agreed to work the land.[36] In this text, Grosseteste, like Petrus Alfonsi, turns to the fall of Jerusalem as the primary narrative that defines the Jews' role: because of the murder of Christ, Titus and Vespasian destroyed Jerusalem, and subsequently, the Jews have been scattered "from their own home" to live as fearful captives throughout various nations until the end of days, when they will be converted and freed.[37] Grosseteste's argument for immediate expulsion is, then, a singularly problematic application of the Augustinian idea of "Jewish witness" in its confrontation with the actual Jews living under his jurisdiction: citing Augustine's exegesis of Psalm 58:12 ("slay them not, lest my people forget"), he forbids the killing of Jews, who in theory remain theologically useful, while at the same time he views Jewish conversion as a consequence of the end of history rather than as a current possibility or even a desire.[38]

Grossesteste's strident letter, with its call for a new exile of Jews, evokes the specific nexus of interpretations of the historical fall of Jerusalem and its relation to Europe addressed in the first chapter. His language evokes *Hegesippus*, which assigns the meaning of Jewish Diaspora to Jesus "whose death is the destruction of the Jews," as well as the immensely influential *Vengeance of the Savior*, which in turn reimagines the bloody end of Jerusalem as a lurid fantasy of European conversion.[39] The Jews confess to killing the Messiah and are punished with exile and slavery. In this strand of historical imagination, the Jews become defined by their refusal to convert even as the Roman Empire miraculously and universally shifts to Christianity.

Among Grossesteste's English predecessors and contemporaries, nevertheless, were monastic chroniclers who found such narrative models entirely inadequate to confront the realities of local anti-Jewish violence and forced conversions. Recounting episodes in which contemporary Jews were baptized by coercion, these writers evidently feared losing their own traditional understanding of the Jews' central hermeneutic and eschato-logical roles. The conversion of Jews becomes, in their accounts, a fraught issue in precisely the way figured by the Pseudo-Augustine sermon: it is both a desire, an object of ardent polemic, and yet at the same time an event coolly projected beyond history. The monastic chroniclers attempt to draw connections, therefore, between the actual "historical" Jews in their midst and the eschatological Jews who will fulfill their role at the end of days.

The chroniclers' narratives of the massacre at York in 1190 speak to their period's new understandings of martyrdom; these monks themselves, however, were actually more interested in conversion as the other side of the story. William of Newburgh's famous account of the events at York during Richard I's preparations for the Third Crusade emphasizes above all the breakdown of the logic of conversion and the ensuing confusion of Jewish and Christian martyrdoms.[40] William foreshadows the bloody event itself with the story of Benedict (*Baruch*), a prominent York money-lender wounded and forced to convert when he was caught in the London anti-Jewish riots following the king's coronation in 1189. Brought before the king and asked whether he was a Christian, Benedict asserted that although he had been baptized by force, he had always been a Jew in his soul (*animo semper fuisse Judaeum*), which is how he wanted to die. In describing this episode, William elaborately plays on the Jew's Latinized name, emphasizing the absolute opposition between Benedict's interior beliefs and his insubstantial words, the ethereal and transgressive product of violence: "He was truly Bene-dictus, having been compelled to receive Christian baptism without accepting what was right in his heart, but only beating the air with the empty confession of his voice" ("Benedictus vero ille, lavacrum Christianum coactus acceperat, corde quidem non credens ad justitiam sed inani tantum oris confessione aerem verberans").[41] As William finally comments, he became a Christian only long enough to die an apostate.

The chronicler's climactic narrative of the slaughter of the York Jews presents an even more vexed sense of conversion and martyrdom. For William, the breakdown comes when the scholar Yom Tov urges his fellow

Jews trapped in the tower of York castle to commit ritual suicide, preferring a glorious death to a most foul life in the hands of impious enemies.[42] The learned canon's polemical use of Josephus's *Jewish War*, imagining Yom Tov as a second Eleazer ben Yair speaking at Masada, underscores his familiarity with the Latin interpretations of the text that emphasize the Jews' punishment for their refusal to convert.[43] William immediately moves from his astonishment at the Jews' "ancient superstition," their killing their own wives and children—which he characterizes as madness (*vesania*)—to his outrage at the York attackers' betrayal of those Jews who, resisting their leader's words, had asked to receive baptism. To these Jews, William also assigns a speech directed to their attackers on the logic of conversion, whereby they proclaim that they had been spared from the murderous *vesania* of their former "brothers" in order to abandon their old rites and join the *ecclesia Christi* as one with their new brothers. Despite their tearful plea, they nonetheless fall into the cruel hands of "Richard, rightly called Mala-Bestia" and his followers. Of these Jews, killed while "all the while begging to convert," William writes: "If there was no falsehood in their request for holy baptism, they were in no way robbed of its effect, but baptized in their own blood."[44] The canon hence takes it upon himself as a historian to supersede the Jewish martyrdom, which he provides with its own "irrational" voice, with a truly Christian martyrdom, dependent, however, upon the absolutely unknowable and doubtful intentions of the dead.

In this recuperative move, William acknowledges the hermeneutic limits of the fall of Jerusalem narrative, in all of its various Christianizing Latin forms, as a paradigm of Jewish–Christian relations.[45] *Vesania*—insanity—is the term William uses earlier in the *Historia* to characterize the Jews' murder of their savior, the event that led to their destruction by the Romans and to the replacement in the Holy Land of the "carnal seed of Abraham" with the true Christian seed.[46] In his *kinnah* concerning the York Massacre, the poet Menachem ben Jacob of Worms reciprocally characterizes the Christians' actions as insane, by reference to the destruction of the Temple:

> Behold O Lord! They would scale the heavens if they could,
> Even as they tore down the curtain in your house, while reveling
>    in blasphemy;

Raving like madmen, they intended evil against you;
They imagined devices which they were powerless to fulfill.

The word Menachem uses for the Christians' madness, *yitholelu*, is taken
from Jeremiah 51:7, where it already implies God's imminent vengeance
against the "nations." [47]

In the same vein, another Augustinian canon, Thomas Wykes,
laments in his chronicle the later murders and forced conversions of
Jews in London, Canterbury, and elsewhere during the baronial wars
of the 1260s. The only chronicler to fervently support the royal cause,
Wykes finds in the abuse of the Jews another source of polemic against
the erstwhile crusader Simon de Montfort and his allies.[48] Outdo-
ing William of Newburgh in pathos, Wykes lingers over descriptions
of slaughtered women and especially children—"screaming in their
cradles, hanging from their mothers' breasts"—yet unlike his fellow
canon, he has no vocabulary with which to redefine this carnage as
martyrdom.[49] For Wykes, William's Jewish *vesania* has now become the
Christian baronial forces' own violence, especially examples like John
Fitz John's murder of Kok f. Abraham, the best-known Jew in London, "with his own hands." Against this apocalyptic backdrop, Wykes
argues that the Jews, "created in God's image," will eventually convert,
citing the Pauline reading of Isaiah 10 that at the end of the world, the
remnant of Israel will be saved; but he also emphasizes the spiritual
danger to those who falsely receive baptism. The frenzy (*vesania*) of
the attacks having passed, he writes, the Jews returned to their nonbe-
lief, renouncing Christianity, to the worse end that they would live in
sin and die as apostates.[50] In Wykes's history, *vesania*, for William of
Newburgh the very essence of Jewish psychology, has not only become
a "Christian" trait but is also the word that best describes the Jewish
experience of insincere conversion.

Robert Stacey has shown that apostasy became a concern of both the
church and crown following the forced conversions, especially of Jewish
women, during the baronial wars and then later conversions occasioned
by Edward I's measures against Jewish moneylending.[51] The Franciscan
archbishop John Pecham took a special interest in Jews who had relapsed,
energetically if unsuccessfully prosecuting thirteen supposed apostates,
eleven of whom were women, in 1281–82 and consistently complaining to

the king about the problem of apostasy in general. Yet, as F. D. Logan has argued, the circumstances of the apostates' supposed original "conversions" were so murky that the charges against them were virtually impossible to prove to juries; in the exemplary case of Swetecote, wife of Moses de Horndon, an enemy alleged that she had converted during the baronial wars, but she countered that she had in fact never been baptized.[52] The authorities' heightened concern about such cases is likewise reflected in Pope Honorius IV's bull of 1286 to Pecham and his clergy, complaining that in England "the Jews try to attract to their sect not only faithful Christians but, by means of inducements, they even approach those who have become converts to Christianity. Indeed they dwell with them in the very parishes where they have been baptized, thus scandalizing the faithful and bringing contumely upon the Christian faith. These people are then sent to other places, where they are unknown, and there they openly revert to Judaism."[53] Stacey concludes that the final implications of apostasy, that no Jewish conversion could be fully trusted—together with the overall failure of Jews to convert to Christianity—helped to justify the 1290 expulsion.[54]

The extraordinary letters that the convert Alice of Worcester sent via her son to both King Edward I and Chancellor Robert Burnell, pleading for monastic charity in the 1270s, offer a trace of how biblical exegesis itself could mold the former Jews' precarious identity. Writing to Burnell, who was also bishop of Bath and Wells, after one priory at Coventry refused to support her, Alice refers to herself as "sua captiva" and compares herself first to the wandering exile Hagar and then to the penitent Mary Magdalene, recipient of God's "maxima misericordia."[55] This typological identification of Hagar with Mary Magdalene positions Alice as a figure of the desert, whether representative of the solitude of unbelief or of the liminality of mystical experience.[56] In the Pauline exegesis of Genesis 21, Hagar, mother of Ishmael, personifies an enslaved Jerusalem and the Old Testament itself, handmaiden to the New. Grosseteste himself summarizes this tradition of reading the Hebrew Hagar as "the stranger" (*ha-ger*) in his *Commentary on Galatians*, 4:

> Since the old law bore children into slavery, it is fittingly signified by the handmaid. It follows also that the meaning of the handmaid's name indicates the slavery of the law: "Agar" is therefore interpreted as "being

a stranger" or "exile," that is, "dwelling in a foreign land" or "passing through"; furthermore, a slave is born without an inheritance and cannot stay in his masters' home.[57]

Alice's fragment, by posing the distance between its two female exemplars, speaks to the insufficiency of exegesis to accommodate the idea of an authentic conversion. In one sense Jews can only exist in an extreme exteriority, as slaves and exiles, Hagar to the Christians' Sarah; their true conversion, however, entails an acceptance of the radically interior, contemplative ideal of Mary Magdalene. Alice's reference to Hagar, moreover, suggests as well a different captive Jerusalem, the city actually held by the Muslims or "Agarenes" and the Christian desire for the Holy Land's conversion that is the subject of so much twelfth- and thirteenth-century imaginative literature.

## Apocrypha as Counternarrative

The Canterbury manuscript represents a different kind of clerical response to the problems of Jewish conversion that were exacerbated by the political and intellectual conditions of the mid-thirteenth century. Recorded among the "Books of Nicholas of Sandwich" in the great library catalog compiled under Prior Henry Estry (ca. 1300), the manuscript includes a partial list of contents: "Glose super Osee, Infancia Salvatoris, Evangelium Nazareorum, Asseneth, Methodius, Prophetia Hildegardi, Epistole Frederici Imperatoris," and "Libellus qualiter Tartari invaserunt regna Christianorum."[58] Unlike either the contemporary polemicists or monastic chroniclers, the compiler of this anthology locates the key to understanding conversion in the resources of fictional invention provided by the category of "apocryphal" texts. In his selections, the compiler attempts to construct a Christian eschatological narrative that responds to both the monastic understanding of a hostile but largely inaccessible Jewish, Hebrew textual tradition and the heightened violence against English Jews, including those in Canterbury itself. As in Grosseteste's theological epistle to the Countess of Winchester, the compiler positions the fall of Jerusalem and the end of the world as the origin and the end of the Jews in history: the brutal

*Vindicta Salvatoris* explains both the conversion of England to Christianity by analogy to pagan Rome and the presence of the exiled Jews
in Europe whom the Pseudo-Augustine sermon then attacks for their
stubborn disbelief; the famous apocalyptic scenario of Pseudo-Methodius claims that the prophets Enoch and Elijah will return during the
time of Antichrist to "lead the Jews into the church."[59] The compiler,
however, parts company from Grosseteste by juxtaposing between these
bookends a series of works of a broadly apologetic nature that address
the relationship between Judaism and Christianity and the dynamics of
conversion within historical time.

The *Infancy Gospel of Thomas*, for example, announces itself as a document of Jewish eyewitness of Jesus's violent pranks and miracles between
the ages of five and eight. Jesus himself in this text is characterized as a
type of convert, a Jew developing an inner awareness of Christian mercy
who also converts others when he restores Jewish children he has killed
with his curses back to life.[60] The *Life of Adam and Eve*, a rewritten
Christian version of a second-century CE Jewish text, traces the story of
the wood of the cross from Seth's journey to paradise to seek the "oil
of mercy" for his father to the three trees that he is told to plant in the
dead Adam's mouth to the miraculous uses of the trees by Moses, David,
and Solomon—including as a beam of the Temple; a prophetess named
Maximilla becomes the first Jewish convert *and* Christian martyr during
Solomon's reign when she names Jesus and is killed by a crowd of Jews.[61]
The story of *Aseneth* deals most directly with the theme of conversion,
recounting the mystical transformation of its Egyptian heroine from idolatry to Judaism.

Vincent of Beauvais's theoretical approach to the Apocrypha provides
insight into the Canterbury monk's method. The texts that he selected
for his encyclopedia, Vincent emphasizes, are "neither true nor false"; he
includes them so that the discerning reader of his polyvocal work can benefit from the good ones.[62] For the Canterbury compiler, apocryphal texts
also retain a useful flexibility between history and fiction. They are not
entirely authoritative but function rather as alternate narratives, potential missing pieces in a textual puzzle that allow him to reconfigure the
meaning of the Jews within the total body of Christian writing. Moreover,
unlike contemporary Jews' own texts, primarily the Talmud as described

and cited by Petrus Alfonsi and his successors, they are also transparent to Christian hermeneutics. Given the apocalyptic texts that occupy the final folios of the manuscript, the compiler's main concern seems to be with the eschatological role of the Jews in the present day, that is, with interpreting the history of the future through a dialogic method much like Vincent's.

The anthology, which was most likely produced in the 1250s or 1260s, demonstrates, therefore, the response of a kind of monastic textual study to the midcentury persecutions of English Jews by the king and the baronial forces. The Canterbury Cathedral Priory had previously had a long and mostly harmonious relationship with Canterbury's Jews. Notably, according to the house's chronicler Gervase of Canterbury, in 1187–88 local Jews had supported the monks of Christ's Church with both food and prayers during their struggle over obedience to Archbishop Baldwin.[63] Moreover, while the priory was in debt to Jewish moneylenders throughout the thirteenth century, it also acquired sizable landholdings by paying off landowners' debts to Jews in what Robin Mundill has called an "uneasy alliance of Jewish finance and local Christian financial aid."[64] While the Canterbury Jews had largely escaped earlier anti-Jewish violence, almost all the Jews in the city, according to the *Canterbury Chronicle*'s rather exaggerated claim, were killed or expelled by Gilbert de Clare's forces in 1264.[65] This is precisely the period when Canterbury's monks were studying the compilation including *Aseneth* and other anthologies like it. Nicholas of Sandwich, the manuscript's donor to the monastery's library, was a rather timid prior from 1244 to 1258, and then precentor very briefly in 1262 before being forced to resign.[66] His book collection shows his particular interest in biblical Apocrypha; in the library catalog compiled under Prior Estry he is listed as the donor of a "Liber Solomon" containing Ecclesiastes and the Song of Songs with other "Wisdom of Solomon" texts. He also had a copy of Grosseteste's Latin translation of the Greek *Testaments of the Twelve Patriarchs*.[67] The manuscript juxtaposes texts in such a way as to suggest Jewish conversion as a current and even urgent problem. The manuscript points to a compiler who, like William of Newburgh, understood the potential for hermeneutic and social crisis (*vesania*) in a narrative of the fall of Jerusalem that not only forecloses the possibility of Jewish conversion but also redefines the Jews' slaughterers as Christians.

### Aseneth's Perfect Conversion

In this regard, the most intriguing work that the compiler includes in his collection is *Aseneth*, a twelfth-century translation of a Greek text of the Diaspora in Egypt that recounts the marriage of Joseph to the Egyptian Aseneth.[68] Christoph Burchard traces the text's probable routes of monastic transmission from ninth-century Byzantium to twelfth-century England and notes that the translation, most likely produced at Canterbury itself, "may well be the first piece of Greek ever translated in Britain."[69] Nine copies of this Latin version survive, and it was widely disseminated in the later thirteenth century by Vincent of Beauvais, who included a condensed version as part of a larger narrative of Joseph's life and exegetical significance in the *Speculum Historiale*.[70] With *Aseneth*, the Canterbury compiler explores the murky intersection of eschatology with psychology in images of how a "real" or sincere conversion emerges—in this case, Aseneth's conversion from pagan idol-worship to her husband's Jewish faith. In its emphasis on the phenomenology of conversion, the *Book of Aseneth* provides a striking contrast to the *Vindicta Salvatoris*'s dominant narrative of Roman-Christian murder that, in its modern reenactments, as William of Newburgh feared, threatened to legitimate Jewish martyrdom. If indeed by the thirteenth century, the monks had heard rumors of the Jewish response to the persecutions in England and France, their worst fears would have been realized in the corpus of Hebrew poems celebrating martyrdom.[71] Moreover, the text's focus on Aseneth as a "type" of the convert is particularly suggestive given the roles that women play as passive victims in representations of both conversions and martyrdoms in contemporary Christian chronicles and legal documents.

In William of Newburgh's and Thomas Wykes's accounts, the main problem with the coerced conversions they describe is that, despite baptism, the Jewish subject remains inwardly Jewish, "a Jew at heart." The process of conversion as a whole therefore becomes unreadable—a matter, the chroniclers suspect, of performance rather than spiritual transformation. *Aseneth*, composed in a style similar to later Hellenic romances and often compared with Apuleius's tale of Cupid and Psyche, addresses the issue of conversion with a portrait of perfect penitential and mystical transformation.[72] Aseneth, the virgin daughter of the Egyptian priest

Putiphar, despises all men including the Pharaoh's agent Joseph, whom she dismisses as a foreign (*alienus*) slave, who moreover was caught in bed with his former master's wife. When she finally sees Joseph from her window, however, she is overcome by his beauty and undergoes an immediate physical experience of penance, trembling all over in her inner recognition of him as the "son of God" ("filius dei"). Although Joseph refuses to kiss Aseneth, a "strange woman" ("mulier alienagena") who blesses idols with her mouth, he holds her away by putting his right hand between her breasts, which "stood upright" ("mamille eius prominebant foras"). Joseph offers a prayer for Aseneth's conversion from "error to truth, death to life" ("ab errore in veritatem, de morte in vitam"), upon which she begins the spiritual ordeal of conversion, destroying her idols, fasting in sackcloth and ashes, and praying at length for divine forgiveness. Aseneth is finally visited by an angel who prepares her for her marriage to Joseph with a mystical initiation ceremony. The angel tells her that in her purity she may remove her veil, for "your head is like a young man's" ("capud tuum est sicut viri adolescentuli") and that "your name will no longer be Aseneth, but instead your name will be 'Refuge of Many'" ("Et nomen tuum non vocabitur ahuc Aseneth, sed erit nomen tuum Multis refugii") or "City of Refuge" ("civitas refugii"). When Joseph returns, he is in turn dazzled by Aseneth's new beauty, and they are joined in a scene of spiritual eroticism: "And Joseph said to Aseneth: 'blessed are you by the most high God and blessed is your name forever. . . . And now come close to me, virgin. Why do you stand so far from me?' And Joseph raised his hand and embraced Aseneth, and they kissed each other."

Aseneth's mystical conversion from Egyptian idolatry to Judaism is, in this Latin Christian version, identically a conversion to Christianity, culminating in marriage to the "son of God." Her temporary symbolic transformation of gender, from woman to young man, is similar to many early Christian saints' transcendence of femininity, including the converted "apostle" Mary Magdalene's assumption of aspects of male authority.[73] *Aseneth* is, above all, a document of interiority, with the heroine's lengthy soliloquies comprising a considerable part of the text. Lawrence Wills argues that in contrast to the late antique Greek romances, "the internalizing has become an end in itself . . . at issue is the inward transformation of the protagonist, and the despair results from the conviction on Aseneth's part that she could never be worthy."[74] Indeed, as many of its readers have noted, the narrative includes almost nothing about the cultic aspects of Judaism, or what Grosseteste called the "legalia" of the Torah, an attribute that particularly lends *Aseneth* to a Christian reading and would have made it attractive to medieval readers who imagined conversion as a spiritual and psychological process.

The interpretation of Joseph as a figural type of Jesus is a commonplace of patristic and medieval commentaries on Genesis, with Joseph's betrayal and sale prefiguring the passion; in Augustine's succinct formulation: " Just as Christ was killed by the Jews and handed over to the gentiles, so Joseph was handed over to the Egyptians by his brothers in order that the remnant of Israel would be saved."[75] The tradition of Joseph's beauty, central in Jewish commentaries and midrashim, is known in Christian literature from Jerome's translation of Jacob's blessing (Gen. 49:22) and his explanation of it in *Hebrew Questions on Genesis*: "O Joseph, I say, you who are so handsome that the whole throng of Egyptian girls looked down from the walls and towers and windows."[76] In the Christian context of *Aseneth*, Joseph's beauty—usually associated with the danger of temptation—represents a spiritual force that transcends the category of *alienus/aliena* by which the pagan Aseneth and Jewish Joseph initially characterize each other. Aseneth's virgin body functions in this narrative as a sign of inner truth, so that the radical physical changes of erotic arousal and penitential mortification transparently reflect her spiritual condition. Unlike the *vesania* that William of Newburgh saw at the heart of the Jews' stubbornness and murderous self-destruction, Aseneth's conversion epitomizes a nonrational, erotic frenzy that nevertheless leads from error to Jewish—or Christian—understanding.

In its position within a thirteenth-century manuscript that also includes the Pseudo-Augustine sermon, with its emphasis on the Jews' refusal to embrace the Christian meaning of the prophecies of Isaiah and Jeremiah and then convert, *Aseneth*'s lengthy descriptions of the interior experiences of a convert's penance are all the more striking since the conversion is literally to Judaism. While within this collection, *Aseneth* stands apart from the other apocryphal texts' greater or lesser emphasis on Jewish error, its portrayal of the romance of conversion is remarkably similar to that in many imaginative works of the Crusade era. *Aseneth*'s reception at Canterbury and popularity elsewhere in the Anglo-Norman world are linked to its intersection with monastic chroniclers' and *chansons de geste*'s narratives of the conversions of Muslim women to Christianity. Both Sharon Kinoshita and Suzanne Akbari emphasize the masculinizing agency of the so-called "enamored Muslim princess" who helps the crusaders to defeat their Saracen enemies.[77] In Orderic Vitalis's account of Bohemond of Antioch's imprisonment by the Danishmend, Melaz, the emir's daughter—out of admiration for the Franks' "true religion" and chivalry—devises a strategy that enables the crusaders to escape. Having led Bohemond to victory over the emir, Melaz proclaims her conversion: "I am a Christian. . . . For the religion of the Christians is holy and honorable, and your religion is full of vanities and polluted with filth"; after she is duly "regenerated by holy baptism," she is married to Bohemond's even "more handsome" cousin Roger.[78] Orderic underlines the eschatological importance of the romance by drawing a comparison between Melaz and an apocryphal Old Testament exemplar: "The prudent Melaz departed from her father's house with her servants and eunuchs and noble household, and . . . was devoutly associated with the Christians, as Bithia, Pharaoh's daughter, accompanied Moses and the Hebrews in safety when the Egyptians perished."[79]

In the twelfth-century *chansons de geste*, the sincerity of the Muslim princess's conversion functions similarly as a sign of the Christians' coherent eschatological narrative. In the *Chanson de Roland*, which glories in the violence of the forced conversions of the "pagans," Queen Bramimonde, as Kinoshita argues, must "actively choose her conversion, as [the emperor Charlemagne] puts it, 'par amur'": "They found for her the name of Juliana. / She is a Christian out of sheer conviction."[80] In other *chansons*, such as *Fierabras* and *La Prise d'Orange*, the Muslim princess converts through erotic desire for a "fetishized" handsome chivalric hero like Gui de Bourgogne or Guillaume d'Orange. Although there is no way of knowing if the Canterbury monks who were the earliest Western readers of *Aseneth* were familiar with any of these texts, they almost certainly did know one early thirteenth-century version of the story: the legend of St. Thomas of Canterbury's Muslim mother. Interpolated into a recension of the *Quadrilogus*, the lives of Becket compiled by Elias of Evesham, the legend recounts how Thomas's father Gilbert Becket is imprisoned and enslaved in the Holy Land by the Saracen prince Amiraldi, and how the prince's daughter falls in love with him and offers to convert to Christianity

if he agrees to marry her.[81] After Gilbert escapes, the princess follows
him to London, receives baptism, and—once he secures the approval of
the bishop of London and six other bishops—weds her beloved; during
their first night together, they conceive "the future archbishop of Canterbury and martyr."[82] The sharp ecclesiastical focus of this version of the
romance, in which a virtual council of bishops deems a conversion based
in both erotic and spiritual desire sincere, points to the interest of the
church in the underlying issues. Not only is such a conversion valid, but it
also actually bestows the charisma generated by the Crusades upon a saint
already elevated by martyrdom.

*Aseneth*'s medieval reception can thus be seen as a literary expression
of what Jeremy Cohen identifies as Christian theologians' "linkage" of
Jews and Muslims in the twelfth and thirteenth centuries as categories
of *infideles* whose conversions, under the influence of crusasder eschatology, become conceptually intertwined.[83] The Christian cultural fantasy at play in the various "enamored Muslim princess" narratives is, in
fact, much like the ideal that *Aseneth* represents in relation to the Jews.
As Ross Kraemer has argued of Aseneth's gender, her experience reflects
the same valorization of the "feminine" sufferer found in both Jewish
and Christian martyrologies.[84] Yet here, the figure of Aseneth inevitably
recalls and counters the representations of Jewish women as radically
passive and unknowable in the narratives of martyrdom and conversion
provided by the English chronicles and records of apostates, the numerous "Milkas" who had been baptized "Matildas" or "Julianas" in name
only. In reponse to these "false converts," Aseneth represents a refigur-
ing of the feminine as knowable, her authenticity voiced finally in a long
penitential psalm, after her marriage and the birth of her sons Manasseh
and Ephraim. In her transparent interiority, Aseneth becomes a kind of
allegory of the soul (*anima*), the otherwise unreadable, indefinite element
in accounts of Jewish conversion like the story of Benedict of York's
dissembling, for instance, where his "soul" remains Jewish. Aseneth's
"temporary" switch in gender from young woman to adolescent man,
as Kraemer suggests, "masculinizes," that is, affirms and transforms, the
traditional role of the feminine sufferer, signaling the inner "truth" of her
conversion from "other to self"; through mystic initiation by an angel
resembling Joseph, she too becomes an androgynous reflection of her
future husband's beauty.[85]

There is evidence that thirteenth-century monastic readers similarly interpreted Aseneth's gender as central to her place in the Christian narrative. In another manuscript from Christ's Church Canterbury, *Aseneth* is inserted between the Old and New Testament "fathers" of Isidore of Seville's *De ortu et obitu patrum*.[86] The text immediately follows the short accounts of Esther and Judith, two other sexually powerful Jewish heroines who similarly undergo a penitential "cleansing and self-abasement" before triumphing over a pagan enemy.[87] The placement suggests the monks' understanding of the role of women as "intertestamental" figures occupying the liminal space between the Old Testament prophets and the fulfillment of their prophecies in the New Testament. Isidore characterizes Judith in her glory over Holofernes as "superior to men" ("virorum praestantior"), a woman worthy of the title of "father."[88] Aseneth, with her androgynous transformation, reinforces the idea of a change from female to male as a perfect sign of the historical conversion from Judaism to Christianity represented by the intertestamental moment in the text. The compiler of the Canterbury manuscript was no doubt drawn as well to the eschatological dimension of Aseneth's "renaming" as "City of Refuge . . . because in you many nations will take shelter with the most high lord God" ("quoniam per te confugient gentes multe ad dominus deum altissimum"). Kraemer notes the similarities between Aseneth and the image of the rebuilt Jerusalem in Isaiah 58:

> Your ancient ruins will be rebuilt
> you will raise up the foundations of many generations;
> You will be called the repairer of the breach,
> the restorer of streets to live in.[89]

Within the sequence of texts in this manuscript, the association of Aseneth and the holy city serves a double function, both reinforcing the ultimate conversion and salvation of the Jews that later appears in Pseudo-Methodius's *Revelations*, and recuperating the historical fallen Jerusalem of the *Vindicta Salvatoris* with an allegorical "New Jerusalem" that encompasses Aseneth's "many nations."

The monastic chroniclers had reported the forced conversions of Jews as "frenzied" events that, by exposing the inner instability of both Christians and Jews, threatened the coherence of providential understanding.

The false convert, or Jewish apostate, becomes in these histories the figure for a current-day spiritual uncertainty that casts all interpretation into question. Rather than secular history, the Canterbury manuscript offers apocryphal texts that in their "fictive" status propose alternate if ultimately conflicting readings of the Jews' historical and allegorical roles. *Aseneth* responds to this historical situation with a counternarrative of an "authentic" conversion that plays out within the collection's eschatological frame. Here Alice of Worcester, self-described "conversa captiva," would no longer be suspended in the spiritual desert between Hagar and Mary Magdalene but welcomed within Aseneth's walls. As any number of English chronicles demonstrate, alas, the "Vengeance of the Savior" prevailed as the governing narrative, with the last word in 1290 as the monks dutifully record the Jews' new "permanent exile" from the island.[90]

# The Testaments of the Twelve Patriarchs in the Shadow of the Ten Lost Tribes

For the year 1242 in his *Chronica Majora*, the English historian Matthew Paris recounts Robert Grosseteste's translation of the apocryphal *Testaments of the Twelve Patriarchs*:

> At that time, Robert the Bishop of Lincoln, a man most expert in Latin and Greek, accurately translated *The Testaments of the Twelve Patriarchs* from Greek into Latin; it had been unknown for a long time and had been concealed due to the envy of the Jews on account of the clear prophecies of the Savior contained within. But the Greeks, the most diligent researchers of all scriptures, were the first to become aware of this text, and translated it from Hebrew into Greek and so preserved it until the present time.[1]

As in the case of Robert of Cricklade's discovery, almost a century earlier, of a Hebrew *Testimonium Flavianum* supposedly written by Josephus himself, Grosseteste's mastery of languages has caught the Jews in their designs to manipulate "secret" ancient Hebrew texts that confirm the truth of Christianity. In emphatic fashion, Matthew puts an idea of translation at the center of the bishop's enterprise: the cultural role of the Greek language, a point he repeats three times, is first to subvert the "original" Hebrew and then to transfer the text to Latin and its rightful place in Western theology. Gerald of Wales had taken a similar position, asserting that the Greek and Latin versions of scripture are more accurate than the Hebrew "originals," while also demonstrating that the Jews never actually succeed in suppressing prophecies of Christ. For Grosseteste himself, as Matthew reports, the *Testaments*, as well as other biblical Apocrypha and pseudepigrapha, represented an element of a larger theological program concerning Jews and issues of translation.

This chapter will show how the medieval Christian reception and transmission of *The Testaments of the Twelve Patriarchs* is intimately related to shifting attitudes toward Jews not only as textual scholars but also literally as the twelve scattered tribes and, as such, representatives of the world beyond Europe's frontiers. The views of these Christian readers, however, also reflect a culture shared with their Jewish counterparts with regard to geography and eschatology. Unlike *Joseph and Aseneth*, the *Testaments* did survive in several different forms in medieval Hebrew, including the full alternate version of *The Testament of Naphtali*. These texts are mostly fragments, yet they provide a glimpse of the world Grosseteste and others imagined with such vitriol in the Jewish afterlife of apocryphal texts. For Grosseteste and Matthew Paris, these were writings that had become Christian, and if not canonical at least, as Vincent of Beauvais argued, potentially illuminating to Christian exegesis. For Jews and Christians alike, the fate of the ten "lost" patriarchs' tribes, wherever they may be, became a newly tangible and urgent issue in the mid-thirteenth century.

At the same time as Grosseteste recovered the *Testaments* for the Christian West from his Greek manuscript, many in Europe believed that the ten lost tribes of Israel had suddenly reappeared in a terrifying form. In 1241–42, the Mongol army led by Batu Khan, Chingiz's grandson, captured the major cities of Poland, Moravia, and Hungary in a bloody onslaught. Batu's men also captured Matthew Paris's vivid imagination. One of Matthew's most striking illustrations in the autograph manuscript of the *Chronica Majora* is of a Mongol roasting one victim on a spit while another devours both legs of a previously cooked

Christian.[2] In the first notice of the Mongols in the year 1240 of the *Chronica*, he associates the Asian invaders with the Paris master Peter Comestor's account of the ten lost tribes, Jews enclosed deep in the Caspian Mountains by Alexander the Great, with the help of "the God of Israel."[3] These mysterious Jews, so different from those he knew in England both in their military and culinary interests, are for Matthew nevertheless fundamentally the same people and crucially both separated and identified by language.

Robert Stacey has called the period from 1240 to 1260 in England a "watershed" in Jewish–Christian relations, with the Jews' financial and social situation becoming increasingly desperate. Henry III's enormous tallages both weakened the Jewish community from within and sparked the resentment of Christian debtors as Jews were forced to collect more quickly.[4] The situation in northern France was no better; Louis IX continued earlier Capetian policies toward Jews, issuing a series of edicts severely limiting Jewish usury while at the same time confiscating debts owed to Jews.[5] Both monarchs also avidly pursued the conversion of Jews under these circumstances, and not only provided support for "new Christians" but also personally sponsored the converts' baptisms.[6] The attack on Jewish belief as well as finance culminated in Louis's support, beginning in 1239, for the church's campaign against the Talmud and other extrabiblical Jewish texts.[7]

Throughout Europe these years also marked, as Israel Yuval has argued, a collision between the respective eschatological hopes of Jews and Christians. The year 1240 was the end of the fifth millennium in the Jewish calendar, and writers since Moshe ha-Darshan in *Bereshit Rabbati* in the early eleventh century and Judah ben Barzillai in his commentary on *Sefer Yetzira* in the twelfth century had predicted that the Messiah would come before or in 5000.[8] Yuval brings together the various fragments of the Jewish messianic movement to demonstrate its novel adaptations of Christian material: for example, he cites an early thirteenth-century text from the Tosafist circle of R. Isaac ben Abrahram (Riẓba), "Homilies of King, Messiah, Gog, and Magog," that calls for an immigration of Torah scholars to the Holy Land, like the one that actually took place in 1212, in order to prepare for the arrival of the Messiah. The text imitates the rhetoric of the crusaders, portraying the Messiah as a kind of Jewish "crusader" king who will destroy both the Christian and Muslim forces: "And the warriors of Israel will be gathered unto him from the four corners of the earth and he will assemble a great army and smite the princes of Ishmael and Edom that are in Jerusalem and evict the gentiles."[9] Yuval cites an equally remarkable text from the same period that includes Jesus himself in the Jewish messianic program, a tripartite scheme that he suggests shows the influence of Joachim of Fiore's three ages (*status*) of the Father, Son, and Holy Spirit. In this account, Jesus has a conversation with a *bat kol* (divine voice) just before his death, which reveals that the crucifixion is positioned in the middle of history, between the giving of the Law to Moses and the coming of the Messiah. The era of Jesus and belief in his doctrines, in other words the rule of Christian Rome, is scheduled to end in 1240/5000.[10]

Yuval contends that such violent messianic ideas among the Jews triggered a reaction from Christians, whose own apocalyptic thinking was informed by the continuing ideals of the Crusades to the Holy Land together with the precise messianic programs of Joachim of Fiore, which predicted the coming of Antichrist and with it the beginning of the "Age of the Holy Spirit" in 1260.[11] Famously, King Richard I had an audience with Joachim in Messina on his way to the Holy Land. In Roger of Howden's fascinating narrative, the abbot and "prophet" expounded at length on the seven heads of the dragon in the Revelation to John, identifying the sixth head as Salah ad-Din and the seventh as the Antichrist to come; he apparently demurred, however, on the success of the Third Crusade.[12] Jeremy Cohen's influential assessment of a major shift in Christian views of Jews through a theological connection to Muslims as "heretical" groups in the twelfth century supports this constellation of ideas.[13] In terms of historical and textual theories, Yuval puts it trenchantly: for Christians "Islam became the political enemy, while Judaism became the eschatological enemy."[14] The writings of Matthew Paris and Robert Grosseteste, eminent English clerics with both great interest and direct involvement in international politics, illuminate how this thirteenth-century "contest" over the end of history played out with regard to ideas about the role of Jewish scripture within Christianity and the meanings of Jewish Diaspora.

Matthew's voluminous history of thirteenth-century Europe and the Crusader States assigns the Mongols a decisive role in shaping a newly negative image of the Jews, based largely on ideas of Diaspora. In his initial account of the Mongols, Matthew Paris admits that while they are said not to use the Hebrew language or follow Mosaic Law, he nevertheless thinks it possible that the fierce, cannibalistic people he describes in gruesome detail are in fact the Jews of the Northern Kingdom who rebelled against their law to follow "alien gods and strange rites."[15] As Robert Lerner has shown, Matthew's imagination in this passage resembles the well-known "Cedar of Lebanon" prophecy that originated with Cistercians in the midst of the Mongol invasion of Hungary; according to this murky text, "the sons of Israel will be liberated from captivity. A certain people called 'without a head,' or reputed to be wanderers will come."[16] From this point in the *Chronica* on, the St. Albans monk weaves together a series of identifications between Mongols and Jews that not only attempts to inscribe the Mongols into a preexisting sense of Europe's borders but also reconfigures European Jews as agents of barely understood Far Eastern powers.[17] Like Peter Comestor's *Historica Scholastica*, both his account and the earlier Hungarian prophecy rework an original historical program in order to assign the ten tribes a cataclysmic role in the final act of history. According to the most widely circulated apocalyptic text in Europe, the seventh-century Byzantine *Revelations of Pseudo-Methodius*, twenty-two grotesque, reptile, and child-eating nations will break out of "the Gates of the North," where Alexander the Great had locked them away, shortly before the coming of the Antichrist and the end of days. By Matthew's time, after dozens of influential Western apocalyptic treatises, these impure nations had become associated with the ten lost tribes of Jews.[18]

In the same vein, Matthew's notice of Grosseteste's translation of *The Testaments of the Twelve Patriarchs* casts Jews in a sinister role and amplifies the importance of the bishop's—and his local helper's—linguistic skills:

> Because of the scheming of the Jews with their ancient malice, the text was unavailable to Christians at the time of St. Jerome and the other blessed interpreters. However, this glorious text—strengthening the Christian faith and greatly confounding the Jews—was translated plainly and clearly by the bishop, word by word from Greek into Latin, with the help of master Nicholas the Greek, a clerk of the abbot of St. Albans.[19]

This passage, couched in the *Chronica* amid the years of Matthew's growing fascination with the Mongols, draws together the concept of Jewish malevolence with an ancient text that itself addresses the eschatological role of the ten lost tribes along with their "known" counterparts, the tribes of Judah and Benjamin. At the same time that the *Chronica* identifies the ten lost tribes with the Eastern invaders, it understands the *Testaments* as a text that reinscribes the figures of the twelve Jewish patriarchs and their descendants into an apocalyptic discourse already concerned with their Diaspora to Far Eastern territories.

Grosseteste's translation participated in the larger ongoing Christian reevaluation of the role of extrabiblical texts in determining their relations with Jews. By the thirteenth century, Franciscan and Dominican friars elaborated on the polemic against Jewish texts introduced by Petrus Alfonsi. The examination and burning of the Talmud in Paris, ordered by Pope Gregory IX, epitomized a rapidly growing suspicion of works that supposedly replaced the Hebrew Bible with errors and blasphemies. The thirty-five articles against the Talmud, drawn up from relevant extracts by the convert Nicholas Donin and presented as evidence at the 1240 trial, provide a condemnation of rabbinic textual practices that focuses on the rabbis' corrupting and hiding "authentic" scripture.[20] Among the charges against the Talmud, along with its blasphemies against Jesus and insults toward Christians, were that it held that rabbinic scholars and scribes were superior to the prophets, that scholars can change the law, and that it prohibits children from studying the bible in favor of the Talmud itself.[21] In both the Latin and Hebrew accounts of the trial, the nature of the Talmud's "scriptural" authority is central; for the Christians, it represents a text that defies the traditional Augustinian narrative of the Jews' role in the Christian historical frame.

Augustine's doctrine of Jewish "witness" establishes the connection between Hebrew texts and the Diaspora:

> [The Jews], having been vanquished by the Romans, completely deprived of their kingdom, and scattered throughout the world so that they are not lacking anywhere, are testimony for us through their own scriptures that we have not contrived the prophecies concerning Christ. . . . For we realize that on account of this testimony, which they unwillingly provide for us by

having and preserving these books, they are scattered among all the nations, wherever the church of Christ extends itself.[22]

The Diaspora is not only the Jews' punishment in that as they are enslaved politically to other nations, but also the Christians' means of proving and circulating the truth of Hebrew prophecies of the Messiah, already fulfilled in Jesus. Elsewhere, Augustine figures the Jews as servants who carry their masters' books; one of the great anxieties that emerges in the Talmud trial is that the Jews actually carry, interpret, and transmit Hebrew books of their own that contain an entirely different Jewish eschatological narrative. Pope Gregory's 1239 letter to the bishop of Paris, William of Auvergne, instructing him to confiscate all copies of the Talmud stresses this view of "the chief cause that holds the Jews obstinate in their perfidy":

> If what is said about the Jews of France and of the other lands is true, no punishment would be sufficiently great or sufficiently worthy of their crime. For they, so we have heard, are not content with the old law which God gave to Moses in writing: they even ignore it completely, and affirm that God gave another law which is called "Talmud," that is "Teaching," which was handed down to Moses orally. Falsely they allege that it was implanted within their minds and, unwritten, was there preserved until certain men came, whom they call "Sages" and "Scribes," who, fearing that this law may be lost from the minds of men through forgetfulness, reduced it to writing, and the volume of this by far exceeds the text of the bible. In this is contained matter so abusive and so unspeakable that it arouses shame in those who mention it and horror in those who hear it.[23]

In the Hebrew account of the Talmud trial, the *Vikuaḥ Rabbenu Yeḥiel* (*Debate of Rabbi Yeḥiel*), the author, Rabbi Joseph ben Nathan Official, represents the famous scholar Yeḥiel of Paris defending the Talmud as an interpretation of the Torah inseparable from the practice of Judaism. The rabbi further claims that the Talmud was familiar to Jerome and therefore not a new threat to Christianity.[24] Donin's attacks, however, reveal that one of the main Christian concerns is that the Talmud asserts a fundamental challenge to the traditional understanding of Hebrew prophecy in the form of an alternative Jewish messianic program. One of the charges against the Talmud in the Latin account is that in various places it claims that "only one who studies the Talmud will inherit the future world."[25] At one point the ecclesiastical judges in the Hebrew account ask R. Yeḥiel if Christians can even be saved according to his religion, and at another, Donin asks why so many Jews had been massacred by crusaders in Brittany, Anjou, and Poitiers if they are God's "chosen people" (or literally "treasured people"—*am segula*).[26] To the latter, R. Yeḥiel replies that at the end of days, God will perform great miracles for the Jews as he did at the exodus from Egypt. As Robert Chazan points out, while this response is "highly traditional," it also emphasizes the Jewish view of a future, perhaps even imminent, messianic redemption.[27] Indeed, in the *Vikuah*'s notice that the examination took place during the week of the Torah reading *Parshat Balak*, Yuval finds a subtle reference to an earlier French messianic prophecy of 1240/5000 based on a vengeful interpretation of Balaam's words to Balak in Numbers 24:14: "let me inform you of what this people will do to your people in the days to come."[28]

In both the proceedings against the Talmud and the writings of Matthew Paris and Robert Grosseteste, the twelfth-century monastic model of the Jewish "informant" who provides Christian exegetes with a translation of the "literal sense" of the Hebrew Bible is overshadowed by the counterimage of the Jew who uses the language of the bible to subvert and conceal the true Christian narrative. Since the time of Jerome himself, an entire corpus of texts has been hidden away. In the school of exegesis championed by Hugh of Saint-Victor, the present-day Jewish interpreter is central to the Christian understanding of the Old Testament. Victorine exegesis, while not free of anti-Jewish invective, often presents rabbinic readings of scripture without comment as a means of providing access to Hebrew learning.[29] In a commentary on Joel, for example, Hugh even cites knowledge of the Talmud as evidence of authority: his source is "a certain Jew, fluent and expert in the fables of Gamaliel."[30]

Matthew regards the local French-speaking Jews that he encountered around St. Albans not as clarifiers of scripture but rather, in keeping with his geographical imagination, part of an international conspiracy connected by Hebrew writing.[31] He makes the precise nature of the Jewish element of the Mongol threat explicit in two texts. The first, from 1242, is a letter that he acquired, sent from a Hungarian bishop to Bishop William of Auvergne in Paris, informing him of the shocking news he had

supposedly learned from two Mongol prisoners. This letter took on a textual life of its own beyond Matthew's *Liber Additamentorum*—the appen-
dix of documents to the *Chronica Majora*—appearing also in the annals
of the Cistercian abbey of Waverley and later in the same manuscript
from the monastery of Christ Church at Canterbury that I discussed in
the previous chapter. The second is the celebrated story of a plot by Jews
of the German-Roman Empire under Frederick II to smuggle weapons
to the Mongol armies in 1241.[32] A suggestion of the practical uses to
which Matthew's work was put appears in the *Chronicle* of St. Benet of
Hulme: in 1258, Simon de Montfort, the Earl of Leicester, received a tract
on the "history and customs of the Mongols," made up of texts from
the *Liber Additamentorum*. The text's emphasis on the Mongols' military
strength supports J. R. Maddicott's suggestion that Grosseteste's proposal
to Montfort in 1251 for a new Crusade "for the liberation of souls" was
aimed at Central Asia.[33]

The Hungarian bishop's letter recounts that the Mongols informed him
that since they have no written language of their own, they use Hebrew
writing (*literas Judaeorum habent*), which they began to learn when they
set out to conquer the world. When he asks who taught them, they reply
that their teachers were "certain pale men who often fasted, wore long
robes, and bothered nobody."[34] He further concludes that these men are
the long-lost Pharisees and Sadducees, since much of what the Mongols
told him accords with what he knows of those groups' "superstitions."
Although he ascertains that the Mongols themselves don't follow any
dietary code and eat frogs, dogs, and snakes, the bishop nevertheless anx-
iously imagines them as converts to a kind of Judaism, now persecut-
ing the friars sent from Hungary to convert them to Christianity. The
so-called Pharisee and Sadducee missionaries, whom Peter Jackson identifies as Uighur Buddhist monks, have reached the Mongols ahead of the
Franciscans and Dominicans and given them not the Mosaic Law but
rather the Hebrew language as their principal tool of world domination.[35]
Despite their many differences, these threatening lost Jews resemble the
stereotypical "pale" melancholic, postexilic Jews of Europe, imagined to
be sick from the blood they lose in an anal flux as punishment for killing Christ.[36] They also, of course, resemble the diasporic "scholars and
scribes" invoked in the Christian documents of the Talmud trial, who
change the law to suit their own purposes.

William of Auvergne, who two years earlier had served as one of the judges in the interrogation of the four French rabbis who formally defended the Talmud, would have likely received this news as a confirmation of his worst fears. In the *Vikuah*, the author deploys a triumphant view of the Jewish Diaspora that relies on a cultural fantasy held in common with the Christians; Rabbi Yeḥiel, addressing the clerical judges and assembled French courtiers, declares: "If you inflict your hatred upon us, our dispersion is spread to the nethermost part of the world. This Torah of ours is in Babylonia, Media, Greece, and the Islamic world. Indeed, it is to be found among the seventy peoples on the nether side of the River Cush. Our bodies lie in your hands but not our souls."[37] The rabbi's geographic imagination, like Matthew Paris's, encompasses both the known and unknown world. The Jewish realms of Ethiopia were familiar in Europe from the fantastical early medieval travel texts of Eldad ha-Dani, the mysterious wanderer who appeared in Kairouan in the late ninth century. In Eldad's account of his distant Jewish world, the warlike tribes of Dan, Gad, Naphtali, and Asher inhabit Ethiopia; on the other side of the legendary river Sambatyon, the Levites or "People of Moses" live in an utopia of perfect faith and equality, speaking Hebrew only.[38] Moshe ha-Darshan of Narbonne refined this idea of the ten tribes in his eleventh-century anthology *Midrash Bereshit Rabbati*, where he emphasizes that the Levites are "learned in Torah, Mishnah, and Aggadah"—in effect, Rabbi Yeḥiel's Talmud far beyond the reach of Christians.[39] Of the tribe of Issachar, Moshe writes "no yoke of sovereignty achieves dominance over them except for the yoke of Torah"; Judah and Benjamin, unfortunately, "are dispersed among all lands."[40] In this cultural context, it is easy to see why the Hebrew *Testament of Naphtali*, with its frustrated messianic progress after the patriarch's shipwreck vision, would be a popular text; even its bleak view of the future could potentially be seen in a more positive light. While the tribe of Naphtali is far away, neither it nor the other nine have actually disappeared.

Akin to *Yosippon*, and part of the same medieval revival of Hebrew language and literature, these geographies constitute a literature of resistance that restores a lost history of Jews with a different relationship to exile and power. While both narratives originate in the Jews' histories of rebellion and sin, they become in the circumstances of exile a means of recovering the lost past and future. The ten tribes, as they appear in this extracanonical literature, will return in the messianic era not just with military might but, above all, with the Torah and a perfected Hebrew language.

Much the same geopolitical logic informs Matthew's account of the so-called "Jewish-Mongol Plot of 1241," which as Sophia Menache has shown, contains an even more plausible echo of actual Jewish eschatological hopes about the Mongol invasion.[41] Matthew takes pains in this narrative to construct an authentic-sounding Jewish voice, a leader who addresses his coconspirators:

> Brothers, you are the seed of illustrious Abraham, the vineyard of the Lord of *Sabaoth*, whom our God *Adonay* has allowed for so long to be oppressed by Christian rule. But now the time of our liberation is here, and by God's judgment we will in turn oppress the Christians so that the remnant of Israel may be saved. For now our brothers, namely those tribes of Israel formerly inclosed, have gone forth to subject the entire world to themselves and to us.[42]

This ventriloquized "Jewishness," among other things, marks Matthew's advance over previous medieval representations of anti-Christian conspiracies, a discourse that culminates in modernity with the nineteenth-century forgery known as *The Protocols of the Learned Elders of Zion*, which records a meeting of representatives of "the twelve tribes of Israel." The Jews' desired end, as in the *Chronica*, is world empire, but here achieved solely by ideological means:

> The intellectuals of the *goyim* will puff themselves up with their knowledge and without any logical verification of them will put into effect all the information available from science, which our *agenteur* specialists have cunningly pieced together for the purpose of educating their minds in the direction we want. . . . In place of the rulers of today, we shall set up a bogey which will be called the Super-Government administration. Its hands will reach out in all directions like nippers and organization will be of such colossal dimensions that it cannot fail to subdue all the nations of the world.[43]

The medieval plot that Matthew describes thickens into the German Jews' attempt to smuggle weapons to the Mongols in barrels, deceiving the Christian rulers by claiming that the Mongols, as good Jews, would only drink their wine; they then promise to poison these "inhuman enemies" and save the Christians from their "imminent tyrannical pillaging."[44] The nefarious plan almost succeeds but is foiled by a bridge keeper suspicious of the Jews' claim to be acting "for the good of the Empire" ("pro utilitate imperii"). Matthew reveals the Jews' lethal hypocrisy as inherent in the way they move between two languages, Hebrew among themselves and the vernacular when trying to ingratiate themselves with the Christians. Matthew here combines elements of what he vaguely knows about English Jews—that is, the halakhic prohibition against wine produced by non-Jews—with the disturbing rumors about the Jews' own messianic expectations that, as Yuval shows, were circulating widely in Christian Europe. For example, in a contemporary letter from Sicily quoted by various scholars as an example of Jewish interpretation of the Mongols, the writer refers to armed "emissaries . . . from the enclosed ones (*ha-genuzim*)," bringing a document written in Hebrew with them: "and the manuscript they brought was written in Hebrew characters and was signed up and down with twelve golden seals. . . . And the King of Spain and the King of Germany and the King of Hungary and the King of France are in fear."[45] In the 1260s the Spanish poet Meshullam ben Solomon da Piera similarly rejoices in the earlier Mongol victories "to the border of Ashkenaz" as the advance of the ten tribes toward a reunion with other Jews.[46] The new victories of Hülegü Khan in the Middle East are a prelude to the messianic time, a signal that the fulfillment of Ezekiel's prophecies about the rebuilding of the Temple in Jerusalem is at hand. Matthew and these Jewish writers shared a sense of their time. The Mongols represent not only an overwhelming military force, but also a specifically Jewish threat to Christian messianic narrative stability. The Mongols' world-conquering ambitions seek to replace a Christian eschatology that encompasses the Jews' final conversion with a Jewish eschatology that celebrates the final gathering of the twelve tribes.

The implications of Matthew's understanding of the Mongols as quasi-Jews for the scriptural economy become clear in a sensational event he relates in 1244: the discovery in London of a murdered boy with Hebrew letters inscribed on the skin of his legs, arms, and chest.

> Many who had gathered to wonder at this spectacle, and not being able to read the letters but knowing that they were Hebrew, called for Jewish

converts who lived in the house founded for them by the king. And they, valuing life and limbs, out of honor, love, and fear of the lord king, revealed this writing without a figment of falsehood. . . . And when these converts had read what was written, and studied and reread it (there were letters which because of the extension and contraction of skin and flesh were stretched here and there and misshapen by various distortions and therefore not legible), they discovered the names of the father and mother of the boy—but without surnames—and that they had sold him to the Jews, but to whom or for what reason they could not figure out.[47]

This bizarre anecdote—with its telling lack of specific identities—transforms the already well-known genre of the ritual murder, or specifically crucifixion, of a Christian child by Jews into a grisly parodic account of interpretation and translation. The boy's body itself is a manuscript—uncomfortably like both the Hebrew Bible and the Mongols' supposed Hebrew writings—covered with a script written by one set of Jews and wholly dependent upon another set for reception and proper "study." The role of the converts from Henry III's *Domus Conversorum* is, to say the least, ambiguous; like the Jews involved in the Mongol plot, they speak in two languages but obscure the truth. Matthew ironically exaggerates their devotion to their king and new faith yet emphasizes their failure to reveal a clear interpretation of the text. While the burden of anxiety falls equally here on both the condition of the manuscript and the sincerity of the newly Christian readers, the lurid story's predominant idea is Jewish textual violence: the relationship between Hebrew writing and the ongoing torments of Christ, the collaboration for profit of Christians with Jews, and the unreliability of Jewish informants. Conversion provides no translation, as could be expected.

The same theme of a malevolent Jewish textual tradition appears in a different guise in Matthew's report of Grosseteste's translation of *The Testaments of the Twelve Patriarchs*. Matthew, most likely following Grosseteste himself, characterizes the text through a fictive genealogy by which it was originally written, like the canonical biblical prophecies, in Hebrew rather than Greek. Greek here is strictly the language of the Christians who have saved the text, which was hidden from the early Latin translators like Jerome, for its full recognition by the Latin West. The chronicler thus anticipates this mysterious work's contentious modern reception, with rival claims for its Christian or Jewish origins. *The*

*Testaments of the Twelve Patriarchs* is a collection of "copies" of the last words of the twelve sons of Jacob, each containing ethical exhortations and accounts of the eschatological events that await the twelve tribes. The individual patriarchs frequently cite the "Books of Enoch" as their source of prophetic knowledge for how their descendants will act against God. In proposing a Jewish scribal subculture as the background of the text's composition in Palestine, David Frankfurter stresses that "the *Testaments* invoke the authority of *literature*: books of Enoch, old literary genres, and the mystique of literary transmission."[48] The *Testaments* is also marked by an emphasis on the importance of Levi, representing the priesthood and the law, to Jewish eschatology. The double rule of Levi and Judah, the priestly and kingly tribes from which the Messiah will emerge, is a central theme. In *The Testament of Dan*, for example, the patriarch declares that after his descendants commit every form of sin with the gentiles, a savior "shall arise for you from the tribe of Judah and [the tribe of] Levi."[49] The Messiah himself, who will bring the gentiles into Israel, is described in several of the *Testaments* in terms that explicitly parallel the Gospels: *The Testaments of Levi* and *Benjamin* refer to a "savior of the world" ("salvator mundi") who will be murdered by the tribes' wicked descendants. *The Testament of Benjamin* also includes a prophecy of a new Temple in which the twelve tribes and all the nations will be gathered until God sends his "only-begotten."[50] Modern critical debate about the *Testaments*'s origins has been fierce, with opposing groups of scholars claiming the text as either exclusively "Jewish" (with a date as early as 150 BCE) with much later "Christian" interpolations or as exclusively "Christian" (with a date as late as 200 CE).[51] Neither of these models is satisfactory, however, as Frankfurter convincingly argues, because the text is actually from a period (late second century CE) and milieu that predates a firm boundary between "Judaism" and "Christianity." The *Testaments*, as he points out, "clearly seek to revitalize some assortment of Jewish values under the aegis of the Twelve Tribes of Israel" but also celebrate Christ as a "priestly savior" of both Jews and gentiles.[52]

The *Testaments* is, therefore, a product of the Hellenic "Jewish Life of the Logos," to use Daniel Boyarin's provocative phrase—a hybrid frozen between the two nascent religions of Rabbinic Judaism and Christianity from the period before they became firm orthodoxies in the third and fourth centuries. The *Testaments* is both thoroughly Jewish in its sources, similar in particular to testamentary material from the Qumran scrolls, *and* depends on the idea of Christ as Messiah and universal savior. In Boyarin's study of the emergence of a distinct Judaism and Christianity, he details at length the common pre-Rabbinic Jewish belief in a divine hypostasis, whether Wisdom, Logos, or, as in the *Testaments*, a son of God. For early Jewish Christians and non-Christians alike, belief in a "second God" became heretical only with the rabbis' rejection of Logos theology as a type of heresy.[53]

Although Christian writers were evidently unaware of it, both translations of the Greek *Testaments* and some of their ancient Hebrew sources had a separate transmission history in Hebrew among European Jews who had rediscovered these texts. Moshe ha-Darshan included material from the testaments of Naphtali, Benjamin, Zebulun, and Judah in *Midrash Bereshit Rabbati* in the eleventh century, including elements from *The Testament of Judah*'s description of the war with Esau and his sons in that anthology's earliest version of the *Midrash Va-Yissau*. Like Grosseteste, Moshe may have connected the testament literature that he had to ten lost tribes that he describes at length in exotic terms of both purity and ferocity. An Aramaic *Testament of Levi* related to the Greek text was discovered in the Cairo Genizah, and the previously mentioned Hebrew *Testament of Naphtali* circulated in later medieval Ashkenaz. Fragments from the Aramaic *Testament of Levi* and a Hebrew *Testament of Naphtali* related to the one known by Moshe ha-Darshan are among the Qumran manuscripts. The reappearance of these texts in Hebrew in the Middle Ages, whether in their original language or translated from Greek, signals another aspect of the larger effort by Jews to reclaim Second Temple and later postbiblical writings from Christian discourse.[54]

For Grosseteste and Matthew Paris, as for many of the text's modern readers, the *Testaments* clearly offered a unique opportunity to reconstruct the role of early "Judaism" in Christian history. Indeed, Grosseteste's decision to translate this particular text fits in well with one of his predominant theological concerns, the role of Mosaic Law in the time following the advent of Christ. In his exegetical tract from the 1230s, *On the Cessation of the Ritual Torah*, Grosseteste seeks to prove that any observance of Jewish ritual law is heretical. To this end, he invokes many of the same prooftexts as contemporary Christian disputations with Jews, in particular the interpretation of Isaiah 53 on the identity of God's "suffering servant": the Messiah Jesus for Christians, the collective people of Israel for most Jewish exegetes. Grosseteste shows that Christ's Incarnation and death fulfills the Jewish prophetic texts.[55] The "seed of Abraham" promised in Genesis 17 is not only Isaac, but, through the line of Isaac, Jacob, Judah, Jesse, and David, it is Jesus, God and man in whom "all peoples are blessed."[56] In the final and most scathingly polemical section of the *Cessation*, Grosseteste rails against those who maintain the "dead works of the law" after the advent of Christ:

> To perform the ritual laws as laws—those things which are only signs of the pious life, and the shadows, testimonies, and prophecies of Christ's coming, and only beneficial as a foretokening of Christ who is the only true savior— is altogether a wicked sin, since it rejects Christ and preaches that there is another messiah yet to come, just as the infidel Jews still do.[57]

It stands to reason, then, that Grosseteste prized *The Testaments of the Twelve Patriarchs* as a work that offers a kind of scriptural evidence that the patriarchs themselves, even as they exhorted their children to adhere to the practices of Jewish Law, recognized the eventual supersession of the Torah and prophesied the coming of Jesus as the awaited Messiah. For Grosseteste and Matthew, the text's survival also demonstrated that from early on, "modern" rabbinic Jews have tried to suppress their own explicitly prophetic texts. Certainly, the *Testaments*'s own thematic emphasis on literary circulation, its representation of the patriarchs as both readers and writers of prophecies, lends itself to their imagination of a deliberate censorship.

The appearance of Grossetste's translation of the *Testaments* in the same year that copies of the Talmud were burned by the cartload in Paris is no coincidence. The bishop's presentation of the text participates in an identical ideological construction to the judges of how the "modern" Jews have essentially rejected their own prophets in favor of a false and heretical text that is unremittingly hostile to the Christian Messiah. Another text that Grosseteste translated from Greek into Latin, the entry on "Jesus" from the tenth-century Byzantine encyclopedia, the *Suidas*, addresses similar suspicions of the Jews' understanding of Christ. In this extraordinary account, set in the time of the emperor Justinian, a Jewish leader admits to his Christian friend that certain Jews actually know that Jesus is the Messiah: "I shall entrust a mystery to you, which is kept hidden by us Hebrews, from which we know full well that the Christ worshipped by you Christians is the very one prophesied by the Law and the Prophets; not only from the ancient writings themselves, but also from the mystery written down and hidden by us."[58] The "mystery," as the text explains, is a codex from the Temple that recorded the names of new priests and both of their parents. The other priests elected Jesus, and his mother was then questioned about his birth. In this story, exactly as in *The Testaments of Gad, Dan,* and *Benjamin,* he comes from a "mixing" of the tribes of Judah and Levi, allowing him to be both the Davidic Messiah and a priest. As the Jew Theodosius tells his Christian friend Philippus, the codex, with its revelation of how Mary gave birth to "a son of the Holy Spirit," was "saved from the Temple with great trouble by . . . the Jews at the time of the capture of Jerusalem, and was deposited in Tiberias." And, he adds, "the mystery is known only to very few and faithful people of our nation."[59] Grosseteste's translation of the *Suidas*'s Jesus entry, which frequently circulated in thirteenth-century manuscripts together with the Latin *Testaments,* reveals how both texts were interpreted; in light of the "Jesus" story, the *Testaments* becomes another secret codex that the Rabbis attempted to conceal after the fall of Jerusalem with their mastery of the Hebrew language and the circumstances of the Diaspora.[60] The great rabbinic academy of Tiberias appears to exist in this text mainly in order to obscure Christian truth.

It is possible that Grosseteste, like Andrew of Saint-Victor and Herbert of Bosham, even learned some Hebrew in order to further his study of scripture. On the authority of the fourteenth-century exegete Henry of Cossey, Beryl Smalley and Raphael Loewe have accepted that he commissioned the Latin-Hebrew Psalter known as the *Superscriptio Lincolniensis,* a new "word for word" literal translation that appears in several English manuscripts. The project was an unusual collaboration between Christian and Jewish scholars; the alterations to the Latin translations from Jerome's "Gallican" and "Hebrew" versions clearly demonstrate the influence of Rashi and other Jewish exegetes.[61] Moreover, Smalley attributes a preface that appears in the earliest of the *Superscriptio* manuscripts to Grosseteste himself. Employing the well-worn metaphor of Jacob and Esau, the text asserts that the point of the translation, and of the collaboration itself, is to convert Jews to Christian belief:

> In order to quiet the collision and conflict of these two in their mother's womb, it profits us . . . to bring the nations together into the unity of faith

under the guidance of Christ, by reconciling their differences through a knowledge of both tongues and both scriptures, and to set them side by side, lest because they differ they should forever fight. The zeal of God's house incites me to edit the Hebrew scripture that it may confirm the faithful and convert the infidel.[62]

The bishop's interest in the *Hebraica Veritas* of the Psalms, like his interest in *The Testaments of the Twelve Patriarchs* or the "codex" that he discusses in the *Suidas*, is as a witness of "authentic" prerabbinic Jewish scripture; the alignment of the two languages will inevitably erase Jewish belief as the new Latin version produces a clear Christian meaning. Even as the *Superscriptio* enlists rabbinic exegesis to clarify the more obscure passages of the psalms, the translation as a whole serves as a foil to the independent Jewish textuality exemplified by the Talmud.

Like the parody of textual study in his 1244 ritual-murder story, Matthew Paris's account of Grosseteste's translation of *The Testaments of the Twelve Patriarchs* in spite of the intractable opposition of the Jews reflects the wider thirteenth-century vilification of the Jewish role in Christian hermeneutics. The twelfth-century Victorine exegetes had frequently reproduced rabbinic interpretations rather than traditional Christian ones, even of messianic passages of the bible.[63] In his remarkable commentary on Isaiah 11, for example, Andrew of Saint-Victor goes so far as to suppress the Christian prooftext in favor of a Jewish messianic reading of the twelve tribes' future: "The Lord shall do as it is said above to free the Two Tribes from danger and care. To restore to their land, to reconcile and reduce to one people both Ten and Two, *there shall come forth a rod out of the root of Jesse.*"[64] Matthew's reception of the *Testaments* reads, in this context, like a kind of polemical response to these earlier exegetes' acceptance of Hebrew authority: far from adding to Christian understanding, Jewish eschatology is a dangerous counternarrative that must be disproved through its own secret Hebrew texts. In a second notice of Grosseteste's translation, which Matthew includes in 1252 at the death of the Greek expert John of Basingstoke, he adds to his description of the hidden *Testaments* that it is of the "substance of the bible" ("de substantia Bibliothecae").[65] By constructing the *Testaments* as genuine Hebrew prophecy, translated at some indefinite ancient time into Greek, Matthew circumvents the problem of Jewish informants in what he imagines as the text's early Hebrew-language transmission and interpretation; indeed, he characterizes Grosseteste and his collaborators, like the Greek monks who provided them with their manuscript, as essentially rescuing the biblical *Testaments* from Jewish oblivion.

Given his repeated portrayals of the invading Mongols as remnants of the ten lost Jewish tribes, Matthew's report of the *Testaments*'s discovery in 1242 seems extremely fortuitous: the individual testaments, after all, are purportedly written by the fathers of all the tribes and include a series of prophecies that speak directly to their messianic future. *The Testament of Levi* contains a prophecy that "the Lord will raise up a new priest to whom all the words of the Lord will be revealed . . . and his star shall rise in heaven like a king."[66] *The Testament of Judah* uses similar messianic terms: "There shall arise from you a star of Jacob in peace: And a man shall arise from my seed like a sun of justice, walking with the sons of men in gentleness and justice, and he will be free of all sin."[67] The latter text also emphatically ends with a prophecy of the reunion of the twelve tribes: "Abraham, Isaac, and Jacob will return to life again . . . and my brothers and I will be chiefs, our scepter in Israel. . . . And there will be one people of the Lord with one language."[68] If for Matthew the underlying threat of the Mongol armies is really a world conquest of Jewish exegesis, a supplanting of the Christian eschatological narrative with that of the Jewish conspirators, the *Testaments* provides a well-timed textual salvo. Even as the language of *The Testament of Judah* comes perilously close to the dialogue about the liberation of the tribes that Matthew attributes to the arms-smuggling Jews, it is here at least reassuringly contained within a frame of Christian messianism.

The 1245 Council of Lyons, which Robert Grosseteste attended, included an entire constitution on the threat posed by the Tartars that describes them as "a wicked race . . . seeking to subdue, or rather utterly destroy the Christian people."[69] It was also at this time that Pope Innocent IV sent the first embassies to the Mongols, which included the Franciscan John of Plano Carpini and the Dominican Simon of Saint-Quentin, who both wrote detailed accounts of their experiences. I would like to suggest that the immediate interest in and wide dissemination of the bishop's Latin *Testaments* is partly a result of the text's sensational connection, via the ten lost tribes, to the Mongols. The *Testaments* almost immediately enjoyed a wide circulation; numerous English manuscripts survive from the thirteenth century, including one from St. Albans that may have belonged to Matthew Paris himself.[70] Moreover, Vincent of Beauvais excerpted the messianic highlights of the *Testaments* in his magisterial *Speculum Historiale*, with an emphasis on the prophecies of Levi, Judah, and Benjamin—but also including Naphtali's promise that "God will appear to save the race of Israel, and to assemble the righteous from among the nations." He also included in the *Speculum* lengthy selections from John of Plano Carpini's and Simon of Saint-Quentin's descriptions of the Mongols.[71] The *Testaments* represents a unique artifact: for its Latin readers, the text emerges as a site of contestation between thirteenth-century Jews and Christians over the end of days and the Messiah, yet unlike in the case of the Hebrew Bible itself, the contest in this "hidden" Jewish text has been decisively won by Christian narrative.

The thirteenth-century collection of texts from the Benedictine monastery of Christ's Church at Canterbury that I discussed in the previous chapter also helps to illuminate the immediate textual afterlife of the Mongol-Jewish connection. It contains copies of four of the letters about the Mongols from Matthew Paris's *Chronica* and *Book of Additions*, including the one from the Hungarian bishop about the Pharisees' and Sadducees' Hebrew lessons. The manuscript brings together texts almost all of which in some way concern the eschatological role of Jews in Christianity including the apocalyptic *Revelations of Pseudo-Methodius*, which lists the nations that Alexander locked away in the mountains.[72] As the monastery's library catalog compiled under Prior Henry Estry reveals, the manuscript's owner, Nicholas of Sandwich, also owned a copy of Grosseteste's Latin *Testaments of the Twelve Patriarchs*. Although this manuscript has not survived, a full copy of the *Testaments* was owned by a fellow monk, Richard de Weynchepe, who was made prior of Dover in 1268.[73] Interestingly, Richard also owned a copy of the popular Latin *Gesta Alexander*, one of the favorite medieval sources for speculation about Asian cultures.[74]

The sense of a direct Mongol threat had subsided in Europe with the withdrawal of Hülegü Khan from Syria and the defeat of his remaining army by the Egyptian Mamluks at Ayn Jalut in 1260.[75] The situation of English Jews, however, had continued to deteriorate. The monastic manuscripts from Canterbury and elsewhere are evidence of an effort to make sense of the local Jews with sources from outside of the Hebrew Bible, that is from biblical Apocrypha, Apocalypse, and—in the case of the Mongol letters—recent history. In the period immediately preceding the expulsion of the Jews in 1290, the compiler of the Canterbury manuscript, as well as other Canterbury monks, sought to interpret the history of the future by means of texts that remained comfortably between scripture and legend. In *Aseneth*, the Jews are exponents of spiritual conversion; in the *Testaments*, they are the twelve tribes who will be rejoined with Jesus as the Messiah. Echoing Vincent of Beauvais's theoretical approach to apocryphal texts, Roger Bacon in his *Opus Maius* defends the *Testaments*, in which "each patriarch taught his tribe" about Christ, as a document of authentic scripture that, while not canonical, was "used by Greek and Latin saints and wise men from the beginning of the church."[76] The transmission of Matthew Paris's anxious reportage of the Mongols' progress through Eastern Europe and the Jews' messianic hopes into the later Canterbury miscellany demonstrates the immediate absorption of the news from distant frontiers into a Latin historical romance fueled by the monastic imagination. The contemporary reception of *The Testaments of the Twelve Patriarchs*, also part of Matthew's narrative, points to the story's desirable ending.

# CONCLUSION

Two voices, one Christian and one Jewish, bring this story to its end. Each figure in his way is a master storyteller of fictions of Diaspora. The first is the famous "John Mandeville, knight," probably actually a French or Anglo-Norman monk, who recalls his journey to everywhere in the world short of the Earthly Paradise. The author of the mid-fourteenth-century French text *Mandeville's Travels* addresses Jewish Diaspora, history, language, and eschatology, all in the most negative possible terms. In homage, perhaps, to Matthew Paris's geographic writings and world maps, as well as his skill as a compiler, Mandeville claims that he was "born and raised in England in the town of St. Albans."[1] He collected and adapted an impressive number of works, and has often been characterized as a traveler who perhaps never traveled further than an excellent library. He had access not only to all of the texts that Vincent of Beauvais had included in his *Speculum Historiale* and *Speculum Naturale*, but also to the recent travel narratives of William of Boldensele and Odoric of Pordenone who provided him with details about the Near East, India, and China. *Mandeville's Travels* quickly became one of the most popular medieval books, translated from its two principal French versions into Latin, German, and English among other languages.[2]

In his introduction, he calls for a new Crusade to the Holy Land: "in the said land, he wished to die so as to leave it as a possession to his children—which is why every good Christian . . . ought to take pains and do great work to conquer our above-mentioned and right inheritance."[3] His second goal is to entertain Christians who "take pleasure" in hearing about the Holy Land. While most recent scholars credit Mandeville with tolerance and universalism in regard to the different peoples he encounters, including the "Saracens" in Palestine, many emphasize that he excludes the Jews from his otherwise novel approach to non-Christians. In an influential article, Benjamin Braude asserts that Mandeville's treatment of the Jews "represents a mirror image of the process by which he constructed the description of every other [culture]"—a rejection of any sense of common humanity.[4] Mandeville ultimately derives his characterization of the Jews from the ubiquitous *Vengeance of the Savior*. Titus, he claims, "laid siege to Jerusalem to destroy the Jews because they had put Our Lord to death without the emperor's leave." After the burning of the Second Temple, eleven hundred Jews were killed and the rest sold.[5] The text's popularity and grotesque elaborations attest to its ongoing role as a source of Christian pleasure. From this point in Mandeville's narrative, he defines the Jews entirely by their landless condition, the perpetual Diaspora that makes them distinct from all other peoples in his geographical scheme from England to Indonesia.

The most arresting aspect of Mandeville's treatment of the Jews, however, is his transformation of Hebrew from a written to a spoken language. When he describes the relics of St. Jerome in Bethlehem, he positions the Vulgate as the end of Hebrew rather than a Latin version of a living *Hebraica Veritas*: "[he] translated the Bible and the Psalter from Hebrew into Latin. And outside the minster is the chair on which he sat as he translated them."[6] There is no need for further engagement with Hebrew scripture, which is a relic like Jerome's furniture, fixed in a historical moment. Hebrew, for Mandeville, is no longer the language of the Old Testament but rather of the Jews' current-day conspiracies against Christians. He includes an inaccurate version of the Hebrew alphabet, but does not privilege it over the others like "Egyptian" and "Saracen" that he records. The Jews in *Mandeville's Travels* no longer hide or subvert scripture as they do in the imaginations of Gerald of Wales, Peter of Blois, and Robert Grosseteste; they are strictly part of a violent conspiracy like Matthew Paris's Jewish-Mongol plot. The geopolitical circumstances have, however, changed to suit Mandeville's travel romance: he himself spends time as a soldier in the service of the Great Khan and says much of his vast empire, immense wealth, and nobility. The ten lost tribes, he affirms, are still locked up in the Caspian hills where Alexander left them; if any of them do manage to get out "they can speak no language but Hebrew and so cannot speak with other people." Yet he also includes the following apocalyptic scenario that hinges on the studies of the other two tribes:

> And therefore all the Jews who live in all lands always learn to speak Hebrew in the hope that when those of the Caspian mountains issue forth, the other Jews will know how to talk to them. And they teach that language to their children in order to destroy Christendom. For the other Jews say they know well by their prophecies that those of Caspie will emerge and spread out through the world and that the Christians will be in subjection to them just as they have been in subjection to the Christians.[7]

Suzanne Akbari astutely notes that this passage makes "the Jews of the cities," whom Mandeville likely never encountered personally, into a "fifth column" who speak both Hebrew and European languages.[8] In Ian Higgins's words, Mandeville's paranoid vision of infiltration through spoken Hebrew makes "neither the Tartars nor the Saracens, but the Jews . . . the enemy par excellence."[9] Their danger to Europe comes not from territorial power but their prophecies of dominating all land; Jewish eschatology is once again just out of the reach of Christians in terms of both language and geography. The *Travels*, nonetheless, is a text that pretends to comprehend both. Long gone from the England of Matthew Paris and Grosseteste, the fictional Sir John's Jews of the 1350s have become in their Diaspora the embodiment of Hebrew, a menacing phantom of the unknown East.

From *Hegesippus*'s rewriting of Josephus's *Jewish War* on, the Holy Land has been understood as Christians' inheritance from God. Eleazer ben Asher ha-Levi's introduction to his *Book of Memory* is also concerned with inheritance in a diasporic inversion that encompasses the loss of Jeru-salem. While this work survives only in a single autograph manuscript, it is in many ways a contemporary fourteenth-century counterpart to Mandeville's grand conception of the world. Eleazer's opening exhorta-tion takes the form of a will to his son, commanding him to keep the book that "unites" the "scattered and dispersed" texts that he found. He further explains his painstaking composition of the anthology in terms of the construction of the Tabernacle: "I was continually busy . . . until I had selected each subject and placed it in its proper position, like a pearl in its setting and like a hook in its eye" (Exod. 26:11). In addition, Eleazer describes his book as a metaphorical piece of land that his son may bequeath to a son or brother but not a daughter who might bring it to another "tribe" ("mateh"). His edicts to his son about how to care for the manuscript even have a similar tone of dread to the prophetic warnings of the eschatological testaments of the patriarchs: "[He] who sells it will soon squander the money on frivolity; then he will immediately repent his transaction but in vain."[10] According to this striking and pessimistic idea, the anthology, like territory or like the Temple, could be lost to immorality and conversion.

In his dizzying series of images of loss and recovery, Eleazer sets up a work that extends from the beginning of the world to the beginning of Diaspora after the destruction of the Second Temple in *Yosippon* to the misery of exile that ends with signs of the end of days and the Messiah. Eleazer, however, balances this historical impulse with several of his enter-taining texts, positioned after the end of days in the manuscript, includ-ing the *Tales of Sendebar* (the Arabic *Sindibad* and Latin *Seven Sages of Rome*) and Berekhiah's *Fox Fables*. The messianic texts are ultimately not as important as the manuscript's inclusiveness. Like its namesake, the *Sefer ha-Zikhronot* in which the insomniac King Ahasuerus reads about Mordecai's loyal service in Esther 6:1, the text is a chronicle but also a bridge of sorts between Jews and the non-Jews who rule over them. Amid the scattered midrashic narratives, the *Sefer Yosippon*, at once Jewish and Christian in origin, anchors the compilation.

*The Testament of Naphtali* is one very short text in this huge collec-tion, but it distills the themes of Diaspora in the *Book of Memory*, a ship potentially facing its wreck at the hands of Eleazer's own children. Ulti-mately Eleazer's only solution is to cultivate Hebrew, the "holy language," as the way to avoid falling into idol worship, here clearly Christianity. In the earlier anthologies of *Yosippon* and Yeraḥmeel, the writing of Diaspora is not only to gather Hebrew texts but also to create new ones by mining Christian literature for things that need to be returned to Jews through translation. Eleazer, in his more extensive work, presents his magisterial manuscript as an embodiment of Hebrew texts' place in the Christian world, a stack of parchment that may not outlive him by too many years. Within the scheme of the *Book of Memory*, *The Testament of Naphtali* speaks to Diaspora as a current condition, with the division of the tribes of Judah and Joseph as a mirror for the more recent struggles among factions of Jews in the civil war that destroyed the Second Temple, and for the continuing internal strife that Berekhiah ha-Nakdan deplores in his *Fox Fables*. The Jews are nowhere nearly as united and organized as Mandeville fears.

In its medieval context, *The Testament of Naphtali* resists some of the redemptive possibilities for the ten tribes offered by rabbinic midrash such as this interpretation from *Genesis Rabbah* 98.3 on "Assemble yourselves, O Jacob, and come and hear" (Gen. 49:2): "R. Berekhiah said—sometimes in the name of R. Ḥiyya, and sometimes in the names of the Rabbis of Babylon: This teaches that they were scattered, and an angel descended and assembled them. R. Tanḥuma said: This teaches that they were scattered, and (Jacob) assembled them by means of the Holy Spirit."[11] In the scenario of *The Testament of Naphtali*, the tribes remain unredeemed. The best that Jacob can do is repair the ship while treading water, presumably so that the twelve tribes can try once again to steer it around the Mediterranean in a cycle of failure until a sign of the future redemption appears. The patriarch, however, offers another kind of plan for life in the Diaspora. Following the account of his shipwreck vision, Naphtali resumes admonishing his sons with an account of how God ordered seventy angels to bring the nations of the world seventy languages: "the holy language, Hebrew" remained only in the house of Abraham who worshiped God, but the other nations chose to worship other gods.[12] Whereas some of the Greek *Testaments of the Twelve Patriarchs* refer to the loss of a single language and its restoration to the twelve tribes in the messianic end of history, the emphasis in this text is that the Hebrew language is currently exclusive to Naphtali and his brothers. Identity through the holy language, while a much more optimistic possibility than the shipwreck, is still fragile. Within Eleazer's anthology, the medieval *Testament* has a polemical quality directed toward those still living in history, a warning against destructive Jews amid Eleazer's recuperative efforts. The positive force in this work of diasporic consciousness is the sanctity of the *Testament*'s and the larger collection's own Hebrew. For Mandeville, Hebrew in the Diaspora has become a spoken language that exists almost solely to destroy Christians by uniting Europe's Jews with the vicious ten tribes. For Eleazer, the Diaspora will end, but until then Hebrew literature can provide memory, consolation, and the pleasure of resisting and absorbing the worldviews of other nations.

# NOTES

For all citations of ancient Hebrew texts and transliterations of Hebrew words, I have followed the guidelines of the Association for Jewish Studies.

## Introduction

1. H. C. Kee, ed. and trans., "Testaments of the Twelve Patriarchs" in *The Old Testament Pseudepigrapha*, vol. 1, *Apocalyptic Literature and Testaments*, ed. James H. Charlesworth (New York: Doubleday, 1983), 813.

2. The Hebrew *Testament of Naphtali* was first edited and translated by Moses Gaster, "The Hebrew Text of One of the Testaments of the Twelve Patriarchs," *Proceedings of the Society of Biblical Archaeology* 16 (1893–94): 33–49, 109–17. Gaster's edition is based on the version in the fourteenth-century *Sefer ha-Zikhronot* of Eleazer ben Asher ha-Levi (Oxford, Bodleian Library, MS Heb. D.11) with variant readings from the twelfth-century manuscript Paris, Bibliothèque Nationale de France, MS Orientaux 75. The Bodleian version has been reedited by Eli Yassif, *Sefer ha-Zikhronot: The Book of Memory; that is, The Chronicles of Jerahme'el* (Tel Aviv: Tel Aviv University, 2001), 143–47. Solomon A. Wertheimer edited two more manuscripts of the Hebrew *Testament of Naphtali* in his collection *Batei Midrashot* (Jerusalem: Mosad ha-Rav Kook, 1950), 1:183–203.

3. *SZ*, ed. Yassif, 146; Gaster republished his translation in *The Chronicles of Jerachmeel* (New York: KTAV, 1971), 87–94. The entire Hebrew *Testament* is remarkable for its unremittingly negative view of Joseph throughout the text, as opposed to the Greek version

in which he is a victim mourned by Jacob and appears only as set apart and enigmatic in the visions. Naphtali's opening advice to his sons is to avoid Joseph, who represents the Northern Kingdom—as opposed to the Southern Kingdom of Judah and Levi and Benjamin—and will be responsible for the idolatry and exile of all the other tribes. See Theodore Korteweg, "The Meaning of Naphtali's Visions," in *Studies on the Testaments of the Twelve Patriarchs: Text and Interpretation*, ed. M. de Jonge (Leiden: Brill, 1975), 261–90.

4. John Reeves, "Exploring the Afterlife of Jewish Pseudepigrapha in Medieval Near Eastern Religious Traditions: Some Initial Soundings," *Journal for the Study of Judaism* 30 (1999): 148–77.

5. Korteweg, "The Meaning of Naphtali's Visions, 270. David Flusser believes the medieval Hebrew text to be a translation of a Greek or Latin original, despite its celebration of the Hebrew language; see Flusser, "Testament of Naphtali," in *Encyclopaedia Judaica*, ed. Michael Berenbaum and Fred Skolnik, 2nd ed. (Detroit: Macmillan Reference, 2007), 14:775.

6. Gershom Scholem, "Toward an Understanding of the Messianic Idea in Judaism," in *The Messianic Idea in Judaism and Other Essays on Jewish Spirituality* (New York: Schocken, 1971), 35.

7. John Reeves discusses the difficulty of classifying many of these texts on the website for his project, "Illuminating the Afterlife of Ancient Apocryphal Jewish Literature": https://clas-pages.uncc.edu/john-reeves/research-projects/illuminating-the-afterlife-of-ancient-apocryphal-jewish-literature/.

8. The secondary literature on Jewish–Christian exegetical debate is voluminous and itself a subject of much debate. The most relevant scholarship here is in the introduction to *The Works of Gilbert Crispin, Abbot of Westminster*, ed. Anna Abulafia and G. R. Evans (Oxford: Oxford University Press, 1986), xi–xli and 8–61; and Anna Abulafia, *Christians and Jews in the Twelfth-Century Renaissance* (London: Routledge, 1995), 77–93.

9. "Rabbinic literature," a term necessary to this discussion, is notoriously difficult to define. The introduction to *The Cambridge Companion to the Talmud and Rabbinic Literature* (Cambridge: Cambridge University Press, 2007), "The Talmud, Rabbinic Literature and Jewish Culture," by Charlotte Elisheva Fonrobert and Martin S. Jaffee (1–14), is an excellent concise historical essay from which I draw this brief summary. The authors begin with the legal traditions (*halakhah*) of the Palestinian sages transmitted in the Mishnah and Tosefta (early 3rd century CE). *Halahkic midrashim* such as the *Mehkilta de-Rabbi Ishmael*, a commentary on Exodus ("*midrash*" here taken to mean "scriptural commentary"), are likewise rabbinic legal texts. They move on to the midrashic compilations of the later Palestinian sages (fourth–sixth centuries CE), concerned with "historical and theological topics" (7). These include, for example, *Genesis Rabbah*, *Leviticus Rabbah*, and *Lamentations Rabbah*. Finally, they discuss the two commentaries on the Mishnah, the "Jerusalem Talmud" or "Palestinian Talmud" likely edited in Tiberias (late fourth or early fifth century) and the Babylonian Talmud, compiled in Persia from the third to seventh centuries CE. The latter, which preserves the tradition of both Palestinian and Babylonian sages, is at the heart of all later rabbinic education. They characterize the Babylonian Talmud as "a summa of the entirety of the rabbinic Oral Torah—*mishnah* and *midrash*, *halakhah* and *'aggadah*, combined into a single 'encyclopedia' of knowledge that subsumed all other textualities within its own corpus" (9). It is often simply called "The Talmud." For a much more detailed guide, see H. L. Strack and Günter Stemberger, *Introduction to the Talmud and Midrash*, trans. Markus Bockmuehl, 2d ed. (Minneapolis: Fortress, 1992). The authors provide detailed descriptions of all rabbinic texts as well as accounts of the generations of Palestinian and Babylonian rabbis. A chapter on "Other Haggadic Works" (326–50) includes texts (including *Sefer Yosippon* and *The Wars of the Sons of Jacob*) that do not easily fit into any "rabbinic" canon.

10. Petrus Alfonsi, *Dialogue against the Jews*, trans. Irven Resnick (Washington, DC: Catholic University of America Press, 2006), 3–36. Resnick's introduction provides an excellent survey of the text's sources and situates it within contemporary controversies between Rabbinic scholars and Karaites as well as among Christian, Jewish, and Muslim polemicists. For the passage on God's grief from B. Berakhot 3a, see ibid., 68.

11. See the classic article by David Berger, "Gilbert Crispin, Alan of Lille, and Jacob ben Reuben: A Study in the Transmission of Medieval Polemic," *Speculum* 49 (1974): 34–47; and Daniel Lasker, "Jewish–Christian Polemics at the Turning Point: Jewish Evidence from the Twelfth Century," *Harvard Theological Review* 89 (1996): 161–73. For a detailed treatment of Jacob ben Reuben in the context of other Jewish anti-Christian polemicists, see Robert Chazan, *Fashioning Jewish Identity in Medieval Western Christendom* (Cambridge: Cambridge University Press, 2004), 98–103 and 281–97.

12. For an inventory of the manuscripts, see the Vincent of Beauvais website curated by Hans Voorbij and Eva Albrecht: http://www.vincentiusbelvacensis.eu/mss/mss1.html.

13. Literally "Book of Memories"; *Book of Memory* captures the actual meaning. See Eli Yassif, "The Hebrew Narrative Anthology in the Middle Ages," in *The Anthology in Jewish Literature*, ed. David Stern (Oxford: Oxford University Press, 2004), 176–95.

14. *Libellus totius operis apologeticus*, ed. Serge Lusignan, in "Preface au *Speculum Maius* de Vincent de Beauvais: Refraction et diffraction," *Cahiers d'études médiévales* 5 (1979): 115–39. For the history of the apocryphal book of *Jannes and Jambres*, first mentioned in written form by Origen, see "Jannes and Jambres (First to Third Century A.D.)," in *The Old Testament Pseudepigrapha*, vol. 2, *Expansions of the "Old Testament" and Legends, Wisdom and Philosophical Literature, Prayers, Psalms, and Odes, Fragments of Lost Judeo-Hellenistic Works*, ed. James H. Charlesworth (New York: Doubleday, 1985), 427–36.

15. "Sic et ego pauca illa de apocrifis huic operi inservi, non vera vel falsa asserendo, sed tantum ea que legi simpliciter recitando, que salva fide possunt et credi et legi. Neque enim aliter a quoquam christiano libri apocrifi sive etiam philosophici vel poetici legendi sunt, nisi in mente iugiter servando, quod dicit apostolus: *omnia probate, quod bonum est tenete*. Unde Iheronimus Contra Vigilantium ita loquitur: *operis, inquit, ac studii mei est multos legere, ut ex plurimis diversos carpam flores, non tam omnia probaturus, quam que bona sunt electurus*." Vincent of Beauvais, *Libellus*, ed. Lusignan, "Preface au *Speculum Maius* de Vincent de Beauvais," 124–25. For a translation of Jerome's Letter 61, see *St Jerome: Letters and Select Works*, trans. W. H. Fremantle (1892; repr. Grand Rapids, MI: Eerdmans, 1989), 131–33. When Vincent lists the Apocrypha in another chapter, he defines them according to canon law.

16. The term "midrashic" can mean many different things; the following are two helpful broad frameworks for considering some of the texts in the medieval compilations. James Kugel defines midrash as "not a genre of interpretation but an interpretive stance, a way of reading the sacred text": as such it includes "translations of the bible such as the early Aramaic *targumim*; retellings of biblical passages and books such as the 'Genesis Apocryphon' (discovered amongst the Dead Sea Scrolls) or the medieval *Sefer Hayashar*; sermons, homilies, exegetical prayers and poems, and other synagogue pieces; and of course the great standard corpora of Jewish exegesis" (91–92). The interpretive stance is, in part, to expound a verse of the bible through its "surface irregularities" or inconsistencies, solving possible problems with reference to other scriptural sources. James Kugel, "Two Introductions to Midrash," in *Midrash and Literature*, ed. Geoffrey Hartman and Sanford Budick (New Haven: Yale University Press, 1986), 77–103. Ithamar Gruenwald's hermeneutic approach emphasizes the creative force of midrash within the community of Jewish readers: "The term *midrashic condition* points to a mental attitude or disposition in which the interpretive attention expressed entails more than a concern for lexicological or plain-sense meaning of a text. . . . What really

matters, therefore, is not the mere act of understanding texts, but the creation of the meaning that is attached to them" (7). New interpretations in this model become "at once the source of further speculations and the basis of new traditions" (19). Ithamar Gruenwald, "Midrash and the 'Midrashic Condition': Preliminary Considerations," in *The Midrashic Imagination: Jewish Exegesis, Thought, and History*, ed. Michael Fishbane (Albany: SUNY Press, 1993), 6–22.

17. Yeraḥmeel's poems and other texts are found both in Oxford, Bodl. Lib., MS Heb D.11 (the *Sefer ha-Zikhronot* of Eleazer ben Asher ha-Levi) and Oxford, Bodleian Library, MS Opp. 697. See A. Neubauer, "Yeraḥmeel ben Shelomoh," *JQR* 11 (1899): 364–86, and *SZ*, ed. Yassif, 23–31.

18. Neubauer, "Yeraḥmeel ben Shelomoh," 368.

19. *SZ*, ed. Yassif, 26–27.

20. Neubauer, "Yeraḥmeel ben Shelomoh," 366. Haim Schwarzbaum, "Prolegomenon," in *Chronicles of Jerahmeel*, trans. Gaster, 8. For the original passage in *Yosippon*, see *Sefer Yosippon*, ed. David Flusser (Jerusalem: Bialik Institute, 1980–81), 1:144.

21. *SZ*, ed. Yassif, 69.

22. *SZ*, ed. Yassif, 37–38. John Reeves, in considering the survival of Jewish pseudepigrapha, notes the "strictures" in rabbinic texts against "external books," above all M. Sanhedrin 10:1 in which R. Akiva says that those who read "sefarim ha-ḥizonim" (books excluded from the canon of scripture) will have no share in the world to come. He lists the other principal texts as well. See "Exploring the Afterlife," 148.

23. Mary Franklin-Brown, *Reading the World: Encyclopedic Writing in the Scholastic Age* (Chicago: University of Chicago Press, 2012), 64–65.

24. Yassif, "The Hebrew Narrative Anthology in the Middle Ages," 187–90.

25. Alan Mintz, *Ḥurban: Responses to Catastrophe in Hebrew Literature* (New York: Columbia University Press, 1984), 49–83, at 65.

26. Naomi Seidman, *Faithful Renderings: Jewish-Christian Difference and the Politics of Translation* (Chicago: Chicago University Press, 2006), 30.

27. Jonathan Boyarin and Daniel Boyarin, *Powers of Diaspora: Two Essays on the Relevance of Jewish Culture* (Minneapolis: University of Minneapolis Press, 2002), 11.

28. *SZ*, ed. Yassif, 69. Trans. Gaster, *Chronicles of Jerachmeel*, 1. Yeraḥmeel" uses the same formulation in an apology preceding his translations of Daniel from Aramaic into Hebrew.

29. On this formulation of homeland, see Boyarin and Boyarin, *Powers of Diaspora*, 11.

30. *SZ*, ed. Yassif, 41–48.

31. Mireille Schmidt-Chazan, "L'idée d'Empire dans le *Speculum Historiale* de Vincent de Beauvais," in *Vincent de Beauvais: Intentions et réceptions d'une oeuvre encyclopédique au Moyen-Âge*, ed. E. Monique Paulmier-Foucart, Serge Lusignan, and Alain Nadeau (Montreal: Bellarmin, 1990), 253–84.

32. The most informative introduction is Robin R. Mundill's *The King's Jews: Money, Massacre, and Exodus in Medieval England* (London: Continuum, 2010). There is an enormous amount of recent work on the 1144 Norwich blood libel: the best place to begin is Rubin's introductory essay in Thomas of Monmouth, *The Life and Passion of William of Norwich*, ed. and trans. Miri Rubin (London: Penguin, 2014).

33. Beryl Smalley, *The Study of the Bible in the Middle Ages* (Notre Dame: Notre Dame University Press, 1964); Andrew of Saint-Victor, *Expositionem in Ezechielem*, ed. Michael Signer, CCCM 53E (Turnhout: Brepols, 1991), ix–xxxvii; Rainer Berndt, "The School of St. Victor in Paris," in *Hebrew Bible/Old Testament: The History of Its Interpretation*, vol. 1, *From the Beginnings to the Middle Ages (until 1300)*, pt. 2, *The Middle Ages*, ed. Magne Saebø (Göttingen: Vandenhoek and Ruprecht, 2000), 467–95.

34. Smalley, *Study of the Bible in the Middle Ages*, 162–74.

35. Raphael Loewe, "The Mediaeval Christian Hebraists of England: Herbert of Bosham and Earlier Scholars," *Transactions of the Jewish Historical Society of England* 17 (1951–52): 225–49. Bosham is the subject of two recent studies: Deborah Goodwin, *Take Hold of the Robe of a Jew: Herbert of Bosham's Christian Hebraism* (Leiden: Brill, 2006) and Eva De Visscher, *Reading the Rabbis: Christian Hebraism in the Work of Herbert of Bosham* (Leiden: Brill, 2014).

36. Judith Olszowy-Schlanger, "The Knowledge and Practice of Hebrew Grammar among Christian Scholars in Pre-Expulsion England: The Evidence of 'Bilingual' Hebrew-Latin Manuscripts," in *Hebrew Scholarship and the Medieval World*, ed. Nicholas de Lange (Cambridge: Cambridge University Press, 2001), 114.

37. Raphael Loewe, "The Medieval Christian Hebraists of England: The Superscriptio Lincolniensis," *Hebrew Union College Annual* 28 (1957): 205–52, and "Latin Superscriptio MSS on Portions of the Hebrew Bible Other than the Psalter," *Journal of Jewish Studies* 9 (1958): 63–71; Gilbert Dahan, "Deux psautiers hébraïques glosés en Latin," *REJ* 158 (1999): 61–87.

38. Louis Feldman, "The Jewish Sources of Peter Comestor's Commentary on Genesis in His *Historia Scholastica*," in *Begegnungen zwischen Christentum und Judentum in Antike und Mittelalter: Festschrift für Heinz Schreckenberg*, ed. Dietrich Koch and Hermann Lichtenberger (Gottingen: Vandenhoeck and Ruprecht, 1993), 93–121. Andrew of Saint-Victor did, however, draw on Peter Comestor's borrowings from Yerahmeel. See Andrew of Saint-Victor, *Expositionem super Danielem*, ed. Mark Zier, CCCM 53F (Turnhout: Brepols, 1990), 19.

39. Ian Short, "Patrons and Polyglots: French Literature in Twelfth-Century England," *Anglo-Norman Studies* 14 (1992): 229–49.

40. Rita Copeland, *Rhetoric, Hermeneutics and Translation in the Middle Ages: Academic Traditions and Vernacular Texts* (Cambridge: Cambridge University Press, 1991), 103–7; Serge Lusignan, "*Translatio studii* and the Emergence of French as a Language of Letters in the Middle Ages," *New Medieval Literatures* 14 (2012): 1–19.

41. R. R. Davies, *The First English Empire: Power and Identities in the British Isles, 1093–1343* (Oxford: Oxford University Press, 2000), 31–53.

42. For an overview of the works produced by the English Jewish community, see Cecil Roth, *The Intellectual Activities of Medieval English Jewry* (London: British Academy, 1948). See also the reassessment of the English Talmud scholars by Pinchas Roth and Ethan Zadoff, "The Talmud Community of Thirteenth-Century England," in *Christians and Jews in Angevin England: The York Massacre of 1190, Narratives and Contexts*, ed. Sarah Rees Jones and Sethina Watson (York: York Medieval Press, 2013), 184–203.

43. Judith Olszowy-Schlanger, "The Money Language: Latin and Hebrew in Jewish Legal Contracts from Medieval England," in *Studies in the History of Culture and Science: A Tribute to Gad Freudenthal*, ed. Resianne Fontaine et al. (Leiden: Brill, 2011), 233–50. Philip Slavin has complied examples of Latin legal, geographic, and other terms translated into Hebrew in *shtarot* or charters, demonstrating "dependence on a contemporary Latin diplomatic tradition" (319). See "Hebrew Went Latin: Reflections of Latin Diplomatic Formulae and Terminology in Hebrew Private Deeds from Thirteenth-Century England," *Journal of Medieval Latin* 18 (2008): 306–25.

44. David J. Wasserstein also advocates a reevaluation of the Jews' relationship to a "multiplicity" of languages, but rejects the idea of a multilingual intellectual culture. "The Written Culture of the Jews of Norman England, 1066–1290," *Parcours Judaïques* 6 (2000): 47–60.

45. Susan Einbinder, "Signs of Romance: Hebrew Prose and the Twelfth-Century Renaissance," in *Jews and Christians in Twelfth-Century Europe*, ed. Michael Signer and John Van Engen (Notre Dame: University of Notre Dame Press, 2001), 223.

46. Kirsten Fudeman, *Vernacular Voices: Language and Identity in Medieval French Jewish Communities* (Philadelphia: University of Pennsylvania Press, 2010), 9–25, 124–50.

47. Hanna Liss, *Creating Fictional Worlds: Peshaṭ-Exegesis and Narrativity in Rashbam's Commentary on the Torah* (Leiden: Brill, 2011), 21–31.

48. *Wace's Roman de Brut: A History of the British; Text and Translation*, ed. and trans. Judith Weiss (Exeter: University of Exeter Press, 2002), xi–xxix.

49. See Wasserstein, "Written Culture of the Jews of Norman England," 54–57, on Berekhiah, Abraham Ibn Ezra, and England's "overseas connections."

50. Israel Jacob Yuval, *Two Nations in Your Womb: Perceptions of Jews and Christians in Late Antiquity and the Middle Ages*, trans. Barbara Harshav and Jonathan Chipman (Berkeley: University of California Press, 2006), 1.

51. Walter Benjamin, "The Task of the Translator," trans. Harry Zohn, in *Illuminations*, ed. Hannah Arendt (New York: Shocken, 1968), 74–75.

52. Bella Brodzki, *Can These Bones Live? Translation, Survival, and Cultural Memory* (Stanford: Stanford University Press, 2007), 6; Jacques Derrida, "Des tours de Babel," trans. Joseph Graham, in *Difference in Translation*, ed. Joseph Graham (Ithaca, NY: Cornell University Press, 1985), 165–207.

## 1. Josephus, Jerusalem, and the Martyrs of Medieval England

1. Gerald of Wales, *De Principis instructione liber*, in *Opera*, ed. George F. Warner, Rerum Britannicarum medii aevi scriptores 21 (London: Longman, 1861–91), 8:65: "Fuit autem iisdem temporibus Jesus, sapiens vir, si tamen virum eum nominare fas est. Erat enim mirabilim operum effector et doctor hominum eorum qui libenter quae vera sunt audiunt, et multos quidem Judaeorum, multos etiam ex gentibus sibi adjunxit. Christus hic erat. Hunc, accusatione primorum nostrae gentis virorum, cum Pilatus in crucem agendum esse decrevisset, non deseruerunt hi qui ab initio eum dilexerunt. Apparuit autem eis iterum tertio die vivens, secundum quod divinitus inspirati prophetae vel haec vel alia de eo innumera miracula futura esse praedixerant. Sed *in odium* [*sic*] Christianorum, qui ab ipso nuncipati sunt, et nomen perseverat et genus." The last line should read "Sed *in hodiernum diem* Christianorum, qui ab ipso dicti sunt, et nomen perseverat, et genus." This is no doubt the fourteenth-century scribe's error: describing the sole manuscript (London, British Library, MS Cotton Julius B xiii), Warner calls him "a bad Latin scholar and a shockingly careless copyist" (ix). I am here following Feldman's translation of the Greek *Testimonium* into English in "*The Testimonium Flavianum*: The State of the Question," in *Christological Perspectives: Essays in Honour of Harvey K. McArthur*, ed. Robert F. Berkey and Sarah A. Edwards (New York: Pilgrim Press, 1982), 179–80.

2. Louis Feldman offers arguments on both sides but suggests that the original passage was altered: "*The Testimonium Flavianum*: The State of the Question," 99. See also Alice Whealey, *Josephus on Jesus: The Testimonium Flavianum Controversy from Late Antique to Modern Times* (New York: Peter Lang, 2003), 1–52. For a provocative account of the issues at stake, see Serge Bardet, *Le Testimonium Flavianum: Examen historique, considérations historiographiques* (Paris: Cerf, 2002).

3. Gerald of Wales, *De Principis instructione*, ed. by Warner, 65–66. On the history of the patristic and medieval claim that Jews altered the bible, see William Adler, "The Jews as

Falsifiers: Charges of Tendentious Emendation in Anti-Jewish Christian Polemic," in *Translation of Scripture*, ed. David Goldenberg (Philadelphia: University of Pennsylvania Press, 1990), 1–27, and Irven M. Resnick, "The Falsification of Scripture and Medieval Christian and Jewish Polemics," *Medieval Encounters* 2 (1996): 344–80. As Adler and Resnick both point out, Jerome actually argued against the position that Hebrew texts were falsified: hence his own return to the *Hebraica Veritas*.

4. Peter of Blois, in *Contra perfidiam Judaeorum*, rehearses the more usual argument about Jews falsifying the Septuagint, as per Jerome's *Prologue to Genesis*, but also claims that Jews continue to tamper with scripture. See Resnick, "Falsification of Scripture," 366. Peter of Blois, *Opera Omnia*, ed. J. Giles (Oxford, 1896), 3:62–63.

5. Smalley, *Study of the Bible in the Middle Ages*, 83–195.

6. *Sefer Yosippon*, ed. Flusser, 2:74–90. Yitzhak Baer, "The Hebrew Sefer *Yosippon*" [in Hebrew], in *Sefer Dinaburg*, ed. Ben Zion Dinur and Yitzhak Baer (Jerusalem: Kiryat Sefer, 1949), 178–205. See also Albert A. Bell Jr., "Josephus and Pseudo-*Hegesippus*," in *Josephus, Judaism and Christianity*, ed. Louis Feldman and Gohei Hata (Detroit: Wayne State University Press, 1987), 349–61. On the episode of Robert of Cricklade and *Yosippon*, see Whealey, *Josephus on Jesus*, 58–62.

7. *The Latin Josephus*, vol. 1, *Introduction and Text, Antiquities I–V*, ed. Franz Blatt (Copenhagen: Aarhaus, 1958), 1–16; he discusses the *Testimonium* on 14. Heinz Schreckenberg, *Die Flavius-Josephus-Tradition in Antike und Mittelalter* (Leiden: Brill, 1972) lists citations from both the Greek and Latin traditions through the sixteenth century. In her important work, "The Uses of Josephus: Jewish History in the Medieval Christian Tradition" (PhD diss., University of North Carolina, Chapel Hill, 2005), Karen Kletter discusses and provides an exhaustive catalog of manuscripts of Josephus's works in English libraries in the twelfth century: 120–60 and 189–224; on the *Testimonium*'s appearance in these manuscripts, see 228–29.

8. Heinz Schreckenberg and Kurt Schubert, *Jewish Historiography and Iconography in Early and Medieval Christianity* (Minneapolis: Fortress, 1992), 71–72.

9. *Hegesippi qui dicitur Historiae libri V*, ed. V. Ussani, 2 vols. (Vienna: Tempsky, 1932–60) [hereafter *Hegesippus*].

10. On the revival of classical literature, see R. W. Hunt, "English Learning in the Late Twelfth Century," *Transactions of the Royal Historical Society* 19 (1936): 19–42.

11. *Roberti Crickladensis Defloratio Naturalis historie Plinii Secundi*, ed. Bodo Naf (Bern: Peter Lang, 2002). His dedication to Henry II as a learned as well as a powerful monarch is at 1–2. Charles Haskins identifies Robert of Cricklade with the "Roboratus fortunae" to whom Henry dedicated of his translation of *Phaedo* on the basis of Robert's account (for a collection of Thomas Becket's miracles) of a journey in Sicily from Catania to Syracuse, ca.1158, as well as the two scholars' common interests. Charles H. Haskins, *Studies in the History of Medieval Science* (Cambridge, MA: Harvard University Press, 1927), 165–70. See also Rodney M. Thomson, "England and the Twelfth-Century Renaissance," *Past and Present*, no. 101 (1983): 3–21.

12. Charles H. Haskins, "Italy and Sicily in the Twelfth Century," *English Historical Review* 26 (1911): 433–47. See also Evelyn Jamison "The Sicilian Norman Kingdom in the Mind of Anglo-Norman Contemporaries," *Proceedings of the British Academy* 24 (1938): 237–85. For a brief discussion of the population of Southern Italian Jews in the twelfth century, see Robert Chazan, *The Jews of Medieval Western Christendom* (Cambridge: Cambridge University Press, 2006), 115–20.

13. Rodney M. Thomson, *William of Malmesbury* (Woodbridge: Boydell, 2003), 7.

14. Robert Bartlett, *Gerald of Wales: A Voice of the Middle Ages* (1982; repr., Stroud: Tempus, 2006), 131–71.

15. Beryl Smalley, "Sallust in the Middle Ages," in *Classical Influences on European Culture A.D. 500–1500*, ed. R. R. Bolgar (Cambridge: Cambridge University Press, 1971), 165–175. Bernard Guenée, *Histoire et culture historique dans l'Occident médiéval* (Paris: Aubier, 1980), 300–305.

16. Jerome, Letter 22 to Eustochium, in *Select Letters of St. Jerome*, ed. and trans. F. A. Wright (Cambridge, MA: Harvard University Press, 1933; repr., 1991), 142–43; Cassiodorus, *Institutions of Divine and Secular Learning and On the Soul*, trans. James W. Halporn (Liverpool: Liverpool University Press, 2004), 149. Guenée writes of medieval "Historical Culture": "A simplifier des choses on peut dire que les XIIe et XIIIe siècles furent les temps de Flavius Josephe et d'Orose d'une part, de Lucain et Salluste d'autre part" (*Histoire et culture historique dans l'Occident médiéval*, 304).

17. Jerome, *On Illustrious Men*, trans. Thomas Halton (Washington, DC: Catholic University of America Press, 1999), 28–29. On the importance of the *Testimonium* and Jerome, see Schreckenberg and Schubert, *Jewish Historiography and Iconography*, 77–79, and Kletter, "Uses of Josephus," 84.

18. For inventories of eleventh to thirteenth-century English manuscripts of Pseudo-Hegesippus, see Richard Gameson, *The Manuscripts of Early Norman England (c.1066–1130)* (Oxford: Oxford University Press, 1999), 172.

19. Antonia Gransden, "Prologues in the Historiography of Twelfth-Century England," in *England in the Twelfth Century*, ed. D. Williams (Woodbridge: Boydell, 1990), 55–81.

20. R. Thomson, *William of Malmesbury*, 66.

21. "Res Anglorum gestas Beda . . . ab adventu eorum in Britanniam usque ad suos dies plano et suaui sermone absoluit." William of Malmesbury, *Gesta Regum Anglorum: The History of the English Kings*, ed. and trans. R. A. B. Mynors, completed by R. M. Thomson and M. Winterbottom (Oxford: Clarendon Press, 1998–99), 1:15; 2:15. This sentence echoes Hegesippus's description of his adaptation of the books of Maccabees in his Prologue: "Macchabaeorum quoque res gestas propheticus sermo paucis absolvit" ("The history of the Maccabees has also been recounted briefly in its prophetic language"): *Hegesippus*, 1:3.

22. Kletter, "Uses of Josephus," 252–66.

23. On William's extraordinary manuscript, the Selden Collection (Oxford, Bodleian Library, MS Arch. Seld. B.16), see R. Thomson, *William of Malmesbury*, 27–28, 66–67.

24. Neil Wright, "Twelfth-Century Receptions of a Text: Anglo-Norman Historians and *Hegesippus*," *Anglo-Norman Studies* 31 (2008): 181–82.

25. Geoffrey of Monmouth, *The History of the Kings of Britain*, ed. Michael Reeve and trans. Neil Wright (Woodbridge: Boydell, 2007), 280–81.

26. William of Newburgh, *Historia rerum Anglicarum Books I–IV*, in *Chronicles of the Reigns of Stephen, Henry II, and Richard I*, ed. Richard Howlett, Rerum Britannicarum medii aevi scriptores 82 (London: Longman, 1884–89), 1:11–12.

27. On William's particular engagement with the Latin Josephus, see Nicholas Vincent, "William of Newburgh, Josephus, and the New Titus," in *Christians and Jews in Angevin England: The York Massacre of 1190, Narratives and Contexts*, ed. Sarah Rees Jones and Sethina Watson (York: York Medieval Press, 2013), 57–90.

28. In the second preface to *The Description of Wales* Gerald misquotes Cicero (*De oratore*) as Seneca. Gerald of Wales, *Itinerarium Kambriae*, in *Opera*, ed. James Dimock, Rerum Britannicarum medii aevi scriptores 21.6 (London: Longman, 1868), 6:164. Lewis Thorpe,

trans., *The Journey through Wales and The Description of Wales* (Harmondsworth: Penguin, 1978), 217.

29. Josephus, *The Jewish War*, trans. H. St. J. Thackeray, 3 vols. (Cambridge, MA: Harvard University Press, 1927–28; repr.1997), book 1, 1–3.

30. Ralph of Diceto, *Abbreviationes Chronicorum*, in *Radulfi de Diceto decani Lundoniensis Opera historia*, ed. William Stubbs, Rerum Britannicarum medii aevi scriptores 68 (London: Longman, 1876), 1:20–24.

31. M.-D. Chenu, *Nature, Man, and Society in the Twelfth Century: Essays on the New Theological Perspectives in the Latin West*, trans. Jerome Taylor and Lester Little (Chicago: University of Chicago Press, 1968), 164–65; John's list is in *Policraticus* VIII.18.

32. *Hegesippus*, 3; Chiara Somenzi argues for Ambrose's authorship of *"Hegesippus*," based on both linguistic and historical grounds, in *Egesippo-Ambrogio: formazione scholastica e cristiana a Roma alla metà del IV secolo* (Milan: Vita e Pensiero, 2009); see especially her point-by-point summary, 183–92. See also Schreckenberg, *Die Flavius-Josephus-Tradition*, 56–58; Schreckenberg and Schubert, *Jewish Historiography and Iconography*, 71–73; and Whealey, *Josephus on Jesus*, 30–34.

33. *Hegesippus*, 373.

34. Paulus Orosius, *Histoires*, ed. and trans. Marie-Pierre Arnaud-Lindet, 3 vols. (Paris: Les Belles Lettres, 1990–91), 3:39; Paulus Orosius, *The Seven Books of History against the Pagans*, trans. Roy J. Deferrari (Washington, DC: Catholic University of America Press, 1964), 303.

35. The Latin *Vindicta Salvatoris* is published in *Evangelia Apocrypha*, ed. Constantin von Tischendorf (Leipzig: H. Mendelssohn, 1876), 471–86. Tischendorf's edition is based on fourteenth- and fifteenth-century manuscripts. I am quoting from the new edition and translation from the ninth-century manuscript Saint-Omer, Bibliothèque Municipale, MS 202 in *The Apocryphal Gospels: Texts and Translations*, ed. and trans. Bart Ehrman and Zlatko Plese (Oxford: Oxford University Press, 2011), 546–49.

36. Walafrid Strabo, *De Subversione Jerusalem*, in *Patrologia Cursus Completus, Series Latina*, edited by J.-P. Migne (Paris: Migne, 1852), 114, cols. 965–74. On this progression of texts, see Schreckenberg and Schubert, *Jewish Historiography and Iconography*, 71–74.

37. *The Oldest Version of the Twelfth-Century Poem "La Venjance Nostre Seigneur,"* ed. Loyal A. T. Gryting (Ann Arbor: University of Michigan Press, 1952).

38. Israel Yuval discusses the famous rabbinic story of the giant gnat that enters Titus's brain after the fall of Jerusalem (B. Gittin 56b) as a possible response to early versions of the "Vengeance of the Savior" motifs. *Two Nations in Your Womb*, 38–49.

39. Yosef Hayim Yerushalmi, *Zakhor: Jewish History and Jewish Memory* (New York: Schocken, 1989), 34–35.

40. Steven Bowman, *"Sefer Yosippon*: History and Midrash," in Fishbane, *The Midrashic Imagination*, 280–94.

41. Flusser's location of Yosippon's author in ducal Naples seems perfectly reasonable given the sheer number of Latin sources he uses and his references to the geography of the area. By the tenth century there was a large enough Jewish community in Naples that a document attests to a "vicus Judaeorum" or Jewish quarter. See Cesare Colafemmina, "Insediamente e condizioni degli ebrei nell'Italia meridionale e insulare," in *Gli ebrei nell'alto medioevo* (Spoleto: Presso la Sede del Centro, 1980), 1:225.

42. *Sefer Yosippon*, ed. Flusser, 2:124. He considers two early southern Italian MSS, written in the Beneventan script, of the type that include books I–XVI of the Latin *Jewish Antiquities* followed by the entire text of *Hegesippus*: Naples, Biblioteca Nazionale, Cod. Lat. V F 34 and Florence, Bibliothecca Medicea Laurenziana, Laur. Plut. 66, 1. *Yosippon*'s author was

clearly working with a similar manuscript from this region. See also *The Latin Josephus*, ed. Blatt, 27–28, 32.

43. Shlomo Simonsohn, "The Hebrew Revival among Early Medieval European Jews," in *The Salo Wittmayer Baron Jubilee Volume on the Occasion of His Eightieth Birthday*, ed. Saul Lieberman (Jerusalem: American Academy for Jewish Research, 1974), 2:831–58.

44. *Der Alexanderroman des Archipresbyters Leo*, ed. Friedrich Pfister (Heidelberg: C. Winter, 1913), 44–46.

45. *Sefer Yosippon*, ed. Flusser, 2:216–52.

46. *Sefer Yosippon*, ed. Flusser, 1:234. Flusser points to M. Taanit 4.8 for this particular formulation of the prayer for the rebuilding of the Temple. Ibid., 2:170.

47. *Sefer Yosippon*, ed. Flusser, 2:169–70.

48. *Sefer Yosippon*, ed. Flusser, 1:143–44.

49. David Stern, "The Anthological Imagination in Jewish Literature," *Prooftexts* 17 (1997), 1–7.

50. Flavius Josephus, *Jewish Antiquities*, trans. Louis Feldman, Ralph Marcus, H. St. J. Thackeray, and Allen Wikgren, 9 vols. (Cambridge, MA: Harvard University Press, 1998), 6:3. Tessa Rajak, *Josephus: The Historian and His Society*, 2nd ed. (London: Duckworth, 2002), 78–103; Shaye J. D. Cohen, "Josephus, Jeremiah, and Polybius," *History and Theory* 21 (1982): 366–81.

51. Steven Bowman notes David Ben Gurion's adoption of this name in a larger discussion of the text's place in the early Zionist movement: "*Yosippon* and Jewish Nationalism," *Proccedings of the American Academy for Jewish Research* 61 (1995): 23–51.

52. Avraham Grossman, *The Early Sages of Ashkenaz* (Jerusalem: Magnes, 1981), 158–65. Grossman identifies four main themes of R. Gershom's *selihot*: the suffering of the Jews in the Diaspora; hatred of his persecutors and polemics against Christians; the justice of suffering as punishment for the Jews' sins; and pleas for an imminent Redemption (*ge'ula*). Flusser notes Gershom's use of *Yosippon* in a *piyyut* that mentions the incident from 2 Maccabees of Antiochus's fall from his chariot (*Sefer Yosippon*, ed. Flusser, 1:84). On Gershom's copying of *Yosippon*, see also *Sefer Yosippon*, ed. Flusser, 2:3; and Avraham Grossman, "The Roots of Qiddush ha-Shem in Early Ashkenaz" [in Hebrew], in *Sanctity of Life and Martyrdom: Studies in Memory of Amir Yekutiel*, ed. Isaiah Gafni and Aviezer Ravitzsky (Jerusalem: Zalman Shazar Center, 1992), 117.

53. Jerome, *Commentariorum in Danielem Libri III (IV)*, ed. F. Glorie, CCSL 75A (Turnhout: Brepols, 1964), 921–22.

54. B. Yoma 9b: "But why was the second Sanctuary destroyed, seeing that in its time they were occupying themselves with Torah, [observance of] precepts, and the practice of charity? Because therein prevailed hatred without cause (*sinat ḥinam*). That teaches you that groundless hatred is considered as of even gravity with the three sins of idolatry, immorality, and bloodshed together. And [during the time of] the first Sanctuary did no groundless hatred prevail? Surely it is written: They are thrust down to the sword with my people; smite therefore upon my thigh, and R. Eleazar said: This refers to people who eat and drink together and then thrust each other through with the daggers of their tongue!—That [passage] speaks of the princes in Israel, for it is written, Cry and wail, son of man; for it is upon my people, etc. [Ezek. 21:17]. [The text reads] 'Cry and wail, son of man.' One might have assumed [it is upon] all [Israel], therefore it goes on, Upon all the princes of Israel." Trans. *Babylonian Talmud: Hebrew/Aramaic-English Edition*, ed. Isidore Epstein and Maurice Simon, 30 vols. (London: Soncino Press, 1965–89).

55. Flusser bases his edition on the earliest recension, in Jerusalem, National Library of Israel, MS 8° 41280. The manuscript is dated to 1282. He includes a stemma of the

complicated manuscript tradition in *Sefer Yosippon*, ed. Flusser, 2:53. Flusser points to the rapid transmission of the text by the eleventh century to Mainz, where it was used by Rabbi Gershom Me'or ha-Golah, and to Spain, where it was already available to Ibn Hazm in an Arabic translation. Ibid., 2:66; 2:3–32.

56. *Sefer Yosippon*, ed. Flusser, 1:435–38; 2:55–59. On the context of this interpolation, see Israel Levi, "Jésus, Caligula et Claude dans une interpolation du Yosiphon," *REJ* 91 (1931–32): 135–54.

57. Josephus, *The Jewish War*, books V–VII, trans. H. St. J. Thackeray (Cambridge, MA: Harvard University Press, 1928), book VII, 320–89. See also Rajak, *Josephus*, especially 78–103.

58. Josephus, *The Jewish War*, books V–VII, trans. Thackeray, book V, 361–424. On Josephus's languages, see Rajak, *Josephus*, 230–32.

59. *Hegesippus*, 321.

60. *Sefer Yosippon*, ed. Flusser, 1:357.

61. Benjamin, "Task of the Translator." See also Brodzki's analysis of this text, *Can These Bones Live?*, 1–15.

62. Benjamin, "Task of the Translator," 80.

63. Guenée, *Histoire et culture historique*, 300–331.

64. Roth, *Intellectual Activities of Medieval English Jewry*. On debates between Christians and Jews in England, see Abulafia, *Christians and Jews in the Twelfth-Century Renaissance*, 77–106.

65. *Sefer Yosippon*, ed. Flusser, 1:9–20; on *Yosippon*'s imagination of Rome, see Bowman, "*Sefer Yosippon*."

66. *Sefer Yosippon*, ed. Flusser, 1:430–31.

67. *Sefer Yosippon*, ed. Flusser, 2:96–97.

68. Gerson D. Cohen, "Hannah and Her Seven Sons in Hebrew Literature," in *Studies in the Variety of Rabbinic Cultures* (Philadelphia: Jewish Publication Society, 1991), 39–60.

69. There is a huge amount of scholarship on the story of the Septuagint and its role in shaping Jewish and Christian ideas of translation. See in particular Abraham Wasserstein and David Wasserstein, *The Legend of the Septuagint: From Classical Antiquity to Today* (Cambridge: Cambridge University Press, 2006), especially 192–216 on the *Yosippon* version. For a meditation on the Talmudic account (B. Megilla 9a–b) and the necessity of Greek as the "language of Europe," see Emmanuel Lévinas, *In the Time of the Nations*, trans. Michael Smith (London: Continuum, 2007), 22–42. See also Seidman, *Faithful Renderings*, 37–72.

70. *Sefer Yosippon*, ed. Flusser, 1:70–75.

71. "Ve-lo tithalel terumat hakodesh be-niddat hagoi'im." *Sefer Yoisppon*, ed. Flusser, 1:429.

72. On Platonic thought in Josephus's depiction of the suicides at Masada, see David Ladouceur, "Masada: A Consideration of the Literary Evidence," *Greek, Roman, and Byzantine Studies* 21 (1980): 245–60. See also Shaye J. D. Cohen on the place of Josephus's account in the tradition of classical narratives of mass suicide, "Masada: Literary Tradition, Archaeological Remains, and the Credibility of Josephus," *Journal of Jewish Studies* 33 (1982): 385–405.

73. *Cain and Abel*, in Ambrose, *Opera*, Part I, ed. Karl Schenkl (Vienna: Tempsky, 1897), 339–409. Translation in Ambrose, *Hexameron, Paradise, and Cain and Abel*, trans. John Savage (Washington, DC: Catholic University of America Press, 1961), 359–437. See also Pierre Courcelle, "Tradition Platonicienne et traditions chrétiennes du corps-prison," *Revue des Études Latines* 43 (1965): 406–43.

74. *De bono mortis,* in Ambrose, *Opera,* Part I, ed. Schenkl, 702–53. Translation in Ambrose, *Seven Exegetical Works,* trans. Michael McHugh (Washington, DC: Catholic University of America Press, 1972), 70–113.

75. *Hegesippus,* 409–10.

76. On the persecution of Jews by the Macedonian emperors in the ninth century, see Andrew Sharf, *Byzantine Jewry: From Justinian to the Fourth Crusade* (New York: Schocken, 1971), 82–105. The oppressions of this era were remembered in *piyyutim* possibly known to Yosippon's author.

77. *Sefer Yosippon,* ed. Flusser, 1:425–26. Flusser traces the expression "great light" (Isaiah 9:1) to the *Vision of Baruch* (2 Baruch) 48:53 and the Slavonic *Enoch* 17:7 in this eschatological sense (ibid., 301 n. 26 and 2:110–11). For other uses, see Elliot Wolfson, *Through a Speculum that Shines: Vision and Imagination in Medieval Jewish Mysticism* (Princeton, NJ: Princeton University Press, 1994), 135–36.

78. Grossman, "Roots of Kiddush ha-Shem." An abridged English version of this argument is in Grossman, "The Cultural and Social Background of Jewish Martyrdom in Germany in 1096," in *Juden und Christen zur Zeit der Kreuzzüge,* ed. Alfred Haverkamp (Sigmaringen: Jan Thorbecke Verlag, 1999), 73–86. See also Jeremy Cohen, *Sanctifying the Name of God: Jewish Martyrs and Jewish Memories of the First Crusade* (Philadelphia: University of Pennsylvania Press, 2004), 13–16 and Robert Chazan, *European Jewry and the First Crusade* (Berkeley: University of California Press, 1987), 148–55.

79. *The Jews and the Crusaders: The Hebrew Chronicles of the First and Second Crusades,* ed. and trans. Shlomo Eidelberg (Hoboken: KTAV, 1996), 31. Hebrew in *Hebräische Berichte über die Judenverfolgungen während der Kreuzzüge,* ed. Adolf Neubauer and Moritz Stern (Berlin: Verlag von Leonhard Simion, 1892), 7.

80. *The Jews and the Crusaders,* ed. and trans. Eidelberg, 40; *Hebräische Berichte,* ed. Neubauer and Stern, 12. See J. Cohen, *Sanctifying the Name of God,* 100–102.

81. *The Jews and the Crusaders,* ed. and trans. Eidelberg, 56; *Hebräische Berichte,* ed. Neubauer and Stern, 21.

82. Grossman, "Roots of Kiddush ha-Shem," 119–21; Shmuel Shepkaru, *Jewish Martyrs in the Pagan and Christian Worlds* (Cambridge: Cambridge University Press, 2006), 174.

83. Grossman, "Roots of Kiddush ha-Shem"; Israel Ta-Shma, "The Attitude of Medieval German Halakhists to Aggadic Sources" [in Hebrew], in *Facing the Cross: The Persecutions of 1096 in History and Historiography,* ed. Yom Tov Assis et al. (Jerusalem: Magnes, 2000), 150–56. The ongoing debate over whether Askenazic communities justified suicide and murder through aggadah considered to have the same authority as halakhah or whether the later Tosafists fit the events of 1096 into their interpretations of halakhah is beyond the scope of this study.

84. The *Midrash of the Ten Martyrs* or *Midrash Eleh Ezkerah* ("These I will remember") exists in numerous versions; there is a critical edition of ten recensions: Gottfried Reeg, ed., *Die Geschichte von den Zehn Märtyrern: synoptische Edition mit Übersetzung und Einleitung* (Tübingen: Mohr, 1985). See also Strack and Stemberger, *Introduction to the Talmud and Midrash,* 338–39. For a translation, see David Stern and Mark Jay Mirsky, *Rabbinic Fantasies: Imaginative Narratives from Classical Hebrew Literature* (Philadelphia: Jewish Publication Society, 1990), 143–65. For a discussion of the legend's development, see Joseph Dan, *The Hebrew Story in the Middle Ages* [in Hebrew] (Jerusalem: Keter, 1974), 62–68. The classic study of medieval martyrological traditions about the sacrifice of Isaac is Shalom Spiegel, *The Last Trial: On the Legends and Lore of the Command to Abraham to Offer Isaac as a Sacrifice, the Akedah* (New York: Schocken, 1967); see also J. Cohen, *Sanctifying the Name of God,* 117–20.

85. Robert C. Stacey, "Crusades, Martyrdoms, and the Jews of Norman England, 1096–1190," in Haverkamp, *Juden und Christen zur Zeit der Kreuzzüge*, 233–51.

86. Gerald of Wales, *The Journey through Wales and the Description of Wales*, 74; *De Principis instructione*, ed. Warner, 200.

87. Jeremy Cohen, "The Muslim Connection, or On the Changing Role of the Jew in High Medieval Theology," in *From Witness to Witchcraft: Jews and Judaism in Medieval Christian Thought*, ed. Jeremy Cohen (Wiesbaden: Harrassowitz, 1996), 141–62.

88. Gerald of Wales, *De Principis instructione liber*, ed. Warner, 183–86. Trans. Joseph Stevenson in *The Church Historians of England*, 5.1 (London: Seeleys, 1858), 155–57. On Henry II, see also Stacey, "Crusades, Martyrdoms, and the Jews," 244.

89. John Cotts, *The Clerical Dilemma: Peter of Blois and Literate Culture in the Twelfth Century* (Washington, DC: Catholic University of America Press, 2009), 229.

90. *Petri Blensesis Epistolae*, in Peter of Blois, *Opera Omnia*, ed. Giles, 1:317. He uses terms very similar to and perhaps taken from John of Salisbury to signify a "shared humanist culture." Cotts, *The Clerical Dilemma*, 113–14.

91. *Contra perfidiam Judaeorum*, in Peter of Blois, *Opera Omnia*, ed. Giles, 3:62–129 (at 104). See also R. W. Southern, "The Two Peters of Blois in the Schools and in Government," in *Scholastic Humanism and the Unification of Europe*, vol. 2, *The Heroic Age* (Oxford: Blackwell, 2001), 178–218.

92. Anna Sapir Abulafia, "Twelfth-Century Christian Expectations of Jewish Conversion: A Case Study of Peter of Blois," *Aschkenas* 8 (1998): 45–70.

93. "In hac spe fortiter universa sustinuit, adventum bellicose gentis expectans, sed vereor ne sic eam prestoletur ut Britones Arturum et Iudei Messiam!" *Passio Raginaldi principis Antiochie*, in Peter of Blois, *Tractatus Duo*, ed. R. B. C. Huygens, CCCM 194 (Turnhout: Brepols, 2002), 32.

94. "Et quid Trenos Ieremie revolvo? Totus Ieremias non sufficeret faciem miserie presentis exprimere!" *Conquestio de Dilatione Vie Ierosolimitane*, in Peter of Blois, *Tractatus Duo*, ed. Huygens, 76. See also R. W. Southern, "Peter of Blois and the Third Crusade," in *Studies in Medieval History Presented to RHC Davis*, ed. H. Mayr-Harting and R. I. Moore (London: Hambledon, 1985), 207–69.

95. "Clamavit sanguis Abel ultionem de terra et invenit ultorem, clamat Christi sanguis auxilium et non invenit adiutorem." *Conquestio de Dilatione Vie Ierosolimitane*, ed. Huygens, 83.

96. *The Oldest Version of the Twelfth-Century Poem "La Venjance Nostre Seigneur,"* ed. Gryting.

97. Avraham Grossman, quoting a *piyyut* of R. Yehuda ben R. Kalonymos in "The Victories of Salah ad-Din and the Awakening in Europe for Aliyah to the Land of Israel," in *Studies in the History of Eretz Israel Presented to Yehuda Ben Porat*, ed. Yehoshua Ben-Arieh and Elchanan Reiner (Jerusalem: Yad Ben Zvi Press, 2003), 374, n. 40.

98. The standard and highly detailed history of the York massacre is R. B. Dobson, *The Jews of Medieval York and the Massacre of March 1190*, Borthwick Papers 45, rev. ed. (York: Borthwick Institute for Historical Research, 1996). Dobson emphasizes the role of the Third Crusade in the heightened anti-Judaism of Richard I's reign.

99. Ibid., 35. See also Robert Stacey's informative entry on Aaron of Lincoln: "Lincoln, Aaron of (d. 1186)," in *Oxford Dictionary of National Biography*, Oxford: Oxford University Press, 2004, http://www.oxforddnb.com/view/article/37090.

100. Dobson, *Jews of Medieval York*, 27. The Tosafists were interpreters of the Talmud whose commentaries (tosafot or "additions") are based on Rashi's commentary.

101. "Malebant enim a propria gente percuti, quam manibus incircumcisorum perire." Ralph of Diceto, *Ymagines Historiarum*, in *Radulfi de Diceto decani Lundoniensis Opera*

*historia*, ed. Stubbs, 2:73–74. On Ralph's learning, see Antonia Gransden, *Historical Writing in England*, vol. 1, *c.550 to c.1307* (Ithaca, NY: Cornell University Press, 1974), 230–36.

102. "Hic erat honorabilis omnibus, et tanquam uni ex prophetis obtemperabatur ei ab omnibus." William of Newburgh, *Historia rerum Anglicarum*, ed. Howlett, 318. There is a translation of the entire passage in Stevenson, *The Church Historians of England* 4.2:565–72.

103. "Deus, cui dici non debet, 'Cur ita facis?' jubet nos pro lege sua mori modo. . . . Cum ergo mortem gloriosam vitae turpissimae praeponere debemus, honestissimum plane atque facillimum mortis genus eligendum est. . . . Hoc enim et multi nostrorum in diversis tribulationibus laudabiliter fecisse noscuntur, formam nobis decentissime electionis praestruentes." William of Newburgh, *Historia rerum Anglicarum*, ed. Howlett, 318–19.

104. Rufinus's Latin translation of Eleazer's speeches at Masada from the *Jewish War* are in Flavius Josephus, *Opera, Quae Reperiri Potuerunt Omnia*, ed. John Hudson (Oxford, 1720), 2:1318–23.

105. "Verum qui Josephi de Judaico bello legit historiam satis intelligit ab antiqua Judaeorum superstitione, cum forte tristior casus incumberet, illam nostri temporis manasse vesaniam." William of Newburgh, *Historia rerum Anglicarum*, ed. Howlett, 320.

106. On the relatively wide availability of Eusebius's *Historia Ecclesiastica* in twelfth-century monastic libraries, usually anonymous but sometimes attributed to his translator Rufinus, see Richard Sharpe, *List of Identifications*, 285–86, available at http://www.history.ox.ac.uk/fileadmin/ohf/documents/projects/List-of-Identifications.pdf. The catalogs of monastic libraries are available at http://mlgb3.bodleian.ox.ac.uk/authortitle/medieval_catalogues/.

107. William of Newburgh, *Historia rerum Anglicarum*, ed. Howlett, 321–22.

108. William of Newburgh, *Historia rerum Anglicarum*, ed. Howlett, 253–54. Vincent, "William of Newburgh," interprets William's use of Josephus as a way to understand the Plantagenet dynasty through the model of the Flavian emperors—with Richard compared to the "heroic" Titus. His reading of the Flavians' twelfth-century reputations encompasses William's English contemporaries as well.

109. J. Cohen, *Sanctifying the Name of God*, 13–30.

110. *The Historia Ierosolimitana of Baudric de Bourgueil*, ed. Steven Biddlecombe (Woodbridge: Boydell, 2014), 8. Translation in *The First Crusade: The Chronicle of Fulcher of Chartres and Other Source Materials*, ed. Edward Peters, 2nd ed. (Philadelphia: University of Pennsylvania Press, 1998), 31.

111. Robert the Monk, *History of the First Crusade: Historia Iherosolimitana*, trans. Carol Sweetenham (Burlington, VT: Ashgate, 2005), 82. It should be said that all of these texts are versions of Urban's speech written by clerics not actually in attendance in 1095. On the differing details, see J. O. Ward, "Some Principles of Rhetorical Historiography in the Twelfth Century," in *Classical Rhetoric and Medieval Historiography*, ed. Ernst Breisach (Kalamazoo: Medieval Institute Publications, 1985), 103–65.

112. William of Malmesbury, *Gesta Regum Anglorum*, ed. and trans. Mynors, 1:604–6. On William's sources, principally *Hegesippus*, see ibid. 2:305–6.

113. Shepkaru, *Jewish Martyrs*, 117–25, 142.

114. Jeremy Cohen, "The Hebrew Crusade Chronicles in Their Christian Cultural Context," in Haverkamp, *Juden und Christen zur Zeit der Kreuzzüge*, 17–34; Ivan Marcus, "From Deus Lo Vult to *The Will of the Creator*" [in Hebrew], in Assis et al., *Facing the Cross*, 92–100.

115. See J. Cohen, *Sanctifying the Name of God*, 61–62, on the shifting valences of the "Spiritual Jerusalem."

116. *The Midrash Rabbah: Eichah*, ed. Yaakov Reinman with a translation by Yaakov Blinder (Jerusalem: Machon HaMidrash HaMevo'ar, 2004). Mintz, *Ḥurban*, 45–83. A

prominent theme that connects *Yosippon* and *Lamentations Rabbah* is the composite figure
of Zechariah, murdered and his blood left in the open (*Sefer Yosippon*, ed. Flusser, 1:341, and
throughout *Lamentations Rabbah*); see Sheldon Blank, "The Death of Zechariah in Rabbinic
Literature," *Hebrew Union College Annual* 12/13 (1937–38): 327–46. In the *Sefer ha-Zikhronot*,
*Sefer Yosippon* is followed closely by *Lamentations Rabbah*, followed by the *Midrash of the
Ten Martyrs*, followed by a version of R. Ephraim of Bonn's *Sefer Zechirah*. On the theme
of memory as inscribed in the name "Zechariah," see J.-D. Dubois, "La mort de Zacharie:
mémoire juive at mémoire chrétienne," *Revue des Études Augustiniennes* 40 (1994): 23–38.

117. On the relationship of the *Sefer Yosippon* to chivalry and *romans de geste*, see *Sefer
Yosippon*, ed. Flusser, 2:159–64.

118. Yael Zerubavel, *Recovered Roots: Collective Memory and the Making of Israeli
National Tradition* (Chicago: University of Chicago Press, 1995), 60–76.

119. R. Ephraim Bar Jacob of Bonn, *Sefer Zekhirah*, ed. A. M. Habermann (Jerusalem:
Bialik Institute, 1970), 35–36. Susan Einbinder discusses Yom Tov of Joigny's martyrdom in
*Beautiful Death: Jewish Poetry and Martyrdom in Medieval France* (Princeton, NJ: Princeton
University Press, 2002), 51.

120. *Sefer Yosippon*, ed. Flusser, 2:108–9.

121. See Einbinder, *Beautiful Death*, 57–59. Yom Tov's poem "Yah Tishpokh Hamatkha"
("Lord Pour Out Your Wrath") is in Haim Schirmann, "Persecution Laments from the Land
of Israel, Africa, Spain, Ashkenaz, and France" [in Hebrew], *Qovez 'al Yad* 3 (1939): 36–37.
Translated by Susan Einbinder in *Medieval Hagiography: An Anthology*, ed. Thomas Head
(New York: Routledge, 2000), 554–55.

122. Joseph of Chartres's *kinnah* for the martyrs of York is edited in both Hebrew and
English in *Tisha b'Av Compendium: Tephilot and Kinot*, ed. and trans. Abraham Rosenfeld
(New York: Judaica Press, 1965), 168–70; Cecil Roth's edition and translation with a detailed
introduction, "A Hebrew Elegy on the York Martyrs of 1190," is in the *Transactions of the
Jewish Historical Society of England* 16 (1945–51): 213–20.

123. Roth identifies Yom Tov of Joigny, Moses (Mosse) son of Sarah, Joseph (Josce of
York), and Elijah "the martyr" of York using contemporary pipe rolls and other documents.
He identifies the latter figure with the Elijah "referred to in Tosafot Yoma 27a and Zebaḥim
14b as an acute rabbinical authority." "A Hebrew Elegy," ed. and trans. Roth, 214–16.

## 2. Diaspora without End and the Renewal of Epic

1. Jacob ben Yehuda Ḥazan of London, *Etz Hayyim* [in Hebrew], ed. Israel Brodie,
vol. 1 (Jerusalem: Mosad ha-Rav Kook, 1962). Jacob includes four penitential poems for the
ten days of repentance between Rosh ha-Shanah and Yom Kippur, three with his signature in
an acrostic and one without. For a comprehensive account of the text, see the two articles by
David Kaufmann, "The Etz Chayim of Jacob B. Jehudah of London, and the History of His
Manuscript," *JQR* 5 (1893): 353–74, and "The Prayer-Book According to the Ritual of England before 1290," *JQR* 4 (1891): 20–63. On the four penitential poems, see Susan Einbinder,
"Meir b. Elijah of Norwich: Persecution and Poetry among Medieval English Jews," *Journal
of Medieval History* 26 (2000): 145–62, especially 154–55.

2. Jacob ben Yehuda Ḥazan, *Etz Hayyim*, ed. Brodie, 130–31. The poem's first line
cites Psalm 62.

3. Interestingly, the word Jacob uses here for "captivity"—*shevi*—usually refers to
Israel; a notable exception is Jeremiah 30:16: "Assuredly, all those who wanted to devour you
shall be devoured / and every one of your foes shall go into captivity (*shevi*)." Ezekiel 35:7
provides another example of this kind of harsh fate in store for Edom: "I will make Mount
Seir an utter waste (*shimema*), and I will keep all passersby away from it."

4. On Edward's Crusade, including its Jewish financing, see Michael Prestwich, *Edward I* (New Haven: Yale University Press, 1997), 66–85. See also Robin Mundill, *England's Jewish Solution: Experiment and Expulsion, 1262–1290* (Cambridge: Cambridge University Press, 1998), 68–69.

5. The poem exemplifies what Israel Yuval characterizes as an idea of "vengeful redemption" in post-1096 Ashkenazic *piyyutim* about the annihilation of Edom. See Yuval, *Two Nations in Your Womb*, 92–109.

6. Gerson D. Cohen too notes that the author "had good sources of information from which he departed on occasion quite deliberately." "Esau as Symbol in Early Medieval Thought," in *Studies in the Variety of Rabbinic Cultures*, 256. *Sefer Yosippon*, ed. Flusser, 1:159.

7. Jupiter reassures Aeneas's mother Venus: "his ego nec metas rerum nec tempora pono; imperium sine fine dedi." *Aeneid* 1, 280–81. Virgil, *Eclogues, Georgics, Aeneid 1–6*, ed. and trans. H. R. Fairclough, rev. G. P. Goold (Cambridge, MA: Harvard University Press, 1999).

8. G. Cohen, "Esau as Symbol," 256.

9. B. Sotah 13a. "At that time was the prophecy of Rebekah fulfilled, as it is written: *Why should I be bereaved of you both in one day?* Although the death of the two of them did not occur on the one day, still their burial took place on the same day."

10. The author here evidently uses Benevento to give his story a local setting, one that also evokes the sometimes tense border between the territories of nominally "Byzantine" Naples and "Lombard" Capua-Benevento. In 953, the prince of Benevento was Landolf II; given the long history of military tensions and occasional alliances between the Lombard Benevento and the autonomous Duchy of Naples it's hard to know if *Yosippon*'s identification of Turnus as the "King of Benevento" is an insult or a compliment. The author also refers to "tombs" of Pallas and Turnus "between Albano and Rome" as local monuments; he evidently regarded the world of the *Aeneid* as a somewhat familiar geographical space. For surveys of the politics of Lombard and Byzantine southern Italy in the tenth century, see Barbara Kreutz, *Before the Normans: Southern Italy in the Ninth and Tenth Centuries* (Philadelphia: University of Pennsylvania Press, 1991), 116–49, and Graham Loud, "Southern Italy in the Tenth Century," in *NCMH*, vol. 3, *c.900–c.1024*, ed. Timothy Reuter (Cambridge: Cambridge University Press, 1995), 624–45.

11. Flusser (*Sefer Yosippon*, 1:14, n. 64) points out that *Yosippon*'s characterization of Latinus as an "inventor" or "corrector" of the Latin language is close to Paul the Deacon's. He suggests that the Hebrew "Latinus, ze bi'er lashon Latino ve-ototav" could be a direct translation of Paul's Latinus: "Qui Latinum regnam correxit et Latinos de suo nomine appellavit." Paul the Deacon, *Historia Romana*, ed. H. Droysen (Berlin: Weidman, 1879), 3.

12. *Sefer Yosippon*, ed. Flusser, 1:9–20. For a partial translation, see Gaster, *Chronicles of Jerachmeel*, 95–100.

13. The best source in connection with *Yosippon* on the copying and transmission of the *Aeneid* is still E. A. Lowe, *Virgil in South Italy: Facsimiles of Eight Manuscripts of Virgil in Beneventan Script* (Turin: G. Chiantore, 1932). Lowe surmises that the illustrated tenth-century Virgil, Naples, Biblioteca Nazionale, Lat. 6, was originally from the ducal library of Naples (see 45–46). See also L. D. Reynolds, ed., *Texts and Transmission: A Survey of the Latin Classics* (Oxford: Clarendon Press, 1983), on Servius, 385–88. Naples, Biblioteca Nazionale, Lat. 5 includes the commentary on *Aeneid* 1–11. For more on Naples as a center of Latin and Greek culture, including the circulation of the Latin Josephus, see E. A. Lowe, *The Beneventan Script: A History of the South Italian Miniscule*, 2nd ed, prepared and enlarged Virginia Brown (Rome: Edizioni di Storia e Letteratura, 1980), 1:54–56. *Yosippon*'s knowledge of the other Latin authors can be drawn from the text and the availability of manuscripts

in southern Italy. For a list of the numerous early medieval manuscripts of Orosius's *Seven Books of History against the Pagans*, see Pierre Arnaud-Lindet's introduction to Orosius, *Histoires*, 1:lxvii–xcix, and also online at http://www.tertullian.org/rpearse/manuscripts/orosius_history.htm. The author's knowledge of Paul the Deacon's continuation of Eutropius, composed at nearby Montecassino, is speculation, but the work would have provided him with information about the Vandals; see Flusser on the figure of Latinus, *Sefer Yosippon*, 2:14, n. 64. Birger Munk Olsen, *L'Étude des auteurs classiques latins aux XIe et XIIe siècles*, 4 vols. (Paris: CNRS, 1982–2009) is an extremely useful study of the manuscripts of Virgil and other Latin classics.

14. G. Cohen, "Esau as Symbol," 256.

15. On the immense importance of Orosius for medieval conceptions of geography, see A. H. Merrills, *History and Geography in Late Antiquity* (Cambridge: Cambridge University Press, 2005), 35–99. *Yosippon*'s author would have been familiar of course with Josephus's long catalog of the geographic dispersion of Noah's descendants in the *Antiquities*; see Josephus, *Jewish Antiquities*, 1: 58–73. A midrashic version of the catalog is in *Midrash Genesis Rabbah* 37.

16. Merrills, *History and Geography in Late Antiquity*, especially 20–34.

17. *Sefer Yosippon*, ed. Flusser, 1:3.

18. Baer, "The Hebrew Sefer *Yosippon*," 179.

19. Janet L. Nelson, "The Frankish Kingdoms, 814–898: The West," in *NCMH*, vol. 2, *c.700–c.900*, ed. Rosamond McKitterick (Cambridge: Cambridge University Press, 1995), 110–68. As Flusser points out, he deliberately doesn't call the sons of Gomer "Gauls" like other historians. *Sefer Yosippon*, ed. Flusser, 1:3, n. 9.

20. *Yosippon*, ed. Flusser, 1:7–8. These are presumably the Vikings that Charlemagne repelled but never ruled or the Danes subjected by Henry I of Saxony in 934; they also seem to be conflated with the Vikings who occupied parts of England in the ninth and tenth centuries. Rosamond McKitterick explains the diplomatic relations between Charlemagne and the Danes in *Charlemagne: The Formation of a European Identity* (Cambridge: Cambridge University Press, 2008), 127–29. Flusser mentions Liutprand of Cremona's exaggerated account of Henry I and the Danes, *Sefer Yosippon*, ed. Flusser, 1:7–8; see also Eckhard Muller-Mertens on Henry's defeat of "a petty Danish king" in "The Ottonians as Kings and Emperors," in *NCMH*, vol. 3, ed. Reuter, 233–66. See especially 242–43. Jordanes's sixth-century *Getica* imagined Scandinavia (*Scandza*) as an island: see Merrills, *History and Geography in Late Antiquity*, 142–49.

21. G. Cohen, "Esau as Symbol," 247.

22. G. Cohen, "Esau as Symbol," 256–57 and 267 n. 76. On the origins of the Kittim, see also Mireille Hadas-Lebel, *Jerusalem against Rome*, trans. Robyn Fréchet (Leuven: Peeters, 2006), 23–26.

23. G. Cohen, "Esau as Symbol," 251–55. Israel Yuval aptly describes the Christian's typology of Esau and Jacob and the rabbis' apologetics about Edom as an ongoing "dialogue." *Two Nations in Your Womb*, 19.

24. G. Cohen, "Esau as Symbol," 258.

25. "Let no love or treaty unite the nations! Arise from my ashes, unknown avenger, to harass the Trojan settlers with fire and sword—today, hereafter, whenever strength be ours!" (*Aeneid* 4, 625–27, ed. and trans. H. R. Fairclough, rev. G. P. Goold [Cambridge, MA: Harvard University Press, 1999]). For a comprehensive history of the Vandals, see Andy Merrills and Richard Miles, *The Vandals* (Oxford: Blackwell, 2010), 116–24. Yosippon's knowledge of the North African Vandals and their destruction of Rome possibly comes from Paul the Deacons's *Historia Romana*, who added the imagined detail that they also ravaged the

country south of Rome—Paul's and *Yosippon*'s native land. See Walter Goffart, *The Narrators of Barbarian History (A.D. 550–800): Jordanes, Gregory of Tours, Bede and Paul the Deacon* (Princeton, NJ: Princeton University Press, 1988), 355.

26. Like the famous Hebrew *Chronicle of Ahima'az* written a century later, the author may have wanted to recall the connections between the families and rabbinic scholars of southern Italy and the urban center of Kairouan. The *Chronicle of Ahima'az*, moreover, refers to al-Mui'z, the Fatimid ruler (953–75) as the "King of Ifriquya" as *Yosippon* calls Agneus. The most recent edition is Robert Bonfil's *History and Folklore in a Medieval Jewish Chronicle: The Family Chronicle of Ahima'az ben Paltiel* (Leiden: Brill, 2009); on al-Mui'z, who elevates R. Paltiel to viceroy in "Ifrikiya," see Bonfil's commentary, 67–71, and the text, 314–20. Both this narrative and Agneus's initial relationship to Zefo likewise mirror Pharaoh's reception of Joseph.

27. Maccabees 1:8 recounts Judah Maccabee's admiration for the Romans' military power and the rule of the Senate as well as the treaty between the Jews and Romans. On the Jews' changing views toward Roman military power, see Hadas-Lebel, *Jerusalem against Rome*, 7–29.

28. In his commentary on 1 Maccabees, Jonathan Goldstein suggests that the author omitted the Romans' victory over Carthage in order to preserve friendly relations with the Phoenicians. He also notes "the sympathetic treatment of Carthage in early rabbinic sources" and in the later Jewish traditions. *The Anchor Bible: 1 Maccabees*, trans. Jonathan A. Goldstein (New York: Doubleday, 1976), 348–49.

29. *Sefer Yosippon*, ed. Flusser, 1:91–96. Translation in Gaster, *Chronicles of Jerachmeel*, 280–82.

30. Sigmund Freud, *Interpreting Dreams*, trans. J. A. Underwood (London: Penguin, 2006), 211–13. See Richard H. Armstrong, *A Compulsion for Antiquity: Freud and the Ancient World* (Ithaca, NY: Cornell University Press, 2005), 222–26.

31. Freud, *Interpreting Dreams*, 212.

32. Ibid., 211; *The Complete Letters of Sigmund Freud to Wilhelm Fliess, 1887–1904*, ed. and trans. Jeffrey Moussaieff Masson (Cambridge, MA: Harvard University Press, 1985), 285. It is no doubt significant that Freud resorted to Yiddish to address his complex concerning Rome, where he dreamed about meeting Fliess. According to Daniel Boyarin's reading, in the letter as a whole Rome represents the "ambivalence of possessing and being possessed that is eroticism itself." See *Unheroic Conduct: The Rise of Heterosexuality and the Invention of the Jewish Man* (Berkeley: University of California Press, 1997), 226. Sebastiano Timpanaro reads these texts in terms of a more problematic Jewish nationalism in "Freud's Roman Phobia," *New Left Review* 1, no. 147 (1984): 4–31.

33. Carthage *with* Dido, needless to say, also represents the origin of an unassimilated foreignness, foremost in the imagination of Augustine's *Confessions*. See Jan Ziolkowski and Michael Putnam, eds., *The Virgilian Tradition: The First Fifteen Hundred Years* (New Haven: Yale University Press, 2008), 511–42. While necessary to mention, the topic is beyond the scope of this study.

34. Muller-Mertens, "The Ottonians as Kings and Emperors," 249.

35. See *Midrash Leviticus Rabbah* 17.6. Jonathan Goldstein provides a comprehensive list of the rabbinic sources in his edition of *The Anchor Bible: 1 Maccabees*, 349.

36. *Sefer Yosippon*, ed. Flusser, 2:120–21; Baer, "The Hebrew Sefer *Yosippon*," 180–91.

37. Dares Phrygius, *De excidio Troiae historia*, ed. Ferdinand Meister (Leipzig: Teubner, 1873); translation in *The Trojan War: The Chronicles of Dictys of Crete and Dares the Phrygian*, trans. R. M. Frazer Jr. (Bloomington: Indiana University Press, 1966), 133–68. Dares's text was very widely circulated, including in tenth-century southern Italy: see Louis Faivre

D'Arcier: *Histoire et géographie d'un mythe: La circulation des manuscripts du "De excidio Troiae" de Darès le Phrygien (XVIIIe–XVe siècles)* (Paris: École des Chartes, 2006), 45–46 and 335–37. Orosius, *Histoires*, ed. and trans. Arnaud-Lindet, 68; *Seven Books of History against the Pagans*, trans. Deferrari, 38. On Dares's *De excidio* as "a dismantling of authority," see Sarah Spence, "Felix Casus: The Dares and Dictys Legends of Aeneas," in *A Companion to Vergil's Aeneid and Its Tradition*, ed. Joseph Farrell and Michael C. J. Putnam (Oxford: Blackwell, 2010), 133–46.

38. Richard Stoneman, *Alexander the Great: A Life in Legend* (New Haven: Yale University Press, 2008), 237.

39. Ronit Nikolsky, "The *History of the Rechabites* and the Jeremiah Literature," *Journal for the Study of the Pseudepigrapha* 13 (2002): 185–207.

40. Steven Bowman, "Alexander and the Mysteries of India," *Journal of Indo-Judaic Studies*, no. 2 (1999): 71–111.

41. Flusser and subsequent scholars surmise that the second Hebrew Alexander interpolation was translated from Latin into Arabic and then into Hebrew. *Sefer Yosippon*, ed. Flusser, 2:218–19.

42. *Sefer Yosippon*, ed. Flusser, 2:225–52; Ruth Nisse, "Diaspora as Empire in the Hebrew Deeds of Alexander (*Ma'aseh Alexandros*)," in *Alexander the Great in the Middle Ages: Transcultural Perspectives*, ed. Markus Stock (Toronto: University of Toronto Press, 2016), 76–87.

43. On Carolingian Italy, see Paolo Delogu, "Lombard and Carolingian Italy," in *NCMH*, vol. 2, ed. McKitterick, 290–319; McKitterick, *Charlemagne*, 113–14.

44. McKitterick, *Charlemagne*, 363–72. On the contents of Charles's and Louis's court libraries, see Bernhard Bischoff, *Manuscripts and Libraries in the Age of Charlemagne*, ed. and trans. Michael Gorman (Cambridge: Cambridge University Press, 1994). See also Giles Brown, "The Carolingian Renaissance: An Introduction," in *Carolingian Culture: Emulation and Innovation*, ed. Rosamond McKitterick (Cambridge: Cambridge University Press, 1994), 38.

45. Peter Godman, ed. and trans., *Poetry of the Carolingian Renaissance* (London: Duckworth, 1985), 8.

46. Matthew Innes, "Teutons or Trojans? The Carolingians and the Germanic Past," in *The Uses of the Past in the Early Middle Ages*, ed. Yitzhak Hen and Matthew Innes (Cambridge: Cambridge University Press, 2000), 235.

47. Peter Godman, *Poets and Emperors: Frankish Politics and Carolingian Poetry* (Oxford: Clarendon Press, 1987), see especially 82–125.

48. Godman, *Poetry of the Carolingian Renaissance*, 202–3.

49. Ermold le Noir, *Poème sur Louis le Pieux et Épîtres au roi Pépin*, ed. and trans. Edmond Faral (Paris: Champion, 1932), 2–4. *Charlemagne and Louis the Pious: The Lives by Einhard, Notker, Ermolus, Thegan, and the Astronomer*, trans. Thomas F. X. Noble (University Park: Pennsylvania State University Press, 2009), 127–29.

50. "Caesareum primus Francorum nomen adeptus / Francis Romuleum nomen habere dedi." Ermold, *Poème*, ed. and trans. Faral, 56. *Charlemagne and Louis the Pious*, trans. Noble, 144.

51. Francine Mora-Lebrun, *L'"Enéide" médiévale et la chanson de geste* (Paris: Champion, 1994), 120–34. See also *Charlemagne and Louis the Pious*, trans. Noble, 120–24.

52. Mora-Lebrun, *L'"Enéide" médiévale*, 182.

53. *Sefer Yosippon*, ed. Flusser, 2:120–21.

54. Loud, "Southern Italy in the Tenth Century." See also Jonathan Shepard, "Byzantium and the West," in *NCMH*, vol. 3, ed. Reuter, 605–23.

55. William Hammer, "The Concept of the New or Second Rome in the Middle Ages," *Speculum* 19 (1944): 50–62.

56. *Poetry of the Carolingian Renaissance*, ed. and trans. Godman, 254–55.

57. Augustine in *The City of God*, 15.5, describes Romulus's murder of his brother as the founding crime of Rome as the "capital of the earthly city" and considers it a "reflection" (*imago*) of the primal crime of Cain's murder of Abel. He quotes Lucan's description of the murder, "Those walls were dripping with a brother's blood" ("Fraterno primi maduerunt sanguine muri"). *De civitate Dei, libri XXII*, ed. B. Dombart and A. Kalb (Stuttgart: Teubner, 1981), 64. *Concerning the City of God against the Pagans*, trans. Henry Bettenson (Harmondsworth: Penguin, 1984), 600–601; Orosius describes Romulus's crimes in similar terms, including "staining the walls of the city with his brother's blood." Orosius, *Histoires*, ed. and trans. Arnaud-Lindet, 90; *Seven Books of History against the Pagans*, trans. Deferrari, 48.

58. Martha Himmelfarb, "R. Moses the Preacher and the Testaments of the Twelve Patriarchs," *AJS Review* 9 (1984): 55–78.

59. Moshe ha-Darshan, *Midrash Bereshit Rabbati*, ed. Chanoch Albeck (1940; repr. Jerusalem: H. Vagshal, 1983). The eighth-century Palestinian compilation *Pirke de Rabbi Eliezer* is the best-known collection of midrashic sources that that incorporates Second Temple texts, including *Jubilees*. On the difficulties of determining how postbiblical literature was transmitted in Hebrew, see Reeves, "Exploring the Afterlife." It is worth noting here the singular theory of Israel Ta-Shma that around the same time that Moshe ha-Darshan was compiling *Bereshit Rabbati* in eleventh-century Provence, growing persecution of the Cathars led Jews to censor any texts that could be associated with dualist ideas. These writings would have included *Jubilees*, with its depiction of "Mastema" as a kind of evil god. For this intriguing Umberto Eco-esque scenario, see Israel Ta-Shma, "Rabbi Moses ha-Darshan and the Apocryphal Literature" [in Hebrew], in *Studies in Jewish History and Literature: Lectures Delivered on the Memorial Day for the Late Prof. Yitzhak Twersky*, ed. Carmi Horowitz (Jerusalem: Touro Graduate School of Jewish Studies, 2001), 5–17.

60. There are two critical editions of the three sections of *Midrash Va-Yissau*: "Midrash Vayissau or Sefer Milḥamot Benai Yaaqov," ed. J. Z. Lauterbach, in *Abhandlungen zur Erinnerung an Hirsch Perez Chajes* (Vienna: Alexander Kohut Memorial Foundation, 1933), 67–76; and "The Complete 'Midrash Vayissau,'" ed. Tamar Alexander and Yosef Dan, in *Folklore Research Center Studies*, vol. 3, ed. Issachar Ben-Ami (Jerusalem: Magnes Press, 1972), 67–76. Part 1 (a later addition) is about a war of the sons of Jacob against the Ninevites; part 2 is about their war with the Amorites; part 3 is about their war with the sons of Esau. Other than in Moshe ha-Darshan's *Bereshit Rabbati*, parts 2–3 of the text also appear in *Sefer Yeraḥmeel*: see SZ, ed. Yassif, 136–43. Later, parts 2–3 appear in the thirteenth-century Ashkenazic *Yalkut Shimoni*, Parshat Va-Yishlach 33.18.

61. Dan, *The Hebrew Story*, 138–40; See also Yassif's notes to the text in *Sefer ha-Zikhronot*, ed. Yassif, 477–80.

62. I am following the *Yeraḥmeel* version of *Midrash Va-Yissau* (where it appears just before *The Testament of Naphtali*) in SZ, ed. Yassif, 137–43. Translation in Gaster, *Chronicles of Jerachmeel*, 84–87.

63. O. S. Wintermute, "Jubilees (Second Century B.C.)," in *The Old Testament Pseudepigrapha*, ed. Charlesworth, 2:35–142. Wintermute describes the author as "a Jew who lived in Palestine" who "probably belonged to a priestly family."

64. Himmelfarb "R. Moses the Preacher and the Testaments of the Twelve Patriarchs," 55–78. See also Martha Himmelfarb, "Midrash Vayissa'u," in *Old Testament Pseudepigrapha: More Noncanonical Scriptures*, vol. 1, ed. Richard Bauckham, James R. Davila, and Alexander Panayotov (Grand Rapids, MI: Eerdmans, 2013), 143–59.

65. *SZ*, ed. Yassif, 141–42. Louis Ginzberg suggests that this intriguing detail about Eli-faz as Jacob's student is possibly the source of the story in *Sefer Hasidim* 19, which describes Jacob teaching the sons of Esau in a Beit ha-Midrash. *The Legends of the Jews*, trans. Hen-rietta Szold, Paul Radin, and Boaz Cohen, 7 vols. (Philadelphia: Jewish Publication Society, 1909–38), 5:315–16.

66. Simonsohn, "Hebrew Revival among Early Medieval European Jews."

67. Himmelfarb, "R. Moses the Preacher and the Testaments of the Twelve Patriarchs"; Reeves, "Exploring the Afterlife." Reeves addresses in great detail the many inconclusive the-ories, involving both Christian and Jewish circles and sects, about how these texts survived after the fall of the Second Temple and reappeared in the Cairo Genizah and elsewhere.

68. Martha Himmelfarb, "Some Echoes of Jubilees in Medieval Hebrew Literature," in *Tracing the Threads: Studies in the Vitality of Jewish Pseudepigrapha*, ed. John Reeves (Atlanta: Scholars Press, 1994), 115–41. The text survives in fourteen fragments of Hebrew MSS from the Qumran scrolls: 215/1307 verses of the text; see James C. VanderKam, *The Book of Jubilees* (Leuven: Peeters, 1989), 16.

69. For an overview of Byzantine oppression of Jews in fourth- to sixth-century Palestine, see Michael Avi-Yonah, *The Jews under Roman and Byzantine Rule: A Political History of Palestine from the Bar Kokhba War to the Arab Conquest* (New York: Schocken, 1976), 208–56. At 274, he cites a Jewish source that characterizes the Arab conquest of Palestine in these terms: "Now that the Holy One, blessed be He, has put an end to the rule of Edom (Byzan-tium as heir to Rome) and has abolished its oppressive decrees."

70. G. Cohen, "Esau as Symbol," 245–48.

71. Hadas-Lebel, *Jerusalem against Rome*, 497–505.

72. Up to the seventh century, Jews in parts of Byzantine southern Italy were trilingual (Greek/Latin/Hebrew), and those living in the Naples-Benevento-Salerno area in the ninth and tenth centuries (as well as at Narbonne for that matter) would have spoken a kind of late Latin or proto-Romance dialect. See Giovanni Tabacco, *The Struggle for Power in Medi-eval Italy: Structures of Political Rule*, trans. Rosalind Brown Jensen (Cambridge: Cambridge University Press, 1989), 142, 147; Chris Wickham, *Early Medieval Italy: Central Power and Local Society, 400–1000* (London: Macmillan, 1981), 146–67.

73. On the intersection of the two accounts of Rome's origins, see T. J. Cornell, "Aeneas and the Twins: The Development of the Roman Foundation Legend," *Proceedings of the Cambridge Philological Society*, n.s. 21 (1975): 1–32.

74. Y. Avodah Zarah 1, 1 (39c), cited by Hadas-Lebel, *Jerusalem against Rome*, 388.

75. *Midrash Esther Rabbah* 3, 4–5. Hadas-Lebel, *Jerusalem against Rome*, 387–89.

76. Louis Feldman, "Abba Kolon and the Founding of Rome," *JQR*, n.s. 81 (1991): 239–66.

77. *Servii Grammatici qui feruntur in Vergilii carmina commentarii*, ed. Georg Thilo and Hermann Hagen (Leipzig: Teubner, 1881–1900), 1:101–02.

78. *SZ*, ed. Yassif, 143.

79. Orosius, *Histoires*, ed. and trans. Arnaud-Lindet, 90; *Seven Books of History against the Pagans*, trans. Deferrari, 48.

80. *SZ*, ed. Yassif, 141. It also follows a midrashic tradition of Judah's anger. See *Gene-sis Rabbah* 93:6 and 93:7 (on Genesis 94:18), passages that describe Judah's extreme wrath in his interactions with Joseph in Egypt.

81. Mundill, *England's Jewish Solution*, 249–85.

82. Dozens of twelfth-century MSS of Geoffrey's work survive: see Geoffrey of Mon-mouth, *History of the Kings of Britain*, ed. Reeve and trans. Wright, xi–li.

83. Ibid., 20–21.

84. Martin Aurell argues for the term "empire" based on territory and ideology: *The Plantagenet Empire, 1154–1224*, trans. David Crouch (Harlow: Longman, 2007), 1–22. See also John Gillingham, *The Angevin Empire* (New York: Holmes and Meier, 1984). Francine Mora-Lebrun uses the term "Espace Plantagenêt" to include lands that were not directly under the rule of Henry II and Eleanor but that were part of their cultural orbit: *"Mettre en Romanz": Les romans d'antiquité du XIIe siècle et leur postérité (XIIIe–XIVe siécle)* (Paris: Champion, 2008), 25–36. On patronage, see Diana Tyson, "Patronage of French Vernacular History Writers in the Twelfth and Thirteenth Centuries," *Romania* 100 (1979): 180–222. For an overstated argument against extensive *direct* patronage by Henry II, see Karen M. Broadhurst, "Henry II of England and Eleanor of Aquitaine: Patrons of Literature in French?" *Viator* 27 (1996): 53–84.

85. "Certes, rivaliser avec le poète de Mantoue, c'est lui rendre homage et reconnaitre, en somme, sa supeiorité; mais en contrepartie, l'utilisation du poème antique confère au message une plus grande efficacité: dans la mesure où la partie de public du XIIe siècle à qui ces textes sont destines est capable d'y repérer les influences classiques, plus l'imitation sera réussie, plus le succes de l'oeuvre sera grand et son contenu susceptible de faire, à son tour, autorite." Jean-Yves Tilliette, "Insula me genuit: L'influence de l'Énéide sur l'épopée latine du XII siècle," in *Lectures médiévales de Virgile: actes du colloque organisé par l'École française de Rome (Rome, 25–28 octobre 1982)* (Rome: École française de Rome, 1985), 139.

86. Christopher Baswell, *Virgil in Medieval England: Figuring the Aeneid from the Twelfth Century to Chaucer* (Cambridge: Cambridge University Press, 1995), 1, 46.

87. Ibid., 178.

88. Baswell treats the "platonizing" commentaries extensively, ibid., 84–135.

89. Copeland, *Rhetoric, Hermeneutics and Translation in the Middle Ages*, 61–62, 103–7. Copeland presents the most incisive formulations of how actual "translation" between languages functions in *translatio imperii* and *translatio studii*. For a careful analysis of the "discourse" of *translatio studii* as it evolved in twelfth- and thirteenth-century France, see Lusignan "*Translatio studii* and the Emergence of French."

90. Thomas de Kent, *Le roman d'Alexandre, ou Le roman de toute chevalrie*, ed. Ian Short and Brian Foster, with trans., introd., and notes by Catherine Gaullier-Bourgassas and Laurence Harf-Lancner (Paris: Champion, 2003), 294–95; Peter Damian-Grint, *The New Historians of the Twelfth-Century Renaissance* (Woodbridge: Boydell, 1999), 21–23.

91. *The History of the Norman People: Wace's Roman de Rou*, trans. Glyn Burgess (Woodbridge: Boydell, 2004), 92. Damian-Grint *New Historians of the Twelfth-Century Renaissance*, 23.

92. Olszowy-Schlanger, "The Money Language."

93. Ibn Ezra's commentary on Psalm 120, in *Mikra'ot Gedolot ha-Keter*, Psalms II, ed. Menachem Cohen (Ramat-Gan: Bar Ilan University Press, 1992–), 186.

94. Copeland, *Rhetoric, Hermeneutics and Translation in the Middle Ages*, 105–6.

95. The *romans d'antiquité* continue to generate scholarship on the dating of the texts in sequence and on the specifics of patronage. Mora-Lebrun, *"Mettre en Romanz"*; *Le roman d'Enéas*, ed. and trans. Aimé Petit (Paris: Librarie générale française, 1997), 7–10. *Enéas: A Twelfth-Century French Romance*, trans. John Yunck (New York: Columbia University Press, 1974), 3–9.

96. Baswell, *Virgil in Medieval England*, 173–84. See also Lee Patterson on the text's privileging of Henry II's dynastic ambitions and the erasing of the disruptions of Anglo-Norman history, *Negotiating the Past: The Historical Understanding of Medieval Literature* (Madison: University of Wisconsin Press, 1987), 157–95.

97. Mora-Lebrun presents an intriguing argument that *Enéas* is also specifically directed against the challenge to the West posed by the Byzantine Empire of the Second Crusade era

and in particular Manuel Comnenus's ambitions to revive an Eastern "Roman Empire." Francine Mora-Lebrun: "Byzance et l'Occident dans *Le roman d'Enéas*: Imaginaire historique dans propagande politique," in *Histoire et littérature au Moyen Âge: Actes du Colloque du Centre d'Études Médiévales de l'Université de Picardie*, ed. Danielle Buschinger (Göppingen: Kümmerle, 1991), 331–44.

### 3. A Fox among Fish?

1. Berekhiah ha-Nakdan, *Dodi ve-Nechdi*, ed. and trans. Hermann Gollancz (Oxford: Oxford University Press, 1920), 16; Hebrew Section, 10; translation revised. See Tamás Visi, "Berechiah ben Naṭronai ha-Naqdan's *Dodi ve-Nekdi* and the Transfer of Scientific Knowledge from Latin to Hebrew in the Twelfth Century," *Aleph* 14, no. 2 (2014): 9–73. Visi associates Berekhiah's idea of translation with the topos of the Jewish origins of "alien wisdom" that would have been familiar to him from the works of Abraham Ibn Ezra. Gollancz edits two of the four manuscripts of Uncle and Nephew: a "long version" (Munich, Bayerische Staatsbibliothek, Cod. Hebr. 42) and a "short version" (MS. Oxford, Bodleian MS Opp. 181) and translates the long version; Visi uses a third manuscript as well (Leiden Universiteitbibliotheek, Cod. Or. 4732) in his discussion of the text.

2. In an exhaustively detailed article, Gad Freudenthal and Jean-Marc Mandosio have convincingly argued that the recently edited *Sefer Ko'aḥ ha-Avanim* (*On the Virtue of the Stones*), which has been attributed to Berekhiah, is in fact one of two lapidaries that derive from a translation made by Berekhiah of an Anglo-Norman *Urtext*. The closest text to the Hebrew versions is the Anglo-Norman "Cambridge Version" of Marbode of Rennes's Latin lapidary. See Gad Freudenthal and Jean-Marc Mandosio, "Old French into Hebrew in Twelfth-Century Tsarfat: Medieval Hebrew Versions of Marbode's Lapidary," *Aleph* 14, no. 1 (2014): 11–187. There is also much useful information in Berekhiah ha-Nakdan, *Sefer Ko'aḥ ha-Avanim (On the Virtue of the Stones)*, ed. and trans. Gerrit Bos and Julia Zwink (Leiden: Brill, 2010).

3. Roth, *Intellectual Activities of Medieval English Jewry*, 48–51; Norman Golb, *The Jews of Medieval Normandy: A Social and Intellectual History* (Cambridge: Cambridge University Press, 1998), 324–47.

4. This term (*'ii ha-yam* or just *'iim*, "islands"), taken from Isaiah 11:11, was used as a name for England in the twelfth and thirteenth centuries. See Ephraim of Bonn, *Sefer Zekhirah*, ed. Haberman, 34; and for Joseph of Chartres's use of the term, see Cecil Roth, ed., "A Hebrew Elegy," 19. For an unrelated contemporary usage of *ha-'ii* as identical with "Angleterra," see Baruch ben Isaac of Worms, *Sefer ha-Terumah*, Halakhot Shabbat (Jerusalem: Yerid ha-Sefarim, 2003), 45. I am grateful to Pinchas Roth for this example. See further Golb on Berekhiah's connection to England, *Jews of Medieval Normandy*, 341–42.

5. Both documents are edited and deciphered by Golb: see *Jews of Medieval Normandy*, 324–33.

6. Several scholars believe that Berekhiah spent time in Angevin Normandy as well as in England. Based on his son Elijah's testimony, Golb argues that Berekhiah was born in Rouen and educated and based in Normandy; he also identifies Berekhiah with a commentary on Job that draws on the work of contemporary northern French exegetes. Jordan Penkower reinforces the argument that Berekhiah is the author of this commentary in "The End of Rashi's Commentary on Job: The Manuscripts and the Printed Editions (with three appendices)," *Jewish Studies Quarterly* 10 (2003): 18–48. The most recent scholars to take up Berekhiah's works follow Golb in situating him primarily in northern France, even though they acknowledge the clearly English milieu of all three of his translations. Visi reconstructs Berekhiah's life into three parts: an early period in Normandy during which he wrote *Uncle and Nephew*; a

period in Provence (ca. 1161–70); and a later period in Normandy and England, during which he wrote the *Fox Fables*.

7. There is also a remote possibility that he could have taken them from the considerable number of books pawned to Jews. See Cecil Roth, *The Jews of Medieval Oxford* (Oxford: Clarendon Press, 1951), 118–19. A working relationship with a Christian fellow scribe is much more plausible: Judith Olszowy-Schlanger has argued that Oxford is the most likely place where Jewish and Christian scribes could have worked together to produce the thirteenth-century Hebrew-Latin glossed psalters and other biblical manuscripts associated with Grosseteste and his circle: See Olszowy-Schlanger, *Les Manuscrits Hébreux*, 66.

8. See R. W. Hunt, *The Schools and the Cloister: The Life and Writings of Alexander Nequam, 1157–1217* (Oxford: Clarendon Press, 1984), 73, on Adelard's influence on Nequam's *De naturis rerum*.

9. In B. Sanhedrin 91b, Rabbi tells Antoninus a parable about a king who appointed two watchmen to his orchard, one lame and the other blind. The lame and blind guards conspire to steal figs by having the lame one climb on the blind one. When the king later asks about the figs, the guards claim that they couldn't have stolen them since the lame one has no feet and the blind one no eyes. The king places the lame upon the blind and judges them together. "So will the Holy One, blessed be He, bring the soul, [re]place it in the body, and judge them together." Berekhiah's version reads: "Our sages remark: If man should imagine that body and soul could mutually free each other from the sentence of justice (each throwing the blame for wicked action on the other), his plea would remind one of the parable of the king who had a park in which he placed two keepers, one lame and the other blind and the rest of the story." *The Ethical Treatises of Berachya Son of Rabbi Natronai ha-Nakdan, Being the Compendium and the Maṣref*, ed. and trans. Hermann Gollancz (London: Nutt, 1902), 95. Raphael Loewe and R. W. Hunt, "Alexander Neckam's Knowledge of Hebrew," *Medieval and Renaissance Studies* 4 (1958): 24.

10. Hunt, *The Schools and the Cloister*, 108–10; Loewe and Hunt, "Alexander Neckam's Knowledge of Hebrew," 26–27. The most striking of Nequam's rabbinic references is to a gematria about the names of Sarah and Abraham.

11. Loewe and Hunt, "Alexander Neckam's Knowledge of Hebrew," 22.

12. Gad Freudenthal, "Transfert culturel à Lunel au milieu du XII siècle," in *Des Tibbonides à Maïmonide: rayonnement des Juifs andalous en pays d'Oc médiéval; colloque international, Montpellier, 13–14 décembre 2004*, ed. Danièle Iancu-Agou and Élie Nicolas (Paris: Cerf, 2009), 95–108.

13. On the twelfth-century manuscript transmission of Adelard's *Quaestiones*, see Burnett's introduction to Adelard of Bath, *Conversations with His Nephew: On the Same and the Different, Questions on Natural Science, and On Birds*, ed. and trans. Charles Burnett (Cambridge: Cambridge University Press, 1998). Most of the surviving twelfth-century manuscripts are from England, though at least two are from France (ibid., xxxi–xxii, xlii–xlvii).

14. *Ethical Treatises of Berachya*, ed. and trans. Gollancz, 90–91.

15. Ibid., 2.

16. James T. Robinson, "The Ibn Tibbon Family: A Dynasty of Translators in Medieval 'Provence,'" in *Be'erot Yitzhak: Studies in Memory of Isadore Twersky*, ed. Jay Harris (Cambridge, MA: Harvard University Press, 2005), 193–224.

17. Isadore Twersky, "Aspects of the Social and Cultural History of Provençal Jewry," *Journal of World History* 11 (1968): 185–207.

18. Gad Freudenthal, "Arabic and Latin Cultures as Resources for the Hebrew Translation Movement: Comparative Considerations, Both Quantitative and Qualitative," in *Science*

*in Medieval Jewish Cultures*, ed. Gad Freudenthal (Cambridge: Cambridge University Press, 2011), 74–105.

19. Translated by Twersky, "Aspects of the Social and Cultural History of Provençal Jewry," 197.

20. Solomon Halkin and Angel Sàenz-Badillos, "Translations and Translators," in Berenbaum and Skolnik, *Encyclopedia Judaica*, 20:95. Bachya ben Joseph Ibn Pakuda, *Duties of the Heart* [in Hebrew], trans. from Arabic by Yehuda Ibn Tibbon, ed. Abraham Zifroni (Tel Aviv: Maḥbarot le-Sifrut, 1959), 56–57. See also Robinson, "The Ibn Tibbon Family," 202–3.

21. Charles Burnett, *The Introduction of Arabic Learning into England* (London: British Library, 1997), 31–32.

22. Angel Sáenz-Badillos, "Abraham Ibn Ezra and the Twelfth-Century European Renaissance," in *Studies in Hebrew Literature and Jewish Culture: Presented to Albert van der Heide on the Occasion of His Sixty-Fifth Birthday*, ed. Martin Baasten and Reinier Munk (Dordrecht: Springer, 2007), 1–20. Shlomo Sela and Gad Freudenthal, "Abraham Ibn Ezra's Scholarly Writings: A Chronological Listing," *Aleph* 6 (2006): 13–55.

23. Adelard of Bath, *Conversations with His Nephew*, ed. and trans. Burnett, xi–xix. For an overview of all of Adelard's scientific activities and translations, see Louise Cochrane, *Adelard of Bath: The First English Scientist* (London: British Museum Press, 1994).

24. Adelard of Bath, *Conversations with His Nephew*, ed. and trans. Burnett, 83.

25. Ibid., 103.

26. Ibid., 91.

27. Ibid., 185, 123.

28. Winthrop Wetherbee, "Philosophy, Cosmology, and the Twelfth-Century Renaissance," in *A History of Twelfth-Century Philosophy*, ed. Peter Dronke (Cambridge: Cambridge University Press, 1988), 21–53.

29. Adelard of Bath, *Conversations with His Nephew*, ed. and trans. Burnett, xxi–xxii.

30. *Ethical Treatises of Berachya*, ed. and trans. Gollancz, 91; Adelard of Bath, *Conversations with His Nephew*, ed. and trans. Burnett, 167. See Cicero, *On the Nature of the Gods. Academics*, ed. and trans. H. Rackham (Cambridge, MA: Harvard University Press, 1933), 257.

31. Ibn Ezra sets out his explanation of the three souls—*neshama-ruah-nefesh*—in his commentary on Exodus 23:25. See *Ibn Ezra's Commentary on the Pentateuch: Exodus*, trans. H. Norman Strickman and Arthur M. Silver (New York: Menorah, 1996), 514–18; Mariano Gómez Aranda discusses Berekhiah's main source for the theory, Ibn Ezra's *Commentary on Qohelet*, in "The Meaning of Qohelet According to Ibn Ezra's Scientific Explanations," *Aleph* 6 (2006): 339–70. See also Mariano Gómez Aranda's critical edition of the text, *El Comentario de Abraham Ibn Ezra al libro del Ecclesiatés* (Madrid: Consejo Superior de Investigaciones Científicas, 1994), 53–64.

32. Berekhiah ha-Nakdan, *Dodi ve-Nechdi*, ed. and trans. Gollancz, Hebrew 10; English 16.

33. Berekhiah ha-Nakdan, *Ethical Treatises of Berachya*, ed. and trans. Gollancz, Hebrew 47; English 92–93.

34. Visi discusses Berekhiah's Arabic and Greek "fictional sources" at length, "Berechiah ben Naṭronai ha-Nakdan's *Dodi ve-Neḳdi*," 62–64.

35. Adelard of Bath, *Conversations with His Nephew*, ed. and trans. Burnett, 192: "Ut autem planiori tractemus Minerva, exemplis agatur res." See Geoffrey of Monmouth, *History of the Kings of England*, book II, chap. 10, on Bladud's dedication of the baths to Minerva.

36. *Gesta Stephani*, ed. and trans. K. R. Potter (Oxford: Clarendon Press, 1976), 59.

37. *Dodi ve-Nechdi*, 52.

38. Joshua Prawer, *The History of the Jews in the Latin Kingdom of Jerusalem* (Oxford: Clarendon Press, 1988), 57. Ibn Ezra mentions the "wise men of Tiberias," copiers of the bible, in his *Commentary on Exodus*, 25.31.

39. *The Itinerary of Benjamin of Tudela*, ed. and trans. Marcus Nathan Adler (London: H. Frowde, 1907), 28–29.

40. Berekhiah ha-Nakdan, *Dodi ve-Nechdi*, ed. and trans. Gollancz, 9.

41. Ibid., 38.

42. Shlomo Sela, *Abraham Ibn Ezra and the Rise of Medieval Hebrew Science* (Leiden: Brill, 2003), 161–62.

43. Ibid., 104–6.

44. Ibid., 107.

45. Adelard of Bath, *Conversations with His Nephew*, ed. and trans. Burnett, 112–23.

46. Ibid., 115.

47. Ibid., 119.

48. Berekhiah ha-Nakdan, *Dodi ve-Nechdi*, ed. and trans. Gollancz, 26.

49. Ibid., 27.

50. Ibid., 28.

51. Ibn Ezra elaborates upon a Neoplatonic view of the human soul in his commentary on Ecclesiastes 3:19–21. "Who knows whether the human spirit (*ruah*) goes upward and the spirit of animals goes downward to the earth?" See *El Comentario*, ed. Gómez Aranda, 367–69.

52. For an overview, see Jill Mann, *From Aesop to Reynard: Beast Literature in Medieval Britain* (Oxford: Oxford University Press, 2009), 1–52. Marie de France's *Fables* have been edited and translated by Harriet Spiegel (Toronto: University of Toronto Press, 1987). On Nequam's fables, see Hunt. *The Schools and the Cloister*. Nequam's six fables from Avianus are in *Novus Avianus*, ed. Thomas Klein, in *Favolisti latini medievali e umanistici*, ed. F. Bertini (Genova: Università di Genova, Facoltà di Lettere, Dipartimento di Archeologia, Filologia Classica e Loro Tradizioni, 1998), 7:99–133; his forty-two fables from the "Romulus" collections are in *Novus Aesopus*, ed. Giovanni Garbugino, vol. 2 of *Favolisti latini medievali e umanistici* (Genova: Università di Genova, Facoltà di Lettere, Dipartimento di Archeologia, Filologia Classica e Loro Tradizioni, 1987). For the unidentified "Walter the Englishman," see *The Fables of "Walter of England,"* ed. Aaron E. Wright (Toronto: Pontifical Institute of Mediaeval Studies, 1997).

53. Berekhiah ha-Nakdan, *Mishle Shu'alim* [in Hebrew], ed. A. M. Haberman (Jerusalem: Schocken, 1946). A. Neubauer and Joseph Jacobs, "Berechiah Naqdan," *JQR* 2 (1890): 520–26.

54. Of the texts most relevant to this study, the *Romulus Nilanti* is collected in the five-volume *Fabulistes Latin depuis le siécle d'Auguste jusqu'à la fin du Moyen Âge*, ed. Léopold Hervieux (Paris: Firmin-Didot, 1893–99), 2:512–63. The *Romulus Vulgaris* is in *Der lateinische Äsop des Romulus und die Prosa-Fassungen des Phädrus*, ed. Georg Thiele (Heidelberg: C. Winter, 1910) and also in Hervieux, *Les Fabulistes Latins*, 2:197–264. The original Phaedrus is edited and translated by Ben Perry in *Babrius and Phaedrus* (Cambridge, MA: Harvard University Press, 1965), 191–417.

55. Tovi Bibring, "'Would that my words were Inscribed': Berechiah ha-Naqdan's *Mishlei Shu'alim* and European Fable Traditions," in *Latin-into-Hebrew: Texts and Studies*, ed. Resianne Fontaine and Gad Freudenthal (Leiden: Brill, 2013), 1:309–29. Bibring makes a convincing argument for Berekhiah's borrowing of details from some of Marie's fables in his own versions.

56. The fables of Avianus are edited and translated by J. W. Duff and Arnold Duff in *Minor Latin Poets* (Cambridge MA: Harvard University Press, 1934), 2:669–749; *Kalila*

*wa-Dimna* has been translated into French by André Miquel: Ibn Al-Muqaffa', *Le livre de Kalila et Dimna* (Paris: Klincksieck, 1957). Berekhiah would have used the twelfth-century Hebrew translation attributed to a certain "Rabbi Joel": *Deux versions hébraïques du livre de Kalilah et Dimnah*, ed. Joseph Derenbourg (Paris: F. Vieweg, 1881), 1–309. Unfortunately, Rabbi Joel's translation only survives in one fragment that begins at chapter 3 of *Kalila wa-Dimnah*. I will quote Petrus's *Disciplina Clericalis* from the translation by Joseph Jones and John Keller as *The Scholar's Guide: A Translation of the Twelfth-Century "Disciplina clericalis" of Pedro Alfonso* (Toronto: Pontifical Institute of Mediaeval Studies, 1969).

57. Berekhiah ha-Nakdan, *Mishle Shu'alim*, ed. Haberman, 1; Berekhiah ha-Nakdan, *Fables of a Jewish Aesop*, trans. Moses Hadas (New York: Columbia University Press, 1967), 1.

58. Robert C. Stacey, "Jewish Lending and the Medieval English Economy," in *A Commercialising Economy: England, 1086 to c. 1300*, ed. R. H. Britnell and Bruce M. S. Campbell (Manchester: Manchester University Press, 1995), 78–101; Joe Hillaby, "The London Jewry: William I to John," *Jewish Historical Studies* 33 (1992–94): 1–44.

59. Hillaby, "The London Jewry," 9.

60. H. G. Richardson, *English Jewry under Angevin Kings* (London: Methuen, 1960), 83–92.

61. Ibid., 121.

62. Mundill, *England's Jewish Solution*, 17–18; See Michael T. Clanchy, *From Memory to Written Record: England, 1066–1307*, 2nd ed. (Oxford: Blackwell, 1993), 213–14, on Jews as foreigners within England.

63. Einbinder, *Beautiful Death*. The standard work on the Tosafists—twelfth-century Talmud commentators and biblical exegetes—is E. E. Urbach, *The Tosafists: Their History, Writings and Methods* [in Hebrew], 2 vols., 5th enlarged ed. (Jerusalem: Bialik Institute, 1986); his chapter on the English Tosafists is in 2:493–520. On the commentaries, see also Israel Ta-Shma, "Tosafot," in Berenbaum and Skolnik, *Encyclopaedia Judaica*, 20:67–70.

64. Einbinder, *Beautiful Death*, 45–69; Yuval, *Two Nations in Your Womb*, 92–109.

65. Walther Zimmerli uses this term in *Ezekiel 1: A Commentary on the Book of the Prophet Ezekiel, Chapters 1–24*, trans. Ronald Clements, ed. Frank Moore Cross and Klaus Baltzer (Philadelphia: Fortress, 1979), 58.

66. *Romulus Nilanti*, in *Les Fabulistes Latins*, ed. Hervieux, 513–14; *Der lateinische Äsop*, ed. Thiele, 2–6.

67. Marie de France, *Fables*, ed. and trans. Spiegel, 29–31; 256–59. Logan E. Whalen, "The Prologues and Epilogues of Marie de France," in Logan Whalen, ed., *A Companion to Marie de France* (Leiden: Brill, 2011), 1–30. See also R. Howard Bloch, *The Anonymous Marie de France* (Chicago: University of Chicago Press, 2003), 114–15. On King Alfred's actual translation projects, see Michael Lapidge, "Scholars at King Alfred's Court (*act.* 880–899)," in *Oxford Dictionary of National Biography* (Oxford: Oxford University Press, 2013), http://www.oxforddnb.com/view/theme/95595.

68. Copeland, *Rhetoric, Hermeneutics and Translation in the Middle Ages*, 106–7.

69. Berekhiah ha-Nakdan, *Mishle Shu'alim*, ed. Haberman, Fox Fables, 1. There is a full English translation by Moses Hadas, *Fables of a Jewish Aesop*. This work, however, has various errors and omissions and is rendered in an inexplicably archaic English. It also makes no references to Berekhiah's hundreds of citations of the bible and rabbinic sources. I cite it here together with Haberman's edition, but I do not always quote from it. Haim Schwarzbaum's exhaustive work examines each fable: *The Mishle Shu'alim (Fox Fables) of Rabbi Berekhiah ha-Nakdan: A Study in Comparative Folklore and Fable Lore* (Kiron: Institute for Jewish and Arab Folklore Research, 1979).

70. The famous catalog of the scholars who have died is an index of decline in Mishnah Sotah 9.15: "When Rabbi Meir died there were no more makers of parables." Rabbi Meir also appears in B. Sanhedrin 38b: "Even as R. Johanan said: When R. Meir used to deliver his public discourses, a third was Halacha, a third Haggadah, and a third consisted of parables. R. Johanan also said: R. Meir had three hundred parables of foxes, and we have only three left." The example of R. Johanan ben Zakkai's learning extending to "the speech of palm-trees, fullers' parables and fox fables" is in B. Sukkah 28a and B. Bava Batra 134a. See Schwarzbaum, *Mishle Shu'alim (Fox Fables) of Rabbi Berechiah ha-Nakdan*, xxii–xxiv, on these passages. See also Galit Hasan-Rokem, "Fable," in Berenbaum and Skolnik, *Encyclopaedia Judaica*, 6:666–70.

71. Berekhiah ha-Nakdan, *Mishle Shu'alim*, ed. Haberman, 1; *Fables of a Jewish Aesop*, trans. Hadas, 1.

72. "Rabbi [Judah ha-Nasi] made a wedding feast for his son. He invited all the Rabbis, but forgot to extend an invitation to Bar Kappara. The latter went and wrote above the door [of the banqueting hall], 'After all your rejoicing is death, so what is the use of your rejoicing?' Rabbi inquired, 'Who has done this to us?' They said, 'It was Bar Kappara whom you forgot to invite. He was concerned about himself.' He thereupon arranged another banquet to which he invited all the Rabbis including Bar Kappara. At every course which was placed before them Bar Kappara related three hundred fox-fables, which were so much enjoyed by the guests that they let the food become cold and did not taste it. Rabbi asked his waiters, 'Why do our courses go in and out without the guests partaking of them?' They answered, 'Because of an old man who sits there, and when a course is brought in, he relates three hundred fox-fables; and on that account the food becomes cold and they eat none of it.' Rabbi went up to him and said, 'Why do you act in this manner? Let the guests eat!' He replied, 'So that you should not think that I came for your dinner, but because you did not invite me with my colleagues. Did not Solomon declare, WHAT PROFIT HATH A MAN OF ALL HIS LABOUR *seeing that One generation passeth away and another generation cometh?*' (Ecc. 1:3)." *Midrash Kohelet Rabbah*, 1.4; *Midrash Rabbah: Ecclesiastes*, trans. A. Cohen (London: Soncino Press 1983), 9–10.; Berekhiah ha-Nakdan, *Mishle Shu'alim*, ed. Haberman, vi–vii.

73. Berekhiah ha-Nakdan, *Mishle Shu'alim*, ed. Haberman, 5; *Fables of a Jewish Aesop*, trans. Hadas, 4. Golb notes Berekhiah's "bitter contempt for his co-religionists" in England, *Jews of Medieval Normandy*, 341.

74. Berekhiah ha-Nakdan, *Mishle Shu'alim*, ed. Haberman, 3–5; *Fables of a Jewish Aesop*, trans. Hadas, 3–4. All of these oppositions involve elaborate plays on words that, pointed differently, mean positive or negative things, exemplifying Berekhiah's linguistic pyrotechnics. The most self-reflexive is, of course, the play on *mashal* (fable) and the verb *mashal* (it rules).

75. Berekhiah ha-Nakdan, *Mishle Shu'alim*, ed. Haberman, 4–5; *Fables of a Jewish Aesop*, trans. Hadas, 4.

76. Berekhiah ha-Nakdan, *Mishle Shu'alim*, ed. Haberman, 36; *Fables of a Jewish Aesop*, trans. Hadas, 53.

77. Berekhiah ha-Nakdan, *Mishle Shu'alim*, ed. Haberman, 4–5; *Fables of a Jewish Aesop*, trans. Hadas, 4. Although excessive, Berekhiah's warnings reflect a side of the English Jews that is occasionally revealed in official government records: their lawsuits (including a duel between two Jews), the rivalries among the king's financiers, and their conspicuous consumption. See Richardson, *English Jewry under Angevin Kings*, 113; Hillaby, "The London Jewry," 19–21; Roth, *Jews of Medieval Oxford*, 42–44. Berekhiah's disgust, however, likely derives just as much from issues that arose in rabbinic courts or from rabbinic judges themselves.

78. Berekhiah ha-Nakdan, *Mishle Shu'alim*, ed. Haberman, 4; *Fables of a Jewish Aesop*, trans. Hadas, 4.

79. There are even some rabbinic examples. A wheel of change (but not a *rota fortunae*) appears in a famous passage on poverty and wealth in B. Shabbat 151.

80. The first reference to the chariot appears in the fifth line of Berekhiah's prologue.

81. *Mikra'ot Gedolot ha-Keter: Ezekiel*, ed. Cohen, 3–4. *The Book of Ezekiel*, trans. A. J. Rosenberg (New York: Judaica Press, 2000), 1:5.

82. Berekhiah ha-Nakdan, *Mishle Shu'alim*, ed. Haberman, 5; *Fables of a Jewish Aesop*, trans. Hadas, 5.

83. Berekhiah ha-Nakdan, *Mishle Shu'alim*, ed. Haberman, 5; *Fables of a Jewish Aesop*, trans. Hadas, 5.

84. Alfonsi, *The Scholar's Guide*, trans. Jones and Keller, 47. For a discussion of Petrus as a culturally "Norman" author in terms of the *Disciplina clericalis*'s popularity and literary influence, see Suzanne Conklin Akbari, "Between Diaspora and Conquest: Norman Assimilation in Petrus Alfonsi's *Disciplina clericalis* and Marie de France's *Fables*," in *Cultural Diversity in the British Middle Ages: Archipelago, Island, England*, ed. Jeffrey Jerome Cohen (New York: Palgrave, 2008), 17–37.

85. Berekhiah ha-Nakdan, *Mishle Shu'alim*, ed. Haberman, 73; *Fables of a Jewish Aesop*, trans. Hadas, 118. It seems reasonable to assume that the learned Berekhiah might have known the tradition mentioned by his Provençal near-contemporary R. Menachem ben Shimon and later R. David Kimchi (Radak) in their Ezekiel commentaries: the prophet Jeremiah can be identified as "Buzi," Ezekiel's father, since he was *nibzeh* (despised, shamed) by the Israelites. *Mikra'ot Gedolot 'ha-Keter': Ezekiel*, ed. Cohen, 3–4.

86. Haberman discusses the manuscripts of the *Fox Fables* and the various inauthentic fables added in later versions. His own edition is based on four manuscripts, the earliest of which is Munich, Bayerische Staatsbibliothek, Cod. Heb. 207, the only surviving French manuscript, dated to 1268. Berekhiah ha-Nakdan. *Mishle Shu'alim*, ed. Haberman, vii–ix. In her paleographic work on English manuscripts, Judith Olszowy-Schlanger argues that the thirteenth-century Oxford, Bodleian Library, MS Or. 135, which contains the *Mahberet* of Solomon ibn Parhon with Latin and French annotations by Christians, as well as the *Fox Fables*, was produced in England: *Les manuscrits hébreux dans l'Angleterre médiévale: étude historique et paléographique* (Paris: Peeters, 2003), 33.

87. See Bloch, *The Anonymous Marie de France*, 175–205. It should be said that Berekhiah is not the sole medieval Jewish writer to transmit parables from the Latin tradition. In one misogynistic example, an enigmatic reference in B. Kiddushin 80b to "a certain woman" prompts a retelling, in the Tosafot, of the bawdy tale of "The woman who hangs her dead husband's body on a tree to save her lover" or "The Widow of Ephesus," which appears in Petronius's *Satyricon*, all of the *Romulus* collections, Marie de France's *Fables* (as "De la femme ki fist pendre sun mari," in which she somewhat tones down the misogyny), and of course Berekhiah's text. See Schwarzbaum, *Mishle Shu'alim (Fox Fables) of Rabbi Berechiah ha-Nakdan*, 399.

88. The original in *Phaedrus* is very different in its punishment of a wrongdoer: there, after the "trial," the sheep finds the wolf, the false witness, dead in a pit a few days later. *Babrius and Phaedrus*, ed. and trans. Perry, 213. Berekhiah's version is closest to the *Romulus Nilanti*, *Les Fabulistes Latins*, ed. Hervieux, 2:515. Marie interestingly treats it in her epimythium as a fable about social injustices perpetrated by the rich (Marie de France, *Fables*, ed. and trans. Spiegel, 40–43. The biblical Hebrew word *nesher* could also mean a vulture, but I prefer to use eagle to capture its association with the Roman Empire.

89. Berekhiah ha-Nakdan, *Mishle Shu'alim*, ed. Haberman, 15; *Fables of a Jewish Aesop*, trans. Hadas, 19.

90. Berekhiah ha-Nakdan, *Mishle Shu'alim*, ed. Haberman, 14–15; *Fables of a Jewish Aesop*, trans. Hadas, 19.

91. *Midrash Bereshit Rabbah*, 82.10. *Midrash Rabbah: Genesis*, vol. 2, ed. and trans. H. Freedman and Maurice Simon (London: Soncino Press, 1983), 759–61.

92. Jerome, *In Hieremiam Prophetam Libri VI*, ed. S. Reiter (Turnhout: Brepols, 1960), 306–8.

93. B. Berakhot 61b. For analogues, see Schwarzbaum, *Mishle Shu'alim (Fox Fables) of Rabbi Berechiah ha-Nakdan*, 25–41.

94. Berekhiah ha-Nakdan, *Mishle Shu'alim*, ed. Haberman, 13; *Fables of a Jewish Aesop*, trans. Hadas, 16.

95. Berekhiah ha-Nakdan, *Mishle Shu'alim*, ed. Haberman, 13–14; *Fables of a Jewish Aesop*, trans. Hadas, 17.

96. M. Sotah 9:15 Berekhiah ha-Nakdan, *Mishle Shu'alim*, ed. Haberman, 14; *Fables of a Jewish Aesop*, trans. Hadas, 17–18.

97. Berekhiah ha-Nakdan, *Mishle Shu'alim*, ed. Haberman, 14; *Fables of a Jewish Aesop*, trans. Hadas, 18.

98. Avianus, ed. and trans. J. W. Duff and Arnold Duff, 716–19.

99. Schwarzbaum, *Mishle Shu'alim (Fox Fables) of Rabbi Berechiah ha-Nakdan*, 468–73.

100. Berekhiah ha-Nakdan, *Mishle Shu'alim*, ed. Haberman, 103; *Fables of a Jewish Aesop*, trans. Hadas, 172.

101. The involvement of Jews with Christian religious items seems to have been fairly common, despite laws against it: see Richardson, *English Jewry under Angevin Kings*, 113.

102. B. Sotah 41b; B. Megillah 16b.

103. "Hinc et hedera coronabatur poetae vel utpote Libero consecrati, qui ut Bacchae insaniunt": *Scriptores rerum mythicarum Latini tres Romae nuper reperti*, ed. Georg Bode (Darmstadt, 1834), 245. The work of the so-called "Third Vatican Mythographer" is attributed in several MSS to Alberic of London; a few scholars believe that the prolific Alexander Nequam himself was the author. *The Vatican Mythographers*, trans. Ronald E. Pepin (New York: Fordham University Press, 2008), 7–9; on Bacchus, 318–22.

## 4. Pleasures and Dangers of Conversion

1. Olszowy-Schlanger, "Knowledge and Practice of Hebrew Grammar."

2. For theories about the original intent of *Joseph and Aseneth* with regard to conversion, see Erich Gruen, *Heritage and Hellenism: The Rejuvenation of Jewish Tradition* (Berkeley: University of California Press, 1998), 89–99; and Howard Clark Kee, "The Socio-Cultural Setting of Joseph and Aseneth," *New Testament Studies* 29 (1983): 394–413.

3. The Chronicle of Solomon bar Simson, in *The Jews and the Crusaders*, ed. and trans. Eidelberg, 31.

4. Ibid., 67–68.

5. Ibid., 35. Jeremy Cohen offers an ingenious and convincing reading of how the chroniclers construct the story of Rachel of Mainz to echo aspects of both Jacob and Esau as well as the Virgin Mary in a rejection of Christianity. Their acknowledgement of Christian influence nevertheless speaks to their status as survivors if not converts. See *Sanctifying the Name of God*, 106–29.

6. *The Jews and the Crusaders*, ed. and trans. Eidelberg, 36; G. Cohen, "Hannah and Her Seven Sons."

7. *The Jews and the Crusaders*, ed. and trans. Eidelberg, 42.

8. Ibid., 127.

9. Ephraim Kupfer, "A Note on the History of R. Moshe b. Yom Tov 'The Mighty' of London" [in Hebrew], *Tarbiẓ* 40 (1971): 385–87; Grossman, "The Roots of Qiddush ha-Shem," 126–27. The text is found in Paris, Bibliothèque Nationale de France, MS 1408, within a copy of R. Meir of Rothenburg's halakhot on mourning.

10. Avraham Grossman, "A Typological Story about the Conversion of R. Gershom Me'or ha-Golah's Son," in *Studies in Jewish Narrative: Ma'aseh Sippur, Presented to Yoav Elstein*, ed. Avidov Lipsker and Rella Kushelevsky (Ramat Gan: Bar Ilan University Press, 2006), 65–75. The manuscript, with a commentary on one of R. Gershom's *piyyutim*, is from 1301; the story is garbled. The account of R. Gershom and his son the Jewish Pope draws on various similar narratives, in particular the famous story of Elchanan, the son of R. Shimon ben Yitzhak ben Avun converting and becoming pope. Grossman links the entire tradition about these tenth- to eleventh-century sages to Ephraim of Bonn and his distress with conversions in the aftermath of the Crusades.

11. William Chester Jordan, "Adolescence and Conversion in the Middle Ages: A Research Agenda," in Signer and Van Engen, *Jews and Christians in Twelfth-Century Europe*, 77–93.

12. Grossman, "Roots of Qiddush ha-Shem," especially 112–21; also Einbinder, *Beautiful Death*, 17–26.

13. Jacob Katz, *Exclusiveness and Tolerance: Studies in Jewish–Gentile Relations in Medieval and Modern Times* (Oxford: Oxford University Press, 1961), 67–70; David Malkiel, "Jews and Apostates in Medieval Europe: Boundaries Real and Imagined," *Past and Present*, no. 194 (2007), 3–34.

14. Malkiel, "Jews and Apostates in Medieval Europe," 31; Jakob Blidstien, "The Personal Status of Apostate and Ransomed Women in Medieval Jewish Law" [in Hebrew], *Shenaton ha-Mishpat ha-Ivri* 3–4 (1976–77): 35–116, especially 55–61.

15. Steven Kruger, *The Spectral Jew: Conversion and Embodiment in Medieval Europe* (Minneapolis: University of Minnesota Press, 2006), 85.

16. Avraham (Rami) Reiner, "L'attitude envers les prosélytes en Allemagne et en France du XIe au XIIIe siècle," *REJ* 167 (2008): 99–119; Shaye Cohen, *The Beginnings of Jewishness: Boundaries, Varieties, Uncertainties* (Berkeley: University of California Press, 1999), 330–40.

17. Reiner, "L'attitude envers les prosélytes," 107; B. Pesachim 87b.

18. On the Hebrew midrashic traditions about Aseneth as an Israelite who, therefore, needed no conversion, see V. Aptowitzer, "Asenath, the Wife of Joseph: A Haggadic Literary-Historical Study," *Hebrew Union College Annual* 1 (1924): 239–306; and Ross Shepard Kraemer, *When Aseneth Met Joseph: A Late Antique Tale of the Biblical Patriarch and His Egyptian Wife, Reconsidered* (Oxford: Oxford University Press, 1998), 307–21. *Midrash Kohelet Rabbah* 8:13 includes a passage on Aseneth as a convert, together with Rahab, Ruth, and Hobab.

19. The manuscript is now Cambridge, Corpus Christi College, MS 288. M. R. James, *A Descriptive Catalogue of the Manuscripts in the Library of Corpus Christi College* (Cambridge: Cambridge University Press, 1912), 2:58–63.

20. The sermon has been edited in various redactions: for its original fifth-century form, Quodvultdeus's "Contra Judaeos, Paganos et Arrianos," see Quodvultdeus, *Opera*, ed. René Braun, CCSL 60 (Turnhout: Brepols, 1976), 227–58; as an autonomous medieval tract against the Jews, see Karl Young, "Ordo Prophetarum," *Transactions of the Wisconsin Academy of Sciences, Arts and Letters* 20 (1922): 1–82. In the Cambridge manuscript, the sermon is copied in the form of a Christmas lectionary (fols. 60–65v).

21. The reference is to Matthew 15:24.

22. Brigitte Miriam Bedos-Rezak, "Les juifs et l'écrit dans la mentalité eschatologique du Moyen Âge chrétien occidental (France 1000–1200)," *Annales: Histoire, Sciences Sociales*, no. 5 (1994): 1049–63.

23. On the manuscript transmission of the *Dialogue*, see John Tolan, *Petrus Alfonsi and His Medieval Readers* (Gainesville: University Press of Florida, 1993), 98–103.

24. On Petrus Alfonsi's direct influence on the twelfth- and thirteenth-century English anti-Jewish polemics, see R. W. Hunt, "The Disputation of Peter of Cornwall against Symon the Jew," in *Studies in Medieval History Presented to Frederick Maurice Powicke*, ed. R. W. Hunt et al. (Oxford: Clarendon Press, 1948), 143–56; both Bartholomew of Exeter and Peter of Cornwall quote the *Dialogue*.

25. See Tolan, *Petrus Alfonsi and His Medieval Readers*, 95–131; Abulafia, *Christians and Jews in the Twelfth-Century Renaissance*, 94–106; Jeremy Cohen, *Living Letters of the Law: Ideas of the Jew in Medieval Christianity* (Berkeley: University of California Press, 1999), 201–18.

26. Petrus Alfonsi, *Dialogus contra Judaeos*, ed. Klaus-Peter Mieth (Huesca: Instituto de Estudios Altoaragoneses, 1996), 61–62; trans. Resnick as *Dialogue against the Jews*. See also Ch. Merchavia, *The Church Versus Talmudic and Midrashic Literature, 500–1248* [in Hebrew] (Jerusalem: Bialik Institute, 1970), 114–15.

27. Judah Rosenthal, "The Talmud on Trial: The Disputation at Paris in the Year 1240." *JQR* 47, nos. 1–2 (1956): 58–76, 145–69.

28. Roth, *Jews of Medieval Oxford*, 122–23.

29. Robert C. Stacey, "The Conversion of Jews to Christianity in Thirteenth-Century England," *Speculum* 67 (1992): 263–83.

30. Ibid., 270.

31. Ibid., 269.

32. Joan Greatrex, "Monastic Charity for Jewish Converts: The Requisition of Corrodies by Henry III," in *Christianity and Judaism*, ed. Diana Wood, special issue, *Studies in Church History* 29 (1992): 133–43; see also Susan Wood, *English Monasteries and Their Patrons in the Thirteenth Century* (Oxford: Oxford University Press, 1955), 110–11.

33. Robert Grosseteste, *De cessatione legalium*, ed. Richard C. Dales and Edward B. King, Auctores Britannici medii aevi 7 (London: Oxford University Press, 1986). See Beryl Smalley, "The Biblical Scholar," in *Robert Grosseteste: Scholar and Bishop*, ed. D. A. Callus (Oxford: Oxford University Press, 1955), 70–97.

34. Grosseteste, *De cessatione legalium*, ed. Dales and King, ix–xv, 168.

35. R. W. Southern, *Robert Grosseteste: The Growth of an English Mind in Medieval Europe* (Oxford: Oxford University Press, 1986), 244–49.

36. For a detailed account of this entire episode, including the underlying conflict between Montfort and his great-aunt Margaret over the partitioned earldom of Leicester, see J. R. Maddicott, *Simon de Montfort* (Cambridge: Cambridge University Press, 1994), 15–16.

37. For the text of this letter, see *Roberti Grosseteste Episcopi quondam Lincolniensis Epistolae*, ed. Henry Luard, Rerum Britannicarum medii aevi scriptores 25 (London: Longman, 1861), 33–38. Of the Jews, Grosseteste writes: "Vagus est populus ille per dispersionem, et profugus a propria sede, scilicet Jerusalem, vagus per mansionis incertidinem et profugus per mortis timorem. Habet tamen ne occidatur Domini praelocutionem at etiam jussionem in Psalmo; namque de illis scriptum est: *Deus ostendit mihi super inimicos meos, ne occidas eos, ne quando obliviscantur populi mei*" (35).

38. Note that this reference is according to the Vulgate's numbering of the Psalms. For a new assessment of the Augustianian doctrine in the Middle Ages, see J. Cohen, *Living Letters of the Law*, especially 19–145.

39. *Hegesippus*, 373.

40. On William of Newburgh as a historiographer, see Nancy Partner, *Serious Entertainments: The Writing of History in Twelfth-Century England* (Chicago: University of Chicago Press, 1977), 51–140. For a provocative reading of William of Newburgh and Thomas Wykes as Augustinian Canons in relation to the fourteenth-century poem *The Siege of Jerusalem*, see Elisa Narin van Court, "*The Siege of Jerusalem* and Augustinian Historians: Writing about Jews in Fourteenth-Century England," *Chaucer Review* 29 (1995): 227–48.

41. William of Newburgh, *Historia rerum Anglicarum*, ed. Howlett, 299.

42. Ibid., 318–20.

43. See Schreckenberg, *Die Flavius-Josephus-Tradition*, especially 110–54.

44. William of Newburgh, *Historia rerum Anglicarum*, ed. Howlett, 321–22.

45. For the development of the narrative of the fall of Jerusalem in Latin, from Hegesippus's Christianizing rewriting of Josephus on, see Stephen K. Wright, *The Vengeance of Our Lord: Medieval Dramatizations of the Destruction of Jerusalem* (Toronto: Pontifical Institute of Mediaeval Studies, 1989), 1–32.

46. "Quas tamen postmodum eo quod non cognoverint tempus visitationis suae, sed detestabili vesania proprium peremerunt Redemptorem, cadem terra, jam in ea patratis divines mysteriis inclita, severiori judicio nunquam revocandas evomuit, Romanis imperatoribus Vespasiano et Tito divinae anamadversionis ministries. Exterminato autem carnali semine Abrahae": William of Newburgh, *Historia rerum Anglicarum*, ed. Howlett, 253.

47. The final ten stanzas of the *kinnah* are edited and translated by S. Schechter, "A Hebrew Elegy," *Transactions of the Jewish Historical Society of England* 1 (1893–94): 8–14. The entire poem, which also laments the martyrs of a riot in Boppard in 1179 is in *Sefer Gezerot Ashkenaz ve-Tsarfat*, ed. A. M. Haberman (Jerusalem: Bialik Institute, 1945), 147–51.

48. Noel Denholm-Young, "Thomas de Wykes and His Chronicle," *English Historical Review* 61 (1946): 157–79. See also Gransden, *Historical Writing in England*, 1:463–70.

49. Thomas Wykes, *Chronicon*, in *Annales Monastici*, ed. Henry R. Luard, Rerum Britannicarum medii aevi scriptores 36 (London: Longman, 1864–69), 4:142.

50. Ibid.

51. Stacey, "Conversion of Jews to Christianity," 270–73.

52. F. Donald Logan, "Thirteen London Jews and Conversion to Christianity: Problems of Apostasy in the 1280s," *Bulletin of the Institute for Historical Research* 45 (1972): 214–29.

53. *The Church and the Jews in the XIIIth Century*, vol 2., *1254–1314*, ed. Solomon Grayzel and Kenneth Stow (New York: Jewish Theological Seminary, 1989), 157–58.

54. Stacey, "Conversion of Jews to Christianity," 282. All of these accounts support Jonathan Elukin's argument that "medieval culture's new emphasis on the interior self" in the twelfth century led to a greater need in conversions for "confirmation that the interior person had really changed," usually in the form of a miracle. Jonathan M. Elukin, "The Discovery of the Self: Jews and Conversion in the Twelfth Century," in Signer and Van Engen, *Jews and Christians in Twelfth-Century Europe*, 63–76.

55. Kew, National Archives, PRO SC 1/24/201. See Greatrex, "Monastic Charity for Jewish Converts," 141. A second letter by Alice, addressed to King Edward I, is transcribed in Michael Adler, *Jews of Medieval England* (London: Jewish Historical Society, 1939), 347–48.

56. On the legends of Mary Magdalene as a desert contemplative (often conflated with details from the life of Mary of Egypt), see Katherine Ludwig Jansen, *The Making of the Magdalen: Preaching and Popular Devotion in the Later Middle Ages* (Princeton, NJ: Princeton University Press, 2000), 116–42.

57. "Cum ergo lex vetus sit generans in servitutem, congruit ut ipsa signaretur per ancillam. Congruit quoque interpretatio nominis ancillae servituti legis: Agar enim interpretatur

alienatio vel paroikia, id est, incolatus sive peregrinatio; et servuus alienus est ab haereditate, nec manet in domo magistrorum." Robert Grosseteste, *Expositio in Epistolam Sanct Pauli ad Galatas*, ed. James McEvoy et al, CCCM 130 (Turnhout: Brepols, 1995), 122.

58. M. R. James, ed., *The Ancient Libraries of Canterbury and Dover* (Cambridge: Cambridge University Press, 1903), 118–19. The original Canterbury manuscript, written on seven quires in two thirteenth-century hands, is volume 4 of the multivolume manuscript in M. R. James's description of CCCC, MS 288, in his *Descriptive Catalogue*, 2:58–63. A terminus ab quo is provided by one of the texts on the Tartars, which is dated 1239; the first and last notices of Nicholas of Sandwich in the records of Canterbury Cathedral Priory are 1243, when he was sent to France to meet archbishop-elect Boniface, and 1262, when he served as precentor.

59. CCCC, MS 288, fol. 101r. This text is Recension 2 of Pseudo-Methodius's *Revelations*, a work very widely circulated in the Middle Ages. For an account of the various recensions, see Marc Laureys and Daniel Verhelst, "Pseudo-Methodius, Revelationes: Textgeschichte und Kritische Edition. Ein Leuven-Groninger Forschungprojekt," in *The Use and Abuse of Eschatology in the Middle Ages*, ed. Werner Verbeke, Daniel Verhelst, and Andries Welkenhuysen (Leuven: Leuven University Press, 1988), 112–36.

60. The *Infancy Gospel of Thomas* is edited in *Evangelia Apocrypha*, ed. Tischendorf, 164–80; perhaps reflecting post-Crusade confusion, the manuscript substitutes "Thomas Ishmaelita" for "Thomas Israelita."

61. The Latin *Vita Adae et Evae* from CCCC, MS 288 has been edited by Mayumi Taguchi, "The Legend of the Cross Before Christ: Another Prose Treatment in English and Anglo-Norman," *Poetica* 45 (1996): 15–61. See also M. D. Johnson's introduction to "Life of Adam and Eve (First Century A.D.)," in Charlesworth, *The Old Testament Pseudepigrapha*, 2:249–57.

62. Quoted from Lusignan, "Preface au *Speculum Maius* de Vincent de Beauvais," 125.

63. *The Historical Works of Gervase of Canterbury*, ed. William Stubbs (London: Longman, 1879–80), 1:405. See Michael Adler, "The Jews of Canterbury," *Transactions of the Jewish Historical Society of England* 7 (1911–14): 19–96.

64. Mundill, *England's Jewish Solution*, 35–38.

65. *Historical Works of Gervase of Canterbury*, ed. Stubbs, 2:235. See also Mundill, *England's Jewish Solution*, 41–42. On the *Canterbury Chronicle*'s probaronial position, see Gransden, *Historical Writing in England*, vol. 1, 422–23.

66. *Historical Works of Gervase of Canterbury*, ed. Stubbs, 2:202, 207, 217. Joan Greatrex, *Biographical Register of the English Cathedral Priories of the Province of Canterbury, c. 1066–1540* (Oxford: Clarendon Press, 1997), 280.

67. James, *Ancient Libraries*, 118–19; Marinus de Jonge, "Robert Grosseteste and the *Testaments of the Twelve Patriarchs*," *Journal of Theological Studies* 42 (1991): 115–25.

68. On the original Diaspora context of *Joseph and Aseneth*, see Christoph Burchard's discussion in "Joseph and Aseneth (First Century B.C.–Second Century A.D.," in Charlesworth, *The Old Testament Pseudepigrapha*, 2:177–247; and John J. Collins, *Between Athens and Jerusalem: Jewish Identity in the Hellenistic Diaspora*, 2nd ed. (Grand Rapids, MI: Eerdmans, 2000), 230–39.

69. See Christoph Burchard's description of Latin MSS in "Der Jüdische Asenethroman und seine Nachwirkung," in *Gesammelte Studien zu Joseph und Aseneth* (Leiden: Brill, 1996), 367–70. Of the earliest six surviving MSS (late twelfth–early thirteenth century), three are traceable to Christ's Church, Canterbury. The translation itself, however, may possibly date to the early twelfth century, when a reference to a text called "Assenech" appears in the catalog of books from Rochester Cathedral Priory (the *Textus Roffensis*), intriguingly bound

with another work that touches on Jewish conversion, Anselm of Canterbury's *Cur Deus Homo.* Burchard also notes an entry in the early twelfth-century catalog of Durham Cathedral to a text called "Putiphar." One implication of this early a date for the Latin *Joseph and Aseneth* is that it could have contributed to the subsequent portrayals of conversion in the *chansons de geste.*

70. Burchard reprints this passage on Joseph from the *Speculum Historiale* in "Der Jüdische Asenethroman," 370–79.

71. Einbinder, *Beautiful Death*, especially 1–69.

72. The text is in CCCC, MS 288, fols. 88r–97r; M. R. James edited the text from this manuscript and the earlier Cambridge, Corpus Christi College, MS 424 in *Studia Patristica: Études d'ancienne littérature chrétienne*, ed. Pierre Batiffol (Paris: E. Leroux, 1890), 89–115. Various critics note the text's similarity to the Greek "novels" and, especially, Apuleius's "romance" of Cupid and Psyche in *The Golden Ass.* On these novels' theme of conversion, see Lawrence Wills, *The Jewish Novel in the Ancient World* (Ithaca, NY: Cornell University Press, 1995), 176–80.

73. The fascinating topic of gender-switching in early Christian literature is beyond the scope of this article, but for an overview, see Elizabeth Castelli, "'I Will Make Mary Male': Pieties of the Body and Gender Transformation of Christian Women in Late Antiquity," in *Body Guards: The Cultural Politics of Gender Ambiguity*, ed. Julia Epstein and Kristina Straub (New York: Routledge, 1991), 29–49; on Mary Magdalene, see Ann Graham Brock, *Mary Magdalene, the First Apostle: The Struggle for Authority* (Cambridge, MA: Harvard University Press, 2003).

74. Wills, *The Jewish Novel in the Ancient World*, 172.

75. "Ad hoc enim occisus est Christus a Iudaeis et traditus gentibus tamquam Joseph Aegyptiis a fratribus, ut et reliquae Israhel salvae fierent." Augustine, *Quaestionum in Heptateuchum libri VII*, ed. I. Fraipont, in *Aurelii Augustini Opera*, part 5, CCSL 33 (Turnhout: Brepols, 1958), 56. The *Glossa Ordinaria* on Genesis 37–38 provides a full allegorization of Joseph's tribulations drawn from patristic sources: see *Biblia Latina cum Glossa Ordinaria: Facsimile Reprint of the Editio Princeps, Adolph Rusch of Strassburg 1480/81*, ed. Karlfried Froehlich and Margaret Gibson (Turnhout: Brepols, 1992), 1:88–90.

76. *Saint Jerome's Hebrew Questions on Genesis*, trans. C. T. R. Hayward (Oxford: Oxford University Press, 1995), 86–87; for a discussion of Joseph's beauty, see James Kugel, *In Potiphar's House: The Interpretive Life of Biblical Texts* (Cambridge, MA: Harvard University Press, 1994), 84–89.

77. Sharon Kinoshita, *Medieval Boundaries: Rethinking Difference in Old French Literature* (Philadelphia: University of Pennsylvania Press, 2006), 46–73; Suzanne Conklin Akbari, "Woman as Mediator in Medieval Depictions of Muslims: The Case of Floripas," in *Medieval Constructions in Gender and Identity: Essays in Honor of Joan M. Ferrante*, ed. Teodolinda Barolini (Tempe: Arizona Center for Medieval and Renaissance Studies, 2005), 151–67.

78. *The Ecclesiastical History of Orderic Vitalis*, ed. and trans. Marjorie Chibnall (Oxford: Oxford University Press, 1969–80), 5:369, 379.

79. Ibid., 377.

80. Sharon Kinoshita, "The Politics of Courtly Love: *La Prise d'Orange* and the Conversion of the Saracen Queen," *Romanic Review* 86 (1995): 275; *The Song of Roland: An Analytical Edition*, ed. and trans. Gerard J. Brault, vol. 2 (University Park: Pennsylvania State University Press, 1978), lines 3986–87.

81. *Materials for the History of Thomas Becket, Archbishop of Canterbury*, ed. James Craigie Robertson and J. Brigstocke Sheppard (London: Longman, 1876–85), 2:453–58. The earliest manuscript containing the legend of Becket's Syrian descent dates from the

mid-thirteenth century, although the legend is probably somewhat earlier. See Anne Duggan, "The Cult of St. Thomas Becket in the Thirteenth Century," in *St. Thomas Cantilupe, Bishop of Hereford: Essays in His Honour*, ed. Meryl Jancey (Hereford: Friends of Hereford Cathedral, 1982), 21–44. For an account of the versions of Elias's *Quadrilogus*, see Anne Duggan, *Thomas Becket: A Textual History of His Letters* (Oxford: Clarendon Press, 1980), 178, 205, 223.

82. *Materials for the History of Thomas Becket*, ed. Robertson and Sheppard, 2:453. See Karl Morrison, *Understanding Conversion* (Charlottesville: University Press of Virginia, 1992), 139–41.

83. J. Cohen, *Living Letters of the Law*, 219–70; and "Muslim Connection."

84. Kraemer, *When Aseneth Met Joseph*, 191–221.

85. Ibid., 197.

86. Cambridge, Trinity College, MS B.1.30.

87. Wills, *The Jewish Novel in the Ancient World*, 13; Isidore of Seville, *De ortu et obitu patrum*, ed. César Chaparro Gómez (Paris: Belles Lettres, 1985), 187–89.

88. Cambridge, Trinity College, MS B.1.30, fol. 11r.

89. Kraemer, *When Aseneth Met Joseph*, 28–29.

90. See, for example the accounts in the *Annals of Osney*, in *Annales Monastici*, ed. Luard, 4:326–27; and the *Annals of Waverley*, ibid., 2:409.

### 5. *The Testaments of the Twelve Patriarchs* in the Shadow of the Ten Lost Tribes

1. "Ipsis quoque temporibus, episcopus Lincolniensis Robertus, vir in Latino et Greco pertissimus, *Testamenta duodecim Patriarcharum* de Greco fideli interpretatione transtulit in Latinum, quae per multa tempora incognita et abscondita fuerunt per invidiam Judaeorum, propter manifestas prophetias de Salvatore in eis contentas. Sed Graeci, omnium scriptorum diligentissimi investigatores, primi in notitiam illius scripti devenientes, illud de Hebraeo in Graecum transtulerunt, et penes eos usque in nostra tempora reservarunt." Matthew Paris, *Chronica Majora*, ed. Henry R. Luard, Rerum Britannicarum medii aevi scriptores 57 (London: Longman, 1872–83), 4:76–78. All translations are mine unless otherwise noted. There is a translation of the *Chronica Majora* by J. A. Giles, *Matthew Paris's English History from the Year 1235 to 1273*, 3 vols. (London: Bohn, 1852–54). For details about the Greek manuscript of the *Testaments* that Grosseteste obtained (now Cambridge University Library, MS Ff I.24, fols. 203r–261v), see De Jonge, "Robert Grosseteste and the Testaments of the Twelve Patriarchs."

2. For a comprehensive treatment of Matthew Paris's views of Jews and Mongols, see Sophia Menache, "Tartars, Jews, Saracens, and the Jewish-Mongol 'Plot' of 1241," *History* 81 (1996): 319–42. On Matthew's grotesque drawings of Mongols, see Suzanne Lewis, *The Art of Matthew Paris in the "Chronica Majora"* (Berkeley: University of California Press, 1987), 283–90. The most thorough consideration of Europe's encounters with the Mongols is Felicitas Schmieder, *Europa und die Fremden: die Mongolen im Urteil des Abendlandes vom 13. bis in das 15. Jahrhundert* (Sigmaringen: Thorbecke, 1994).

3. Matthew Paris, *CM Chronica Majora*, 4:76–78. The ten lost tribes refer to all except Judah and Benjamin, exiled "beyond the Euphrates" during the Assyrian and Babylonian captivities; Levi is only occasionally included as a tribe. The classic article is A. Neubauer's "Where Are the Ten Tribes?" *JQR* 1, nos. 1–4 (1888–89): 14–28, 95–114, 185–201, 408–23. For the many medieval versions of the story of Alexander's enclosure of Eastern nations in the Caucasian Mountains, see Andrew Runni Anderson, *Alexander's Gate: Gog and Magog and the Inclosed Nations* (Cambridge, MA: Medieval Academy, 1932). The "inclosed nations" also feature prominently in some of the literature associated with Prester John, the legendary

Christian king said to rule in the East; the ten tribes of Jews are his subjects and pay taxes to him. See Micha Perry, "The Imaginary War between Prester John and Eldad the Danite and Its Real Implications," *Viator* 41 (2010): 1–23.

4. Robert C. Stacey, "1240–60: A Watershed in Anglo-Jewish Relations?" *Historical Research* 61, no. 145 (1988): 135–50.

5. William Chester Jordan, *The French Monarchy and the Jews: From Philip Augustus to the Last Capetians* (Philadelphia: University of Pennsylvania Press, 1989), 128–41; Robert Chazan, *Medieval Jewry in Northern France: A Political and Social History* (Baltimore: Johns Hopkins University Press, 1973), 100–153.

6. Jordan, *The French Monarchy and the Jews*, 149–50. Stacey, "Conversion of Jews to Christianity."

7. Chazan, *Medieval Jewry in Northern France*, 124–31.

8. Yuval, *Two Nations in Your Womb*, 257–95. See also Israel Jacob Yuval, "Jewish Messianic Expectations Towards 1240 and Christian Reactions," in *Toward the Millennium: Messianic Expectations from the Bible to Waco*, ed. Peter Schafer and Mark Cohen (Leiden: Brill, 1998), 105–21.

9. Yuval, "Jewish Messianic Expectations," 107; *Two Nations in Your Womb*, 278–79.

10. Yuval, *Two Nations in Your Womb*, 264–65, 291–94. The text that Yuval cites is found in a thirteenth-century commentary on *Pirke Avot*; he also discusses another text, from an Oxford manuscript, that situates Jesus in a Jewish messianic narrative.

11. Yuval, *Two Nations in Your Womb*, 293–95; see also Marjorie Reeves, *The Influence of Prophecy in the Later Middle Ages: A Study in Joachimism* (Oxford: Oxford University Press, 1969), 45–58; Felicitas Schmieder, "*Nota sectam maometicam atterendam a tartaris et christianis*: The Mongols as Non-believing Apocalyptic Friends around the Year 1260," *Journal of Millennial Studies* 1 (1998), http://www.mille.org/publications/summer98/fschmieder.pdf.

12. Marjorie Reeves sorts out Howden's two versions of this story, one that he attributed to Benedict of Peterborough and a revised account. Howden, who accompanied Richard on the Third Crusade, records Joachim's prediction of the crusaders' failure to overthrow Saladin. See *Influence of Prophecy*, 6–10.

13. J. Cohen, *Living Letters of the Law*, 159–66.

14. Yuval, *Two Nations in Your Womb*, 290.

15. *CM*, IV, 77–78.

16. Robert E. Lerner, *The Powers of Prophecy: The Cedar of Lebanon Vision from the Mongol Onslaught to the Dawn of the Enlightenment* (Berkeley: University of California Press, 1983), 16. See also Lerner's discussion of Matthew Paris's own version of this prophecy, which is not explicitly linked to the Mongols, 26–31.

17. The connection between the Mongols and Jews appears to have been debated in monastic circles. Like Matthew, Richer of Sens mentions the idea of the Mongols as the Jews enclosed by Alexander the Great in close proximity to accounts of local Jewish atrocities, including his unique version of a ritual murder accusation at Hagenau in 1236 that involved Jews killing three Christian boys during Passover. *Richeri Gesta Senoniensis Ecclesiae*, ed. G. Waitz, in Monumenta Germaniae Historica, Scriptores 25 (Hannover: Hahn, 1880), 249–345.

18. On Pseudo-Methodius and his Syrian precursor Jacob of Serugh, see Bernard McGinn, *Visions of the End: Apocalyptic Traditions in the Middle Ages* (New York: Columbia University Press, 1998), 56–59, 70–76.

19. "Nec tempore beati Jeronomi vel alicuius sancti interpretis ad notitiam Christianorum, machinante Judaeorum antiquorum malitia, potuit quomodolibet devenire. Illum igitur gloriosum tractatum, ad robur fidei Christianae et ad majorem Judaeorum confusionem,

transtulit plene et evidenter episcopus memoratus de Graeco, verbo ad verbum in Latinum, coadjuvante magistro Nicholao Graeco, clerico abbatis Sancti Albani." *CM*, 4:232–33.

20. The thirty-five articles against the Talmud were collected later (1248) by another convert, Thibaut de Sezanne, as *Extractiones de Talmud*; the document is published in Isidore Loeb, "La controverse de 1240 sur le Talmud," *REJ* 1 (1880): 247–61; 2 (1881): 248–70; 3 (1882): 39–57.

21. Rosenthal, "Talmud on Trial." Rosenthal compares the Latin accusations against the original Hebrew/Aramaic passages from the Talmud. See also J. Cohen, *Living Letters of the Law*, 317–63.

22. Augustine, *De civitate Dei* XVIII: 46. J. Cohen translates the passage in *Living Letters of the Law*, 32; for more on Augustine's understanding of Jewish Diaspora, see Paula Frediksen, "*Excaecati Occulta Justitia Dei*: Augustine on the Jews and Judaism," *Journal of Early Christian Studies* 3 (1995): 299–324.

23. *The Church and the Jews in the XIIIth Century*, ed. Grayzel and Stow, 1:241.

24. *Vikuaḥ Rabbenu Yeḥiel mi-Pariz* [in Hebrew], ed. Reuben Margoliot (Lwow, 1928); Robert Chazan, "The Hebrew Report on the Trial of the Talmud: Information and Consolation," in *Le brûlement du Talmud à Paris 1242–1244*, ed. Rene-Samuel Sirat (Paris: Cerf, 1999), 79–93.

25. Rosenthal, "Talmud on Trial," 154–55.

26. *Vikuah*, ed. Margoliot, 22.

27. Chazan, "The Hebrew Report on the Trial of the Talmud," 91.

28. Yuval, *Two Nations in Your Womb*, 258–62. This interpretation of Balaam's prophecy depends on a numerological play of words between "the days to come" and "after 5 days" (read as a thousand years for each day, as in Psalm 90:4: "For in Your sight a thousand years are like yesterday that has passed"). In a further gesture of defiance described in the *Vikuah*, Rabbi Yeḥiel ends the debate by recalling the martyrdom of R. Haninah ben Teradion, who was burned wrapped in a torah scroll.

29. Smalley, *Study of the Bible in the Middle Ages*, especially 83–195.

30. Ibid., 103. On the use of the term "Gamaliel" by medieval Christian writers to refer to the Talmud, see Merchavia, *The Church Versus Talmudic and Midrashic Literature*, 208–12.

31. Sophia Menache, "Matthew Paris's Attitudes toward Anglo-Jewry," *Journal of Medieval History* 23 (1997): 139–62.

32. For an overview, see J. J. Saunders, "Matthew Paris and the Mongols," in *Essays in Medieval History Presented to Bertie Wilkinson*, ed. T. A. Sandquist and M. R. Powicke (Toronto: University of Toronto Press, 1969), 116–32.

33. *Chronica Johannis de Oxenedes*, ed. Henry Ellis (London: Longman, Brown, Green, Longmans, and Roberts, 1859), 197. Maddicott, *Simon de Montfort*, 98–99.

34. "Quaesivi qui essent illi qui docent eos literas; dixerunt quod essent hominess pallidi qui multum jejunant, vestes longas portant, et nullos offendunt." *CM*, 6 (*Additamenta*): 75–76.

35. Peter Jackson, *The Mongols and the West, 1221–1410* (Harlow: Longman, 2005), 145–46.

36. Willis Johnson discusses the cultural construct of pale, melancholy Jews in an important article, "The Black Sickness" (unpublished manuscript).

37. Chazan, "The Hebrew Report on the Trial of the Talmud," 92.

38. Dan, *The Hebrew Story*, 47–61.

39. John Reeves, *Trajectories in Near Eastern Apocalyptic: A Postrabbinic Jewish Apocalypse Reader* (Atlanta: Society of Biblical Literature, 2005), 213.

40. Ibid., 215–16.

41. Menache, "Tartars, Jews, Saracens."

42. "Fratris, qui estis semen Abrahae praeclari, vinea domini Sabaoth, Deus noster Adonay nos diu sub potestate Christianorum permisit affligi. Sed nunc venit tempus quo liberamur, ut nos vice versa Dei judicio et ipsos opprimamus, ut salvi fiant reliquae Israel. Exierunt namque fratres nostri, tribus scilicet Israel, quondam inclusae, ut subdant sibi et nobis mundum universum." *CM*, 4:131–32.

43. The full text of this astonishing passage voiced by the twelve tribes in the nineteenth-century *Protocols* is as follows: "The intellectuals of the *goyim* will puff themselves up with their knowledge and without any logical verification of them will put into effect all the information available from science, which our *agenteur* specialists have cunningly pieced together for the purpose of educating their minds in the direction we want. Do not suppose for a moment that these statements are empty words: think carefully of the successes we arranged for Darwinism, Marxism, Nietzsche-ism. To us Jews at any rate, it should be plain to see what a disintegrating importance these directives have had. . . . By all these means we shall so wear down the *goyim* they will be compelled to offer us international power of a nature that by its position will enable us without any violence gradually to absorb all the state forces of the world and to form a super-government. In place of the rulers of today, we shall set up a bogey which will be called the Super-Government administration. Its hands will reach out in all directions like nippers and organization will be of such colossal dimensions that it cannot fail to subdue all the nations of the world." From *The Protocols of the Learned Elders of Zion*, trans. Victor E. Marsden, quoted in Stephen Eric Bronner, *A Rumor about the Jews: Reflections on Antisemitism and the "Protocols of the Learned Elders of Zion"* (New York: St. Martin's, 2000), 13.

44. Matthew again "records" the Jews' speech here: "Nos autem ipsos inhumanos et hostes publicos auferre de medio cupientes, et vos Christianos ab imminenti eorum tyrannical depopulatione liberare." *CM*, 4:132.

45. Menache, "Tartars, Jews, Saracens," 334; Yuval, *Two Nations in Your Womb*, 284–88. A concise version of rabbinic tradition about the ten tribes is in *Midrash Genesis Rabbah* 72:6 : "R. Judah b. R. Simon said: the tribes of Judah and Benjamin were not exiled to the same place as were the other ten tribes. The ten tribes were exiled beyond the river Sambatyon, whereas the tribes of Judah and Benjamin are dispersed in all countries." *Midrash Rabbah Genesis*, vol. 1, ed. and trans. Freedman and Simon, 84.

46. Haim Schirmann, *Hebrew Poetry in Spain and Provence* [in Hebrew] (Tel Aviv: Bialik Institute, 1956), 2:317–18. Excerpts from this poem and other materials on the Mongols are in A. Z. Aescholy, *Jewish Messianic Movements* [in Hebrew] (Jerusalem: Bialik Institute, 1956), 212–20. See also Moshe Idel, *Messianic Mystics* (New Haven: Yale University Press, 1998), 58–100. On Meshullam, see James Lehmann, "Polemic and Satire in the Poetry of the Maimonidean Controversy," *Prooftexts* 1 (1981): 133–51.

47. "Ad quod spectaculum cum plures convenirent admirentes, et nescirent literas legere, scientes quia literae Hebraicae fuerunt, advocabant conversos Judaeos, qui domum, quam dominus rex Londoniis fundaverat, inhabitabant; ut ipsi sicut vitam aut membra dilegebant, pro honore, amore, et timore domini Regis, sine figmento falsitatis scripturam illam aperirent. . . . Et cum adducerentur dicti conversi ad legendum quae inscripta errant, et studerent ut perlegerent, (errant enim literae propter extensionem at contractionem cutis et carnis huc illucque projectae et multipliciter exagitate, deformate, et iam non legibiles,) verum nomen patris et matris pueruli, suppressis cognominibus, inscriptum reperierunt, et quod venditus fuit puer Judaeis, sed quibus, vel ad quid, non poterant investigare." *CM*, IV, 377.

48. David Frankfurter, "Beyond 'Jewish Christianity': Continuing Religious Sub-Cultures of the Second and Third Centuries and Their Documents," in *The Ways that Never Parted:*

*Jews and Christians in Late Antiquity and the Early Middle Ages*, ed. Adam H. Becker and Annette Yoshiko Reed (Tübingen: Mohr Siebeck, 2003), 141.

49. "Orietur vobis ex tribu juda et levi salutare domini et ipse faciet adversus belial prelium." *Testamenta duodecim patriarcharum filiorum Jacob: e Greco in Latinum versa Roberto Lincolniensi Episcopo interprete* (Augsburg: Johan Miller, 1520), fol. D iii. For a translation of the original Greek text, see Kee, "Testaments of the Twelve Patriarchs," 809.

50. "Verutamen in parte vestra fiet templum dei et gloriosum erit in vobis. Quam ipse dominus accipiet regnum. Et duodecim tribus ille congregabunt. Et omnes gentes usque quo altissimus mittat salutare suum in visitatione unigeniti." Grosseteste, *Testamenta*, fol. F iii. See Kee, "Testaments of the Twelve Patriarchs," 788, 827.

51. For an overview of scholarship, see Robert A. Kugler, *The Testaments of the Twelve Patriarchs*; see also Collins, *Between Athens and Jerusalem*, 174–85.

52. Frankfurter, "Beyond 'Jewish Christianity,'" 140–41.

53. Daniel Boyarin, *Border Lines: The Partition of Judaeo-Christianity* (Philadelphia: University of Pennsylvania Press, 2004), especially 112–27.

54. See Himmelfarb, "R. Moses the Preacher and the Testaments of the Twelve Patriarchs"; "The Hebrew Text of One of the Testaments of the Twelve Patriarchs," ed. and trans. Gaster; and Reeves, "Exploring the Afterlife."

55. Grosseteste, *De cessatione legalium*, ed. Dales and King, 95–96. See also Abulafia, *Christians and Jews in the Twelfth-Century Renaissance*, 94–106.

56. Grosesteste, *De cessatione legalium*, ed. Dales and King, 89.

57. "Facere itaque legalia tanquam legalia hoc est tanquam vivencia vita pie significationis, et tanquam umbram et testamonia et prophetalia Christi venturi, et tanquam salutifera per Christi presignationem, qui solus est vera salus, omnino nefas est post Christum, quia hoc est abnegare Christim et predicare alium adhuc venturum, quemadmodum adhuc faciunt infideles Judei." Ibid., 168.

58. David J. Wasserstein, "Grosseteste, the Jews, and Medieval Christian Hebraism," in *Robert Grosseteste: New Perspectives on His Thought and Scholarship*, ed. James McEvoy (Turnhout: Brepols, 1995), 357–76. See also A. C. Dionisotti, "On the Greek Studies of Robert Grosseteste," in *The Uses of Greek and Latin: Historical Essays*, ed. A. C. Dionisotti, Anthony Grafton, and Jill Kraye (London: Warburg Institute, 1988), 19–38.

59. Wasserstein's translation of the *Suidas* entry is at "Grosseteste, the Jews, and Medieval Christian Hebraism," 367–71.

60. The surviving thirteenth-century manuscripts that include both texts are London, British Library, Add. MS 18210, BL, MS Royal 4.D.vii, and Cambridge, St. John's, MS 184. See S. Harrison Thomson, *The Writings of Robert Grosseteste, Bishop of Lincoln, 1235–1253* (Cambridge: Cambridge University Press, 1940), 64–65.

61. Loewe, "Medieval Christian Hebraists of England"; Beryl Smalley, *Hebrew Scholarship among Christians in XIIIth Century England as Illustrated by some Hebrew-Latin Psalters* (London: Shapiro, Valentine, 1939). The Psalters are part of a much larger group of thirteenth-century bilingual manuscripts of biblical books (and rabbinic commentaries) that were evidently intended for Christians learning Hebrew with Jewish masters. See Loewe, "Latin Superscriptio MSS"; Dahan, "Deux psautiers hébraïques glosés en Latin."

62. Smalley, *Hebrew Scholarship*, 8. The manuscript is Cambridge, Corpus Christi College, MS Oxford 10, which Smalley dates to the 1230s–40s.

63. Andrew of Saint-Victor, *Expositionem in Ezechielem*, ed. Signer, xxvii–xxxvii.

64. Smalley, *Study of the Bible in the Middle Ages*, 138; on Richard of Saint-Victor's outrage at Andrew's "Judaizing" commentaries, see 110–11.

65. *CM*, V, 285. See de Jonge, "Robert Grossesteste and the Testaments of the Twelve Patriarchs," 123, and "The Transmission of the Testaments of the Twelve Patriarchs by Christians," *Vigilae Christianae* 47 (1993): 1–28.

66. "Tunc suscitabit deus sacerdotem novum cui omnes sermones domini revelabuntur . . . et orietur astrum ipsius in celo sicut rex." Grossesteste, *Testamenta*, fol. B iv.

67. "Et post hec orietur vobis astrum ex jacob in pace et exurget homo ex semine meo ut sol justicie ambulans cum filiis hominem in mansuetudine et justicia et omne peccatum non invenietur in eo." Ibid., fol. C iii.

68. "Et post hoc resurget Abraham Isaac et Jacob in vitam; et ego et fratres mei principes in Israel erimus. . . . Et erit unus populus domini et lingua una." Ibid., fol. C. iii–iv.

69. *Decrees of the Ecumenical Councils*, vol. 1, *Nicea I–Lateran V*, ed. Norman P. Tanner (Washington, DC: Georgetown University Press, 1990), 297. For a comprehensive account of the background of the First Council of Lyons and the participation of Grossesteste, see Davide Bigalli, *I Tartari e l'Apocalisse: Ricerche sull'escatologia in Adamo Marsh e Ruggero Bacone* (Florence: La Nuova Italia, 1971); see also James McEvoy, *Robert Grosseteste* (Oxford: Oxford University Press, 2000), 31–50.

70. S. Harrison Thomson lists fifteen thirteenth-century MSS in *Writings of Robert Grosseteste*, 42–44; the St. Albans manuscript is now BL, Royal MS 4.D.vii.

71. Vincent of Beauvais, *Speculum Historiale* (Nürnberg: Anton Koberger 1483), cxxv–cxxix. Claude Kappler, "L'image des Mongols dans le *Speculum Historiale* de Vincent de Beauvais," in Paulmier-Foucart, Lusignan, and Nadeau, *Vincent de Beauvais*, 219–40.

72. *Die Apokalypse des Pseudo-Methodius*, ed. W. J. Aerts and G. A. A. Kortekaas, Corpus Scriptorum Christianorum Orientalium 569–70 (Leuven: Peeters, 1998), 1:117–19. Translated in McGinn, *Visions of the End*, 73.

73. Now Cambridge, Corpus Christi College, MS 441.

74. James, *Descriptive Catalogue*, 2:349–55. For an account of Richard's tumultuous career as prior of Dover and his removal by Archbishop Robert Kilwardby in 1273, see the *Gesta Regum Continuata*, in *Historical Works of Gervase of Canterbury*, ed. Stubbs, 2:247–83.

75. Jackson *The Mongols and the West*, 165–95. David Morgan, *The Mongols* (Oxford: Blackwell, 1990), 145–58.

76. Quoted by de Jonge, "Robert Grossesteste and the Testaments of the Twelve Patriarchs," 124–25.

## Conclusion

1. Deluz's critical edition of the insular version reads: "neez et norrriz d'Engleterre de la ville de Seint Alban." John Mandeville, *Le livre des merveilles du monde*, ed. Christiane Deluz (Paris: CNRS, 2000), 92. The current standard account of *Mandeville's Travels*'s background and sources is M. C. Seymour's monograph *Sir John Mandeville* (Aldershot: Variorum, 1993). Seymour, however, far overstates the argument against an English origin for the text's author.

2. Iain Macleod Higgins, *Writing East: The "Travels" of Sir John Mandeville* (Philadelphia: University of Pennsylvania Press, 1997), 1–27.

3. *The Book of John Mandeville with Related Texts*, ed. and trans. Iain Macleod Higgins (Indianapolis: Hackett, 2011), 4.

4. Benjamin Braude, "Mandeville's Jews among Others," in *Pilgrims and Travelers to the Holy Land*, ed. Bryan Le Beau and Menachem Mor (Omaha: Creighton University Press, 1996), 133–58.

5. *The Book of John Mandeville*, ed. and trans. Higgins, 50–51.

6. Ibid., 43.

7. Higgins, *Writing East*, 184. Higgins translates the Continental version here. The insular version omits the detail that Jews teach their children Hebrew: "Et come bien qe ascuns issent ascun foiz, ils ne scievent langaige forsqe ebrieu, si ne scievent parler as gentz. Et nient purtant l'em dit q'ils isseront fors de temps que Antecrist et q'uils ferront grant occisioun de Christiens. Et pur ceo touz les Iuys qe demoerent par toutes terres aprenndent toutdis a parler ebrieu, sur celle esperaunce qe quant cils des montaygnes de Caspie quant isseront fors, qe ly autres Juys sachent parler a eux et les conduire en Christienetés pur christiens destruire. Qar les autres Iuys dient q'ils scievent bien par lour prophecies qe cils de Caspille isseront et s'espaunderont par my le mounde, et qe unqore seront cristiens en lour subjeccioun atant et plus qe ils ont esté en subjeccioun des cristiens." Mandeville, *Le livre des merveilles*, ed. Deluz, 430.

8. Suzanne Akbari, *Idols of the East: European Representations of Islam and the Orient, 1100–1450* (Ithaca, NY: Cornell University Press, 2009), 139.

9. Higgins, *Writing East*, 183.

10. *SZ*, ed. Yassif, 69–71; Gaster, *Chronicles of Jerachmeel*, 1–4.

11. *Bereshit Rabbah* 98.3. *Midrash Rabbah: Genesis*, vol. 2, ed. and trans. H. Freedman, 947.

12. *SZ*, ed. Yassif, 146; Gaster, *Chronicles of Jerachmeel*, 92. The seventy languages of the nations are a common theme in rabbinic literature in many different contexts. B. Sotah 36b recounts how Gabriel taught Joseph the seventy languages so that he could rule in Egypt. In other texts, he is the ultimate translator. See Ginzberg, *Legends of the Jews*, 2:151–52 and 5:371. Seidman presents an insightful discussion of the seventy languages in relation to translatability in *Faithful Renderings*, 24–26.

# BIBLIOGRAPHY

**Primary Sources**

Adelard of Bath. *Conversations with His Nephew: On the Same and the Different, Questions on Natural Science, and On Birds*. Edited and translated by Charles Burnett. Cambridge: Cambridge University Press, 1998.

*Der Alexanderroman des Archipresbyters Leo*. Edited by Friedrich Pfister. Heidelberg: C. Winter, 1913.

Alfonsi, Petrus. *Dialogue against the Jews*. Translated by Irven Resnick. Washington, DC: Catholic University of America Press, 2006.

——. *Diálogo contra los judíos*. Edited by John Victor Tolan, Klaus-Peter Mieth, Esperanza Ducay, and Maria Jesús Lacarra. Huesca: Instituto de Estudios Altoaragoneses, 1996.

——. *The Scholar's Guide: A Translation of the Twelfth-Century "Disciplina clericalis" of Pedro Alfonso*. Translated by Joseph Ramon Jones and John Esten Keller. Toronto: Pontifical Institute of Mediaeval Studies, 1969.

Ambrose. *Hexameron, Paradise, and Cain and Abel*. Translated by John Savage. Washington, DC: Catholic University of America Press, 1961.

——. *Opera*, Part 1. Edited by Karl Schenkl. Vienna: Tempsky, 1897.

——. *Seven Exegetical Works*. Translated by Michael McHugh. Washington, DC: Catholic University of America Press, 1972.

Andrew of Saint-Victor, *Expositionem in Ezechielem*. Edited by Michael Signer. CCCM 53E. Turnhout: Brepols, 1991.

———. *Expositionem super Danielem*. Edited by Mark Zier. CCCM 53F. Turnhout: Brepols, 1990.

*Annales Monastici*. Edited by Henry R. Luard. Rerum Britannicarum medii aevi scriptores 36. 5 vols. London: Longman, 1864–69.

*The Apocryphal Gospels: Texts and Translations*. Edited and translated by Bart Ehrman and Zlatko Plese. Oxford: Oxford University Press, 2011.

Augustine. *Concerning the City of God against the Pagans*. Translated by Henry Bettenson. Harmondsworth: Penguin, 1984.

———. *De civitate Dei, libri XXII*. Edited by B. Dombart and A. Kalb. 1909. Reprint, Stuttgart: Teubner, 1981.

———. *Quaestionum in Heptateuchum libri VII*. Edited by I. Fraipont. In *Aurelii Augustini Opera*, part 5. CCSL 33. Turnhout: Brepols, 1958.

*Babrius and Phaedrus*. Edited and translated by Ben Perry. Cambridge, MA: Harvard University Press, 1965.

*Babylonian Talmud: Hebrew/Aramaic-English Edition*. Edited by Isidore Epstein and Maurice Simon. 30 vols. London: Soncino Press, 1965–89.

Baruch ben Isaac of Worms. *Sefer ha-Terumah*. Jerusalem: Yerid ha-Sefarim, 2003.

*Batei Midrashot*. Edited by Solomon A.Wertheimer. 2 vols. Reprint, Jerusalem: Mosad ha-Rav Kook, 1950–53.

Baudric de Dol. *The Historia Ierosolimitana of Baudric de Bourgueil*. Edited by Steven Biddlecombe. Woodbridge: Boydell, 2014.

Benjamin of Tudela. *The Itinerary of Benjamin of Tudela*. Edited and translated by Marcus Nathan Adler. London: H. Frowde, 1907.

Berekhiah ha-Nakdan. *Dodi ve-Nechdi (Uncle and Nephew)*. Edited and translated by Hermann Gollancz. Oxford: Oxford University Press, 1920.

———. *The Ethical Treatises of Berachya, Son of Rabbi Natronai ha-Nakdan, Being the Compendium and the Maṣref*. Edited and translated by Hermann Gollancz. London: Nutt, 1902.

———. *Fables of a Jewish Aesop*. Translated by Moses Hadas. New York: Columbia University Press, 1967.

———. *Mishle Shu'alim* [in Hebrew]. Edited by A. M. Haberman. Jerusalem: Schocken, 1946.

———. *Sefer Ko'aḥ ha-Avanim (On the Virtue of the Stones)*. Edited and translated by Gerrit Bos and Julia Zwink. Leiden: Brill, 2010.

*Bereshit Rabbah*. Edited by J. Theodor and Chanoch Albeck. 3 vols. Revised ed. Jerusalem: Wahrmann Books, 1965.

*Biblia Latina Cum Glossa Ordinaria: Facsimile Reprint of the Editio Princeps, Adolph Rusch of Strassburg 1480/81*. Edited by Karlfried Froehlich and Margaret Gibson. 4 vols. Turnhout: Brepols, 1992.

*Biblia sacra iuxta vulgatam versionem*. Edited by Robert Weber. Stuttgart: Deutsche Bibelgesellschaft, 1983.

*The Book of Ezekiel*. Translated by A. J. Rosenberg. New York: Judaica Press, 2000.

Cassiodorus. *Institutions of Divine and Secular Learning and On the Soul*. Translated by James W. Halporn. Liverpool: Liverpool University Press, 2004.

*Charlemagne and Louis the Pious: The Lives by Einhard, Notker, Ermolus, Thegan, and the Astronomer.* Translated by Thomas F. X. Noble. University Park: Pennsylvania State University Press, 2009.

*Chronica Johannis de Oxenedes.* Edited by Henry Ellis. London: Longman, Brown, Green, Longmans, and Roberts, 1859.

*The Church and the Jews in the XIIIth Century.* Edited by Solomon Grayzel and Kenneth Stow. 2 vols. New York: Jewish Theological Seminary, 1989.

Cicero. *On the Nature of the Gods. Academics.* Edited and translated by H. Rackham. Cambridge MA: Harvard University Press, 1933.

"The Complete 'Midrash Vayissau.'" Edited by Tamar Alexander and Yosef Dan. In *Folklore Research Center Studies*, vol. 3, edited by Issachar Ben-Ami, 67–76. Jerusalem: Magnes Press, 1972.

Crispin, Gilbert. *The Works of Gilbert Crispin, Abbot of Westminster.* Edited by Anna Abulafia and G. R. Evans. Oxford: Oxford University Press, 1986.

Dares Phrygius. *De excidio Troiae historia.* Edited by Ferdinand Meister. Leipzig: Teubner, 1873.

———. *The Trojan War: The Chronicles of Dictys of Crete and Dares the Phrygian.* Translated by R. M. Frazer Jr. Bloomington: Indiana University Press, 1966.

*Decrees of the Ecumenical Councils.* Edited by Norman P. Tanner. 2 vols. Washington, DC: Georgetown University Press, 1990.

*Deux versions hébraïques du livre de Kalilah et Dimnah.* Edited by Joseph Derenbourg. Paris: F. Viewig, 1881.

*Enéas: A Twelfth-Century French Romance.* Translated by John Yunck. New York: Columbia University Press, 1974.

Ephraim Bar Jacob of Bonn. *Sefer Zekhirah.* Edited by A. M. Haberman. Jerusalem: Bialik Institute, 1970.

Ermold le Noir. *Poème sur Louis le Pieux et Épitres au roi Pépin.* Edited and translated by Edmond Faral. Paris: Champion, 1932.

*Evangelia Apocrypha.* Edited by Constantin von Tischendorf. Leipzig: H. Mendelssohn, 1876.

*The Fables of "Walter of England."* Edited by Aaron E. Wright. Toronto: Pontifical Institute of Mediaeval Studies, 1997.

*Les Fabulistes Latins depuis le siécle d'Auguste jusqu'à la fin du Moyen Âge.* Edited by Léopold Hervieux. 5 vols. Paris: Firmin-Didot, 1893–99.

*The First Crusade: The Chronicle of Fulcher of Chartres and Other Source Materials.* Edited by Edward Peters. 2nd ed. Philadelphia: University of Pennsylvania Press, 1998.

*Gesta Stephani.* Edited and translated by K. R. Potter. Oxford: Clarendon Press, 1976.

Geoffrey of Monmouth. *The History of the Kings of Britain.* Edited by Michael Reeve and translated by Neil Wright. Woodbridge: Boydell, 2007.

Gerald of Wales. *De Principis instructione liber.* Translated by Joseph Stevenson. In *The Church Historians of England*, 5.1. London: Seeleys, 1858.

———. *The Journey through Wales and the Description of Wales.* Translated by Lewis Thorpe. Harmondsworth: Penguin, 1978.

——. *Opera*. Edited by J. S. Brewer, James F. Dimock, and George F. Warner. Rerum Britannicarum medii aevi scriptores 21. 8 vols. London: Longman, 1861–91.

Gervase of Canterbury. *The Historical Works of Gervase of Canterbury*. 2 vols. Edited by William Stubbs. London: Longman, 1879–80.

Grosseteste, Robert. *De cessatione legalium*. Edited by Richard C. Dales and Edward B. King. Auctores Britannici Medii Aevi 7. London: Oxford University Press, 1986.

——. *Roberti Grosseteste Episcopi quondam Lincolniensis Epistolae*. Edited by Henry Luard. Rerum Britannicarum medii aevi scriptores 25. London: Longman, 1861.

——. *Expositio in Epistolam Sanct Pauli ad Galatas*. Edited by James McEvoy et al. CCCM 130. Turnhout: Brepols, 1995.

——. *Testamenta duodecim patriarcharum filiorum Jacob: e Greco in Latinum versa Roberto Lincolniensi Episcopo interprete*. Augsburg: Johan Miller, 1520.

*Hebräische Berichte über die Judenverfolgungen während der Kreuzzüge*. Edited by Adolf Neubauer and Moritz Stern. Berlin: Verlag von Leonhard Simion, 1892.

"A Hebrew Elegy on the York Martyrs of 1190." Edited and translated by Cecil Roth. *Transactions of the Jewish Historical Society of England* 16 (1945–51): 213–20.

"The Hebrew Text of One of the Testaments of the Twelve Patriarchs." Edited and translated by Moses Gaster. *Proceedings of the Society of Biblical Archaeology* 16 (1893–94): 33–49, 109–17.

Himmelfarb, Martha, ed. "Midrash Vayissa'u." In *Old Testament Pseudepigrapha: More Noncanonical Scriptures*, vol. 1, edited by Richard Bauckham, James R. Davila, and Alexander Panayotov, 143–59. Grand Rapids, MI: Eerdmans, 2013.

Ibn Al-Muqaffa'. *Le livre de Kalila et Dimna*. Translated by André Miquel. Paris: Klincksieck, 1957.

Ibn Ezra, Abraham ben Meir. *El Comentario de Abraham Ibn Ezra al libro del Ecclesiatés*. Edited by Mariano Gómez Aranda. Madrid: Consejo Superior de Investigaciones Científicas, 1994

——. *Ibn Ezra's Commentary on the Pentateuch* [in Hebrew]. Translated by H. Norman Strickman and Arthur M. Silver. 5 vols. New York: Menorah 1988–2004.

Ibn Pakuda, Bachya ben Joseph. *Duties of the Heart* [in Hebrew]. Translated from Arabic by Yehuda ibn Tibbon. Edited by Abraham Zifroni. Tel Aviv: Maḥbarot le-Sifrut, 1959.

Isidore of Seville. *De ortu et obitu patrum*. Edited by César Chaparro Gómez. Paris: Belles Lettres, 1985.

Jacob ben Yehuda Hazan of London. *Etz Hayyim* [in Hebrew]. Edited by Israel Brodie. 3 vols. Jerusalem: Mosad Ha-Rav Kook, 1962–67.

Jerome. *Commentariorum in Danielem Libri III (IV)*. Edited by F. Glorie. CCSL 75A. Turnhout: Brepols, 1964.

——. *Saint Jerome's Hebrew Questions on Genesis*. Translated by C. T. R. Hayward. Oxford: Oxford University Press, 1995.

——. *In Hieremiam Prophetam Libri VI*. Edited by S. Reiter. Turnhout: Brepols, 1960.

——. *St Jerome: Letters and Select Works*. Translated by W. H. Fremantle. Nicene and Post-Nicene Fathers, Series 2. 1892. Reprint, Grand Rapids, MI: Eerdmans, 1989.

——. *On Illustrious Men*. Translated by Thomas Halton. Washington, DC: Catholic University of America Press, 1999.

——. *Select Letters of St. Jerome*. Edited and translated by F. A. Wright. Cambridge, MA: Harvard University Press, 1933. Reprint, 1991.

*The Jews and the Crusaders: The Hebrew Chronicles of the First and Second Crusades.* Edited and translated by Shlomo Eidelberg. Hoboken: KTAV, 1996.

Josephus, Flavius. *Jewish Antiquities*. Translated by Louis Feldman, Ralph Marcus, H. St. J. Thackeray, and Allen Wikgren. 10 vols. Cambridge, MA: Harvard University Press, 1998.

——. *The Jewish War*. Translated by H. St. J. Thackeray. 3 vols. Cambridge, MA: Harvard University Press, 1927.

——. *The Latin Josephus*, vol. 1, *Introduction and Text, Antiquities I–V*. Edited by Franz Blatt. Copenhagen: Aarhus, 1958.

——. *Opera, Quae Reperiri Potuerunt Omnia*. 2 vols. Edited by John Hudson. Oxford, 1720.

*Der lateinische Äsop des Romulus und die Prosa-Fassungen des Phädrus*. Edited by Georg Thiele. Heidelberg: C. Winter, 1910.

Mandeville, John. *The Book of John Mandeville, with Related Texts*. Translated by Iain Macleod Higgins. Indianapolis: Hackett, 2011.

——. *Le livre des merveilles du monde*. Edited by Christiane Deluz. Paris: CNRS, 2000.

Marie de France. *Fables*. Edited and translated by Harriet Spiegel. Toronto: University of Toronto Press, 1987.

*Materials for the History of Thomas Becket, Archbishop of Canterbury*. Edited by James Craigie Robertson and J. Brigstocke Sheppard. 7 Vols. London: Longman, 1876–85.

Matthew Paris. *Chronica Majora*. Edited by Henry R. Luard. Rerum Britannicarum medii aevi scriptores 57. 7 vols. London: Longman, 1872–83.

——. *Matthew Paris's English History from the Year 1235 to 1273*. Translated by J. A. Giles. 3 vols. London: Bohn, 1852–54.

*Medieval Hagiography: An Anthology*. Edited by Thomas Head. New York: Routledge, 2000.

*The Midrash Rabbah: Eichah*. Edited by Yaakov Reinman. Translated by Yaakov Blinder. Jerusalem: Machon HaMidrash HaMevo'ar, 2004.

*Midrash Rabbah*. Edited and translated by H. Freedman and Maurice Simon. 10 vols. London: Soncino Press, 1983.

"Midrash Vayissau or Sefer Miḥamot Benai Yaaqov." Edited by J. Z. Lauterbach. In *Abhandlungen zur Erinnerung an Hirsch Perez Chajes*, 67–76. Vienna: Alexander Kohut Memorial Foundation, 1933.

*Mikra'ot Gedolot ha-Keter*. Edited by Menachem Cohen. Ramat-Gan: Bar Ilan University Press, 1992–.

*Minor Latin Poets*. Translated by J. Wight Duff and Arnold M. Duff. 2 vols. Cambridge, MA: Harvard University Press, 1934.

Moshe Ha-Darshan. *Midrash Bereshit Rabbati*. Edited by Chanoch Albeck. 1940. Reprint, Jerusalem: H. Vagshal, 1983.

Nequam, Alexander. *Novus Aesopus*. Edited by Giovanni Garbugino. Vol. 2 of *Favolisti latini medievali e umanistici*. Genova: Università di Genova, Facoltà di Lettere, Dipartimento di Archeologia, Filologia Classica e Loro Tradizioni, 1987.

———. *Novus Avianus.* Edited by Thomas Klein. In *Favolisti latini medievali e umanistici,* edited by F. Bertini, 7:99–133. Genova: Università di Genova, Facoltà di Lettere, Dipartimento di Archeologia, Filologia Classica e Loro Tradizioni, 1998.

*The Old Testament Pseudepigrapha.* Edited by James Charlesworth. 2 vols. New York: Doubleday, 1983

*The Oldest Version of the Twelfth-Century Poem "La Venjance Nostre Seigneur."* Edited by Loyal A. T. Gryting. Ann Arbor: University of Michigan Press, 1952.

Orderic Vitalis. *The Ecclesiastical History of Orderic Vitalis.* Edited and translated by Marjorie Chibnall. 6 vols. Oxford: Oxford University Press, 1969–80.

Orosius, Paulus. *Histoires.* Edited and translated by Marie-Pierre Arnaud-Lindet. 3 vols. Paris: Les Belles Lettres, 1990–91.

———. *The Seven Books of History against the Pagans.* Translated by Roy J. Deferrari. Washington, DC: Catholic University of America Press, 1964.

Paul the Deacon. *Historia Romana.* Edited by H. Droysen. Berlin: Weidman, 1879.

Peter of Blois. *Opera Omnia.* Edited by J. Giles. 4 volumes. Oxford: Parker, 1846–47.

———. *Tractatus Duo.* Edited by R. B. C. Huygens. CCCM 194. Turnhout: Brepols, 2002.

*Poetry of the Carolingian Renaissance.* Edited and translated by Peter Godman. London: Duckworth, 1985.

Pseudo-Hegesippus. *Hegesippi qui dicitur Historiae libri V.* Edited by V. Ussani. 2 vols. Vienna: Tempsky, 1932–60.

Pseudo-Methodius. *Die Apokalypse des Pseudo-Methodius.* Edited by W. J. Aerts and G. A. A. Kortekaas. 2 vols. Corpus Scriptorum Christianorum Orientalium 569–70. Leuven: Peeters, 1998.

Quodvultdeus. *Opera.* Edited by René Braun. CCSL 60. Turnhout: Brepols, 1976.

Ralph of Diceto. *Radulfi de Diceto decani Lundoniensis Opera historica.* Edited by William Stubbs. Rerum Britannicarum medii aevi scriptores 68. 2 vols. London: Longman, 1876.

Richer of Sens. *Richeri Gesta Senoniensis Ecclesiae.* Edited by G. Waitz. In Monumenta Germaniae Historica, Scriptores 25, 249–345. Hannover: Hahn, 1880.

Robert of Cricklade. *Roberti Crickladensis Defloratio Naturalis historie Plinii Secundi.* Edited by Bodo Naf. Bern: Peter Lang, 2002.

Robert the Monk. *History of the First Crusade: Historia Iherosolimitana.* Translated by Carol Sweetenham. Burlington, VT: Ashgate, 2005.

*Le roman d'Eneas.* Edited and translated by Aimé Petit. Paris: Librarie générale française, 1997.

Schirmann, Haim. *Hebrew Poetry in Spain and Provence* [in Hebrew]. 4 vols. Tel Aviv: Bialik Institute, 1956.

———. "Persecution Laments from the Land of Israel, Africa, Spain, Ashkenaz, and France" [in Hebrew]. *Qovez 'al Yad* 3 (1939): 23–74.

*Scriptores rerum mythicarum Latini tres Romae nuper reperti.* Edited by Georg Bode. Darmstadt, 1834.

*Sefer Gezerot Ashkenaz ve-Tsarfat.* Edited by A. M. Haberman. Jerusalem: Bialik Institute, 1945.

*Sefer ha-Zikhronot: The Book of Memory; that is, The Chronicles of Jerahme'el.* Edited by Eli Yassif. Tel Aviv: Tel Aviv University, 2001.

——. Partial translation by Moses Gaster. In *The Chronicles of Jerachmeel*. New York: KTAV, 1971.

*Sefer Yosippon* [in Hebrew]. Edited by David Flusser. 2 vols. Jerusalem: Bialik Institute, 1980–81.

Servius. *Servii Grammatici qui feruntur in Vergilii carmina commentarii*. Edited by Georg Thilo and Hermann Hagen. 3 vols. Leipzig: Teubner, 1881–1900.

*The Song of Roland: An Analytical Edition*. Edited and translated by Gerard J. Brault. 2 vols. University Park: Pennsylvania State University Press, 1978.

*Studia Patristica: Études d'ancienne littérature chrétienne*, ed. Pierre Batiffol (Paris: E. Leroux, 1890)

Thomas de Kent. *Le roman d'Alexandre, ou Le roman de toute chevalrie*. Edited by Ian Short and Brian Foster with translation, introduction, and notes by Catherine Gaullier-Bourgassas and Laurence Harf-Lancner. Paris: Champion, 2003.

Thomas of Monmouth. *The Life and Passion of William of Norwich*. Edited and translated by Miri Rubin. London: Penguin, 2014.

*Tisha b'Av Compendium: Tephilot and Kinot*. Edited and translated by Abraham Rosenfeld. New York: Judaica Press, 1965.

*The Vatican Mythographers*. Translated by Ronald E. Pepin. New York: Fordham University Press, 2008.

*Vikuah Rabbenu Yehiel mi-Pariz* [in Hebrew]. Edited by Reuben Margoliot. Lwow, 1928.

Vincent of Beauvais. *Speculum Historiale*. Nürnberg: Anton Koberger, 1483.

Virgil. *Eclogues, Georgics, Aeneid 1–6*. Edited by H. R. Fairclough. Revised by G. P. Goold. Cambridge, MA: Harvard University Press, 1999.

*The Virgilian Tradition: The First Fifteen Hundred Years*. Edited by Jan Ziolkowski and Michael Putnam. New Haven: Yale University Press, 2008.

Wace. *The History of the Norman People: Wace's Roman de Rou*. Translated by Glyn Burgess. Woodbridge: Boydell, 2004.

——. *Wace's Roman de Brut: A History of the British; Text and Translation*. Edited and translated by Judith Weiss. Exeter: University of Exeter Press, 2002.

Walafrid Strabo. *De Subversione Jerusalem*. In *Patrologia Cursus Completus, Series Latina*, edited by J.-P. Migne, 114, cols. 965–74. Paris: Migne, 1852.

William of Malmesbury, *Gesta Regum Anglorum: The History of the English Kings*. Edited and translated by R. A. B. Mynors. Completed by R. M. Thomson and M. Winterbottom. 2 vols. Oxford: Clarendon Press, 1998–99.

William of Newburgh. *Historia Rerum Anglicarum*. Translated by Joseph Stevenson. In *The Church Historians of England*, 4.2:565–72. London: Seeleys, 1856.

——. *Historia rerum Anglicarum Books I–IV*. In *Chronicles of the Reigns of Stephen, Henry II, and Richard I*, edited by Richard Howlett. Rerum Britannicarum medii aevi scriptores 82, vol. 1. London: Longman, 1884.

**Secondary Sources**

Abulafia, Anna Sapir. *Christians and Jews in the Twelfth-Century Renaissance*. London: Routledge, 1995.

——. "Twelfth-Century Christian Expectations of Jewish Conversion: A Case Study of Peter of Blois." *Aschkenas* 8 (1998): 45–70.

Adler, Michael. "The Jews of Canterbury." *Transactions of the Jewish Historical Society of England* 7 (1911–14): 19–96.

——. *Jews of Medieval England.* London: Jewish Historical Society, 1939.

Adler, William. "The Jews as Falsifiers: Charges of Tendentious Emendation in Anti-Jewish Christian Polemic." In *Translation of Scripture*, edited by David Goldenberg, 1–27. Philadelphia: University of Pennsylvania Press, 1990.

Aescholy, A. Z. *Jewish Messianic Movements* [in Hebrew]. Jerusalem: Bialik Institute, 1956.

Akbari, Suzanne Conklin. "Between Diaspora and Conquest: Norman Assimilation in Petrus Alfonsi's *Disciplina clericalis* and Marie de France's *Fables.*" In *Cultural Diversity in the British Middle Ages: Archipelago, Island, England*, edited by Jeffrey Jerome Cohen, 17–37. New York: Palgrave, 2008.

——. *Idols of the East: European Representations of Islam and the Orient, 1100–1450.* Ithaca, NY: Cornell University Press, 2009.

——. "Woman as Mediator in Medieval Depictions of Muslims: The Case of Floripas." In *Medieval Constructions in Gender and Identity: Essays in Honor of Joan M. Ferrante*, edited by Teodolinda Barolini, 151–67. Tempe: Arizona Center for Medieval and Renaissance Studies, 2005.

Anderson, Andrew Runni. *Alexander's Gate: Gog and Magog and the Inclosed Nations.* Cambridge, MA: Medieval Academy, 1932.

Aptowitzer, V. "Asenath, the Wife of Joseph: A Haggadic Literary-Historical Study." *Hebrew Union College Annual* 1 (1924): 239–306.

Aranda, Mariano Gómez. "The Meaning of Qohelet According to Ibn Ezra's Scientific Explanations." *Aleph* 6 (2006): 339–70.

Armstrong, Richard H. *A Compulsion for Antiquity: Freud and the Ancient World.* Ithaca, NY: Cornell University Press, 2005.

Aurell, Martin. *The Plantagenet Empire, 1154–1224.* Translated by David Crouch. Harlow: Longman, 2007.

Avi-Yonah, Michael. *The Jews under Roman and Byzantine Rule: A Political History of Palestine from the Bar Kokhba War to the Arab Conquest.* New York: Schocken, 1976.

Baer, Yitzhak. "The Hebrew Sefer *Yosippon*" [in Hebrew]. In *Sefer Dinaburg*, edited by Ben Zion Dinur and Yitzhak Baer, 178–205. Jerusalem: Kiryat Sefer, 1949.

Bardet, Serge. *Le Testimonium Flavianum: Examen historique, considérations historographiques.* Paris: Cerf, 2002.

Bartlett, Robert. *Gerald of Wales: A Voice of the Middle Ages.* 1982. Reprint, Stroud: Tempus, 2006.

Baswell, Christopher. *Virgil in Medieval England: Figuring the Aeneid from the Twelfth Century to Chaucer.* Cambridge: Cambridge University Press, 1995.

Bedos-Rezak, Brigitte Miriam. "Les juifs et l'écrit dans la mentalité eschatologique du Moyen Âge chrétien occidental (France 1000–1200)." *Annales: Histoire, Sciences Sociales*, no. 5 (1994): 1049–63.

Bell, Albert A., Jr. "Josephus and Pseudo-*Hegesippus*." In *Josephus, Judaism and Christianity*, edited by Louis Feldman and Gohei Hata. Detroit: Wayne State University Press, 1987, 349–61.

Benjamin, Walter. *Illuminations*. Edited by Hannah Arendt. Translated by Harry Zohn. New York: Schocken, 1968.

Berger, David. "Gilbert Crispin, Alan of Lille, and Jacob ben Reuben: A Study in the Transmission of Medieval Polemic." *Speculum* 49 (1974): 34–47.

Berndt, Rainer. "The School of St. Victor in Paris." In *Hebrew Bible/Old Testament: The History of Its Interpretation*, vol. 1, *From the Beginnings to the Middle Ages (until 1300)*, pt. 2, *The Middle Ages*. Edited by Magne Saebø. Göttingen: Vandenhoek and Ruprecht, 2000, 467–95.

Bibring, Tovi, "'Would that my words were Inscribed': Berechiah Ha-Naqdan's *Mishlei Shu'alim* and European Fable Traditions." In *Latin-into-Hebrew: Texts and Studies*, edited by Resianne Fontaine and Gad Freudenthal, 1:309–29. Leiden: Brill, 2013.

Bigalli, Davide. *I Tartari e l'Apocalisse: Ricerche sull'escatologia in Adamo Marsh e Ruggero Bacone*. Florence: La Nuova Italia, 1971.

Bischoff, Bernhard. *Manuscripts and Libraries in the Age of Charlemagne*. Edited and Translated by Michael Gorman. Cambridge: Cambridge University Press, 1994.

Blank, Sheldon. "The Death of Zechariah in Rabbinic Literature." *Hebrew Union College Annual* 12/13 (1937–38): 327–46.

Blidstien, Jacob. "The Personal Status of Apostate and Ransomed Women in Medieval Jewish Law" [in Hebrew]. *Shenaton ha-Mishpat ha-Ivri* 3–4 (1976–77): 35–116.

Bloch, R. Howard. *The Anonymous Marie de France*. Chicago: University of Chicago Press, 2003.

Bonfil, Robert. *History and Folklore in a Medieval Jewish Chronicle: The Family Chronicle of Ahima'az ben Paltiel*. Leiden: Brill, 2009.

Bowman, Steven. "Alexander and the Mysteries of India." *Journal of Indo-Judaic Studies*, no. 2 (1999): 71–111.

——. "*Sefer Yosippon*: History and Midrash." In *The Midrashic Imagination: Jewish Exegesis, Thought, and History*, edited by Michael Fishbane, 280–94. Albany: SUNY Press, 1993.

——. "*Yosippon* and Jewish Nationalism." *Proceedings of the American Academy for Jewish Research* 61 (1995): 23–51.

Boyarin, Daniel. *Border Lines: The Partition of Judaeo-Christianity*. Phildelphia: University of Pennsylvania Press, 2004.

——. *Unheroic Conduct: The Rise of Heterosexuality and the Invention of the Jewish Man*. Berkeley: University of California Press, 1997.

Boyarin, Jonathan, and Daniel Boyarin. *Powers of Diaspora: Two Essays on the Relevance of Jewish Culture*. Minneapolis: University of Minnesota Press, 2002.

Braude, Benjamin. "Mandeville's Jews among Others." In *Pilgrims and Travelers to the Holy Land*, edited by Bryan Le Beau and Menachem Mor, 133–58. Omaha: Creighton University Press, 1996.

Broadhurst, Karen M. "Henry II of England and Eleanor of Aquitaine: Patrons of Literature in French?" *Viator* 27 (1996): 53–84.

Brock, Ann Graham. *Mary Magdalene, the First Apostle: The Struggle for Authority*. Cambridge, MA: Harvard University Press, 2003.

Brodzki, Bella. *Can These Bones Live? Translation, Survival, and Cultural Memory*. Stanford: Stanford University Press, 2007.

Bronner, Stephen Eric. *A Rumor about the Jews: Reflections on Antisemitism and the "Protocols of the Learned Elders of Zion."* New York: St. Martin's, 2000.

Brown, Giles. "The Carolingian Renaissance: An Introduction." In *Carolingian Culture: Emulation and Innovation,* edited by Rosamond McKitterick, 1–51. Cambridge: Cambridge University Press, 1994.

Burchard, Christoph. *Gesammelte Studien zu Joseph und Aseneth.* Leiden: Brill, 1996.

Burnett, Charles. *The Introduction of Arabic Learning into England.* London: British Library, 1997.

Castelli, Elizabeth. "'I Will Make Mary Male': Pieties of the Body and Gender Transformation of Christian Women in Late Antiquity." In *Body Guards: The Cultural Politics of Gender Ambiguity,* edited by Julia Epstein and Kristina Straub, 29–49. New York: Routledge, 1991.

Chazan, Robert. *European Jewry and the First Crusade.* Berkeley: University of California Press, 1987.

——. *Fashioning Jewish Identity in Medieval Western Christendom.* Cambridge: Cambridge University Press, 2004.

——. "The Hebrew Report on the Trial of the Talmud: Information and Consolation." In *Le brûlement du Talmud à Paris, 1242–1244,* edited by Rene-Samuel Sirat, 79–93. Paris: Cerf, 1999.

——. *Medieval Jewry in Northern France: A Political and Social History.* Baltimore: Johns Hopkins University Press, 1973.

Chenu, M.-D. *Nature, Man, and Society in the Twelfth Century: Essays on the New Theological Perspectives in the Latin West.* Translated by Jerome Taylor and Lester Little. Chicago: University of Chicago Press, 1968.

Clanchy, Michael T. *From Memory to Written Record: England, 1066–1307.* 2nd ed. Oxford: Blackwell, 1993.

Cochrane, Louise. *Adelard of Bath: The First English Scientist.* London: British Museum Press, 1994.

Cohen, Gerson D. *Studies in the Variety of Rabbinic Cultures.* Philadelphia: Jewish Publication Society, 1991.

Cohen, Jeremy. "The Hebrew Crusade Chronicles in Their Christian Cultural Context." In *Juden und Christen zur Zeit der Kreuzzüge,* edited by Alfred Haverkamp, 17–34. Sigmaringen: Jan Thorbeck Verlag, 1999.

——. *Living Letters of the Law: Ideas of the Jew in Medieval Christianity.* Berkeley: University of California Press, 1999.

——. "The Muslim Connection or On the Changing Role of the Jew in High Medieval Theology." In *From Witness to Witchcraft: Jews and Judaism in Medieval Christian Thought,* edited by Jeremy Cohen, 141–62. Wiesbaden: Harrassowitz, 1996.

——. *Sanctifying the Name of God: Jewish Martyrs and Jewish Memories of the First Crusade.* Philadelphia: University of Pennsylvania Press, 2004.

Cohen, Shaye J. D. *The Beginnings of Jewishness: Boundaries, Varieties, Uncertainties.* Berkeley: University of California Press, 1999.

——. "Josephus, Jeremiah, and Polybius." *History and Theory* 21 (1982): 366–81.

——. "Masada: Literary Tradition, Archaeological Remains, and the Credibility of Josephus." *Journal of Jewish Studies* 33 (1982): 385–405.

Colafemmina, Cesare. "Insediamente e condizioni degli ebrei nell'Italia meridionale e insulare." In *Gli ebrei nell'alto medioevo*, 1:197–228. Spoleto: Presso la Sede del Centro, 1980.

Collins, John J. *Between Athens and Jerusalem: Jewish Identity in the Hellenistic Diaspora*. 2nd ed. Grand Rapids, MI: Eerdmans, 2000.

Copeland, Rita. *Rhetoric, Hermeneutics and Translation in the Middle Ages: Academic Traditions and Vernacular Texts*. Cambridge: Cambridge University Press, 1991.

Cornell, T. J. "Aeneas and the Twins: The Development of the Roman Foundation Legend." *Proceedings of the Cambridge Philological Society*, n.s. 21 (1975): 1–32.

Cotts, John. *The Clerical Dilemma: Peter of Blois and Literate Culture in the Twelfth Century*. Washington, DC: Catholic University of America Press, 2009.

Courcelle, Pierre. "Tradition Platonicienne et traditions chrétiennes du corps-prison." *Revue des Études Latines* 43 (1965): 406–43.

Dahan, Gilbert. "Deux psautiers hébraïques glosés en Latin." *REJ* 158 (1999): 61–87.

Damian-Grint, Peter. *The New Historians of the Twelfth-Century Renaissance*. Woodbridge: Boydell, 1999.

Dan, Joseph. *The Hebrew Story in the Middle Ages* [in Hebrew]. Jerusalem: Keter, 1974.

D'Arcier, Louis Faivre. *Histoire et géographie d'un mythe: La circulation des manuscripts du "De excidio Troiae" de Darès le Phrygien (XVIIIe–XVe siècles)*. Paris: École des Chartes, 2006.

Davies, R. R. *The First English Empire: Power and Identities in the British Isles, 1093–1343*. Oxford: Oxford University Press, 2000.

De Jonge, Marinus. "Robert Grosseteste and the Testaments of the Twelve Patriarchs." *Journal of Theological Studies* 42 (1991): 115–25.

——. "The Transmission of the Testaments of the Twelve Patriarchs by Christians." *Vigilae Christianae* 47 (1993): 1–28.

Delogu, Paolo. "Lombard and Carolingian Italy." In *NCMH*, vol. 2, *c.700–c.900*, edited by Rosamond McKitterick, 290–319. Cambridge: Cambridge University Press, 1995.

De Visscher, Eva. *Reading the Rabbis: Christian Hebraism in the Work of Herbert of Bosham*. Leiden: Brill, 2014.

Denholm-Young, Noel. "Thomas de Wykes and His Chronicle." *English Historical Review* 61 (1946): 157–79.

Derrida, Jacques. "Des tours de Babel." Translated by Joseph Graham. In *Difference in Translation*, edited by Joseph Graham, 165–207. Ithaca, NY: Cornell University Press, 1985.

Dionisotti, A. C. "On the Greek Studies of Robert Grosseteste." In *The Uses of Greek and Latin: Historical Essays*, edited by A. C. Dionisotti, Anthony Grafton, and Jill Kraye, 19–38. London: Warburg Institute, 1988.

Dobson, R. B. *The Jews of Medieval York and the Massacre of March 1190*. Borthwick Papers 45. Rev. ed. York: Borthwick Institute for Historical Research, 1996.

Dubois, Jean-Daniel. "La mort de Zacharie: mémoire juive at mémoire chrétienne." *Revue des Études Augustiniennes* 40 (1994): 23–38.

Duggan, Anne. "The Cult of St. Thomas Becket in the Thirteenth Century." In *St. Thomas Cantilupe, Bishop of Hereford: Essays in His Honour*, edited by Meryl Jancey, 21–44. Hereford: Friends of Hereford Cathedral, 1982.

———. *Thomas Becket: A Textual History of His Letters*. Oxford: Clarendon Press, 1980.

Einbinder, Susan. *Beautiful Death: Jewish Poetry and Martyrdom in Medieval France*. Princeton, NJ: Princeton University Press, 2002.

———. "Meir b. Elijah of Norwich: Persecution and Poetry among Medieval English Jews." *Journal of Medieval History* 26 (2000): 145–62.

———. "Signs of Romance: Hebrew Prose and the Twelfth-Century Renaissance." In *Jews and Christians in Twelfth-Century Europe*, edited by Michael Signer and John Van Engen, 221–33. Notre Dame: University of Notre Dame Press, 2001.

Elukin, Jonathan. "The Discovery of the Self: Jews and Conversion in the Twelfth Century." In *Jews and Christians in Twelfth-Century Europe*, edited by Michael Signer and John Van Engen, 63–76. Notre Dame: University of Notre Dame Press, 2001.

Feldman, Louis. "Abba Kolon and the Founding of Rome." *JQR*, n.s. 81(1991): 239–66.

———. "The Jewish Sources of Peter Comestor's Commentary on Genesis in His *Historia Scholastica*." In *Begegnungen zwischen Christentum und Judentum in Antike und Mittelalter: Festschrift für Heinz Schreckenberg*, edited by Dietrich Koch and Hermann Lichtenberger, 93–121. Gottingen: Vandenhoeck and Ruprecht, 1993.

———. "*The Testimonium Flavianum*: The State of the Question." In *Christological Perspectives: Essays in Honour of Harvey K. McArthur*, edited by Robert F. Berkey and Sarah A. Edwards, 179–99, 288–93. New York: Pilgrim Press, 1982.

Flusser, David. "Naphtali, Testament of." In *Encyclopaedia Judaica*, edited by Michael Berenbaum and Fred Skolnik, 14:775. 2nd ed. Detroit: Macmillan Reference, 2007.

Fonrobert, Charlotte Elisheva, and Martin S. Jaffee, eds. *The Cambridge Companion to the Talmud and Rabbinic Literature*. Cambridge: Cambridge University Press, 2007.

Frankfurter, David. "Beyond 'Jewish Christianity': Continuing Religious Sub-Cultures of the Second and Third Centuries and Their Documents." In *The Ways that Never Parted: Jews and Christians in Late Antiquity and the Early Middle Ages*, edited by Adam H. Becker and Annette Yoshiko Reed, 131–43. Tübingen: Mohr Siebeck, 2003.

Franklin-Brown, Mary. *Reading the World: Encyclopedic Writing in the Scholastic Age*. Chicago: University of Chicago Press, 2012.

Fredriksen, Paula. "*Excaecati Occulta Justitia Dei*: Augustine on the Jews and Judaism." *Journal of Early Christian Studies* 3 (1995): 299–324.

Freud, Sigmund. *The Complete Letters of Sigmund Freud to Wilhelm Fliess, 1887–1904*. Edited and translated by Jeffrey Moussaieff Masson. Cambridge, MA: Harvard University Press, 1985.

———. *Interpreting Dreams*. Translated by J. A. Underwood. London: Penguin, 2006.

Freudenthal, Gad. "Arabic and Latin Cultures as Resources for the Hebrew Translation Movement: Comparative Considerations, Both Quantitative and Qualitative." In *Science in Medieval Jewish Cultures*, edited by Gad Freudenthal, 74–105. Cambridge: Cambridge University Press, 2011.

———. "Transfert culturel à Lunel au milieu du XII siècle." In *Des Tibbonides à Maïmonide: rayonnement des Juifs andalous en pays d'Oc médiéval; colloque international, Montpellier, 13–14 décembre 2004*, edited by Danièle Iancu-Agou and Élie Nicolas, 95–108. Paris: Cerf, 2009.

Freudenthal, Gad, and Jean-Marc Mandosio. "Old French into Hebrew in Twelfth-Century Tsarfat: Medieval Hebrew Versions of Marbode's Lapidary." *Aleph* 14, no. 1 (2014): 11–187.

Fudeman, Kirsten. *Vernacular Voices: Language and Identity in Medieval French Jewish Communities*. Philadelphia: University of Pennsylvania Press, 2010.

Gameson, Richard. *The Manuscripts of Early Norman England (c. 1066–1130)*. Oxford: Oxford University Press, 1999.

Gillingham, John. *The Angevin Empire*. New York: Holmes and Meier, 1984.

Ginzberg, Louis. *The Legends of the Jews*. Translated by Henrietta Szold, Paul Radin, and Boaz Cohen. 7 vols. Philadelphia: Jewish Publication Society, 1909–38.

Godman, Peter. *Poets and Emperors: Frankish Politics and Carolingian Poetry*. Oxford: Clarendon Press, 1987.

Goffart, Walter. *The Narrators of Barbarian History (A.D. 550–800): Jordanes, Gregory of Tours, Bede and Paul the Deacon*. Princeton, NJ: Princeton University Press, 1988.

Golb, Norman. *The Jews of Medieval Normandy: A Social and Intellectual History*. Cambridge: Cambridge University Press, 1998.

Goldstein, Jonathan, trans. *The Anchor Bible: 1 Maccabees*. New York: Doubleday, 1976.

Goodwin, Deborah. *Take Hold of the Robe of a Jew: Herbert of Bosham's Christian Hebraism*. Leiden: Brill, 2006.

Gransden, Antonia, *Historical Writing in England, c.550 to c.1307*. Ithaca, NY: Cornell University Press, 1974.

——. "Prologues in the Historiography of Twelfth-Century England." In *England in the Twelfth Century*, edited by D. Williams, 55–81. Woodbridge: Boydell, 1990.

Greatrex, Joan. *Biographical Register of the English Cathedral Priories of the Province of Canterbury, c. 1066–1540*. Oxford: Clarendon Press, 1997.

——. "Monastic Charity for Jewish Converts: The Requisition of Corrodies by Henry III." In *Christianity and Judaism*, edited by Diana Wood, special issue, *Studies in Church History* 29 (1992): 133–43.

Grossman, Avraham. "The Cultural and Social Background of Jewish Martyrdom in Germany in 1096." In *Juden und Christen zur Zeit der Kreuzzüge*, edited by Alfred Haverkamp, 73–86. Sigmaringen: Jan Thorbecke Verlag, 1999.

——. *The Early Sages of Ashkenaz* [in Hebrew]. Jerusalem: Magnes, 1981.

——. "The Roots of Qiddush Ha-Shem in Early Ashkenaz" [in Hebrew]. In *Sanctity of Life and Martyrdom: Studies in Memory of Amir Yekutiel*, edited by Isaiah Gafni and Aviezer Ravitzsky, 99–130. Jerusalem: Zalman Shazar Center, 1992.

——. "A Typological Story about the Conversion of R. Gershom Me'or Ha-Golah's Son." In *Studies in Jewish Narrative: Ma'aseh Sippur, Presented to Yoav Elstein*, edited by Avidov Lipsker and Rella Kushelevsky, 65–75. Ramat Gan: Bar Ilan University Press, 2006.

——. "The Victories of Salah-ad-Din and the Awakening in Europe for Aliyah to the Land of Israel." In *Studies in the History of Eretz Israel Presented to Yehuda Ben Porat*, edited by Yehoshua Ben-Arieh and Elchanan Reiner, 362–82. Jerusalem: Yad Ben Zvi Press, 2003.

Gruen, Erich. *Heritage and Hellenism: The Rejuvenation of Jewish Tradition*. Berkeley: University of California Press, 1998.

Gruenwald, Ithamar. "Midrash and the 'Midrashic Condition': Preliminary Considerations." In *The Midrashic Imagination: Jewish Exegesis, Thought, and History*, edited by Michael Fishbane, 6–22. Albany: SUNY Press, 1993.

Guenée, Bernard. *Histoire et culture historique dans l'Occident médiéval*. Paris: Aubier, 1980.

Hadas-Lebel, Mireille. *Jerusalem against Rome*. Translated by Robyn Fréchet. Leuven: Peeters, 2006.

Halkin, Solomon, and Angel Sàenz-Badillos. "Translations and Translators." In *Encyclopedia Judaica*, edited by Michael Berenbaum and Fred Skolnik, 20:94–102. 2nd ed. Detroit: Macmillan Reference, 2007.

Hammer, William. "The Concept of the New or Second Rome in the Middle Ages." *Speculum* 19 (1944): 50–62.

Hasan-Rokem, Galit. "Fable." In *Encyclopaedia Judaica*, edited by Michael Berenbaum and Fred Skolik, 6:666–70. 2nd ed. Detroit: Macmillan Reference, 2007.

Haskins, Charles H. "Italy and Sicily in the Twelfth Century." *English Historical Review* 26 (1911): 433–47.

——. *Studies in the History of Medieval Science*. Cambridge, MA: Harvard University Press, 1927.

Higgins, Iain Macleod. *Writing East: The "Travels" of Sir John Mandeville*. Philadelphia: University of Pennsylvania Press, 1997.

Hillaby, Joe. "The London Jewry: William I to John." *Jewish Historical Studies* 33 (1992–94): 1–44.

Himmelfarb, Martha. "R. Moses the Preacher and the Testaments of the Twelve Patriarchs." *AJS Review* 9 (1984): 55–78.

——. "Some Echoes of Jubilees in Medieval Hebrew Literature." In *Tracing the Threads: Studies in the Vitality of Jewish Pseudepigrapha*, edited by John Reeves, 115–41. Atlanta: Scholars Press, 1994.

Hunt, R. W. "The Disputation of Peter of Cornwall against Symon the Jew." In *Studies in Medieval History Presented to Frederick Maurice Powicke*, edited by R. W. Hunt et al., 143–56. Oxford: Clarendon Press, 1948.

——. "English Learning in the Late Twelfth Century." *Transactions of the Royal Historical Society* 19 (1936): 19–42.

——. *The Schools and the Cloister: The Life and Writings of Alexander Nequam, 1157–1217*. Oxford: Clarendon Press, 1984.

Idel, Moshe. *Messianic Mystics*. New Haven: Yale University Press, 1998.

Innes, Matthew. "Teutons or Trojans? The Carolingians and the Germanic Past." In *The Uses of the Past in the Early Middle Ages*, edited by Yitzhak Hen and Matthew Innes, 226–49. Cambridge: Cambridge University Press, 2000.

Jackson, Peter. *The Mongols and the West, 1221–1410*. Harlow: Longman, 2005.

James, M. R., ed. *The Ancient Libraries of Canterbury and Dover*. Cambridge: Cambridge University Press, 1903.

——. *A Descriptive Catalogue of the Manuscripts in the Library of Corpus Christi College, Cambridge*. 2 vols. Cambridge: Cambridge University Press, 1912.

Jamison, Evelyn. "The Sicilian Norman Kingdom in the Mind of Anglo-Norman Contemporaries." *Proceedings of the British Academy* 24 (1938): 237–85.

Jansen, Katherine Ludwig. *The Making of the Magdalen: Preaching and Popular Devotion in the Later Middle Ages.* Princeton, NJ: Princeton University Press, 2000.

Johnson, Willis. "The Black Sickness" (unpublished manuscript).

Jordan, William Chester. "Adolescence and Conversion in the Middle Ages: A Research Agenda." In *Jews and Christians in Twelfth-Century Europe,* edited by Michael Signer and John Van Engen, 77–93. Notre Dame: University of Notre Dame Press, 2001.

——. *The French Monarchy and the Jews: From Philip Augustus to the Last Capetians.* Philadelphia: University of Pennsylvania Press, 1989.

Kappler, Claude. "L'image des Mongols dans le *Speculum Historiale* de Vincent de Beauvais." In *Vincent de Beauvais: Intentions et réceptions d'une oeuvre encyclopédique au Moyen-Âge,* edited by E. Monique Paulmier-Foucart, Serge Lusignan, and Alain Nadeau, 219–40. Montreal: Bellarmin, 1990.

Katz, Jacob. *Exclusiveness and Tolerance: Studies in Jewish–Gentile Relations in Medieval and Modern Times.* Oxford: Oxford University Press, 1961.

Kaufmann, David. "The Etz Chayim of Jacob B. Jehudah of London, and the History of His Manuscript." *JQR* 5 (1893): 353–74.

Kaufmann, David. "The Prayer-Book According to the Ritual of England before 1290." *JQR* 4 (1891): 20–63.

Kee, Howard Clark. "The Socio-Cultural Setting of Joseph and Aseneth." *New Testament Studies* 29 (1983): 394–413.

Kinoshita, Sharon. *Medieval Boundaries: Rethinking Difference in Old French Literature.* Philadelphia: University of Pennsylvania Press, 2006.

——. "The Politics of Courtly Love: *La Prise d'Orange* and the Conversion of the Saracen Queen." *Romanic Review* 86 (1995): 265–88.

Kletter, Karen. "The Uses of Josephus: Jewish History in the Medieval Christian Tradition" (PhD diss., University of North Carolina, Chapel Hill, 2005).

Korteweg, Theodore. "The Meaning of Naphtali's Visions." In *Studies on the Testaments of the Twelve Patriarchs: Text and Interpretation,* edited by M. de Jonge, 261–90. Leiden: Brill, 1975.

Kraemer, Ross Shepard. *When Aseneth Met Joseph: A Late Antique Tale of the Biblical Patriarch and His Egyptian Wife, Reconsidered.* Oxford: Oxford University Press, 1998.

Kreutz, Barbara. *Before the Normans: Southern Italy in the Ninth and Tenth Centuries.* Philadelphia: University of Pennsylvania Press, 1991.

Kruger, Steven. *The Spectral Jew: Conversion and Embodiment in Medieval Europe.* Minneapolis: University of Minnesota Press, 2006.

Kugel, James. *In Potiphar's House: The Interpretive Life of Biblical Texts.* Cambridge MA: Harvard University Press, 1994.

——. "Two Introductions to Midrash." In *Midrash and Literature,* edited by Geoffrey Hartman and Sanford Budick, 77–103. New Haven: Yale University Press, 1986.

Kugler, Robert A. *The Testaments of the Twelve Patriarchs.* Sheffield: Sheffield Academic Press, 2001.

Kupfer, Ephraim. "A Contribution to the Chronicles of the Family of R. Moshe Ben R. Yom-Tov 'The Noble' of London" [in Hebrew]. *Tarbiz* 40 (1971): 385–87.

Ladouceur, David. "Masada: A Consideration of the Literary Evidence." *Greek, Roman, and Byzantine Studies* 21 (1980): 245–60.

Lapidge, Michael. "Scholars at King Alfred's Court (*act.* 880–899)." In *Oxford Dictionary of National Biography*. Oxford: Oxford University Press, 2013. http://www.oxforddnb.com/view/theme/95595.

Lasker, Daniel. "Jewish–Christian Polemics at the Turning Point: Jewish Evidence from the Twelfth Century." *Harvard Theological Review* 89 (1996): 161–73.

Laureys, Marc, and Daniel Verhelst, "Pseudo-Methodius, Revelationes: Textgeschichte und Kritische Edition. Ein Leuven-Groninger Forschungprojekt." In *The Use and Abuse of Eschatology in the Middle Ages*, edited by Werner Verbeke, Daniel Verhelst, and Andries Welkenhuysen, 112–36. Leuven: Leuven University Press, 1988.

Lehmann, James. "Polemic and Satire in the Poetry of the Maimonidean Controversy." *Prooftexts* 1 (1981): 133–51.

Lerner, Robert E. *The Powers of Prophecy: The Cedar of Lebanon Vision from the Mongol Onslaught to the Dawn of the Enlightenment.* Berkeley: University of California Press, 1983.

Levi, Israel. "Jésus, Caligula et Claude dans une interpolation du Yosiphon." *REJ* 91 (1931–32): 135–54.

Lévinas, Emmanuel. *In the Time of the Nations.* Translated by Michael Smith. London: Continuum, 2007.

Lewis, Suzanne. *The Art of Matthew Paris in the "Chronica Majora."* Berkeley: University of California Press, 1987.

Liss, Hanna. *Creating Fictional Worlds: Peshaṭ-Exegesis and Narratvity in Rashbam's Commentary on the Torah.* Leiden: Brill, 2011.

Loeb, Isidore. "La controverse de 1240 sur le Talmud." *REJ* 1 (1880): 247–61; 2 (1881): 248–70; 3 (1882): 39–57.

Loewe, Raphael. "Latin Superscriptio MSS on Portions of the Hebrew Bible Other than the Psalter." *Journal of Jewish Studies* 9 (1958): 63–71.

——. "The Mediaeval Christian Hebraists of England: Herbert of Bosham and Earlier Scholars." *Transactions of the Jewish Historical Society of England* 17 (1951–52): 225–49.

——. "The Medieval Christian Hebraists of England: The Superscriptio Lincolniensis." *Hebrew Union College Annual* 28 (1957): 205–52.

Loewe, Raphael, and R. W. Hunt, "Alexander Neckam's Knowledge of Hebrew." *Medieval and Renaissance Studies* 4 (1958): 17–34.

Logan, F. Donald. "Thirteen London Jews and Conversion to Christianity: Problems of Apostasy in the 1280s." *Bulletin of the Institute for Historical Research* 45 (1972): 214–29.

Loud, Graham. "Southern Italy in the Tenth Century." In *NCMH*, vol. 3, *c.900–c.1024*, edited by Timothy Reuter, 624–45. Cambridge: Cambridge University Press, 1995.

Lowe, E. A. *The Beneventan Script: A History of the South Italian Miniscule.* 2nd ed. Prepared and enlarged by Virginia Brown. 2 vols. Rome: Edizioni di Storia e Letteratura, 1980.

———. *Virgil in South Italy: Facsimilies of Eight Manuscripts of Virgil in Beneventan Script*. Turin: G. Chiantore, 1932.

Lusignan, Serge. "Preface au *Speculum Maius* de Vincent de Beauvais: Refraction et diffraction." *Cahiers d'études medievales* 5 (1979): 115–39.

———. "*Translatio studii* and the Emergence of French as a Language of Letters in the Middle Ages." *New Medieval Literatures* 14 (2012): 1–19.

Maddicott, J. R. *Simon de Montfort*. Cambridge: Cambridge University Press, 1994.

Malkiel, David. "Jews and Apostates in Medieval Europe: Boundaries Real and Imagined." *Past and Present*, no. 194 (2007): 3–34.

Mann, Jill. *From Aesop to Reynard: Beast Literature in Medieval Britain*. Oxford: Oxford University Press, 2009.

Marcus, Ivan. "From Deus Lo Vult to the 'Will of the Ceator': Extremist Religious Ideologies and Historical Reality in 1096 and Hasidei Ashkenaz" [in Hebrew]. In *Facing the Cross: The Persecutions of 1096 in History and Historiography*, edited by Yom Tov Assis et al., 92–100. Jerusalem: Magnes, 2000.

McEvoy, James. *Robert Grosseteste*. Oxford: Oxford University Press, 2000.

McGinn, Bernard. *Visions of the End: Apocalyptic Traditions in the Middle Ages*. New York: Columbia University Press, 1998.

McKitterick, Rosamond. *Charlemagne: The Formation of a European Identity*. Cambridge: Cambridge University Press, 2008.

Menache, Sophia. "Matthew Paris's Attitudes Toward Anglo-Jewry." *Journal of Medieval History* 23 (1997): 139–62.

———. "Tartars, Jews, Saracens, and the Jewish-Mongol 'Plot' of 1241." *History* 81 (1996): 319–42.

Merchavia, Ch. *The Church Versus Talmudic and Midrashic Literature, 500–1248* [in Hebrew]. Jerusalem: Bialik Institute, 1970.

Merrills, A. H. *History and Geography in Late Antiquity*. Cambridge: Cambridge University Press, 2005.

Merrills, Andy, and Richard Miles. *The Vandals*. Oxford: Blackwell, 2010.

Mintz, Alan. *Ḥurban: Responses to Catastrophe in Hebrew Literature*. New York: Columbia University Press, 1984.

Mora-Lebrun, Francine. "Byzance et l'Occident dans *Le roman d'Enéas*: Imaginaire historique dans propagande politique." In *Histoire et littérature au Moyen Âge: Actes du Colloque du Centre d'Études Médiévales de l'Université de Picardie*, edited by Danielle Buschinger, 331–44. Göppingen: Kümmerle, 1991.

———. *L'"Enéide" médiévale et la chanson de geste*. Paris: Champion, 1994.

———. "*Mettre en Romanz*": Les romans d'antiquité du XIIe siècle et leur postérité *(XIIIe–XIVe siécle)*. Paris: Champion, 2008.

Morgan, David. *The Mongols*. Oxford: Blackwell, 1990.

———. *Understanding Conversion*. Charlottesville: University Press of Virginia, 1992.

Muller-Mertens, Eckhard. "The Ottonians as Kings and Emperors." In *NCMH*, vol. 3, *c.900–c.1024*, edited by Timothy Reuter, 233–66. Cambridge: Cambridge University Press, 1999.

Mundill, Robin. *England's Jewish Solution: Experiment and Expulsion, 1262–1290*. Cambridge: Cambridge University Press, 1998.

——. *The King's Jews: Money, Massacre, and Exodus in Medieval England*. London: Continuum, 2010.

Munk Olsen, Birger. *L'Étude des auteurs classiques latins aux XIe et XIIe siècles*. 4 vols. Paris: CNRS, 1982–2009.

Narin van Court, Elisa. "*The Siege of Jerusalem* and Augustinian Historians: Writing about Jews in Fourteenth-Century England." *Chaucer Review* 29 (1995): 227–48.

Nelson, Janet L. "The Frankish Kingdoms, 814–898: The West." In *NCMH*, vol. 2, *c.700–c.900*, edited by Rosamond McKitterick, 110–68. Cambridge: Cambridge University Press, 1995.

Neubauer, A. "Where Are the Ten Tribes?" *JQR* 1, nos. 1–4 (1888–89): 14–28, 95–114, 185–201, 408–23.

——. "Yeraḥmeel ben Shelomoh." *JQR* 11 (1899): 364–86.

Neubauer, A., and Joseph Jacobs. "Berechiah Naqdan." *JQR* 2 (1890): 520–26.

Nikolsky, Ronit. "The *History of the Rechabites* and the Jeremiah Literature." *Journal for the Study of the Pseudepigrapha* 13 (2002): 185–207.

Nisse, Ruth. "Diaspora as Empire in the Hebrew Deeds of Alexander (*Ma'aseh Alexandros*)." In *Alexander the Great in the Middle Ages: Transcultural Perspectives*, edited by Markus Stock, 76–87. Toronto: University of Toronto Press, 2016.

Olszowy-Schlanger, Judith. "The Knowledge and Practice of Hebrew Grammar among Christian Scholars in Pre-Expulsion England: The Evidence of 'Bilingual' Hebrew-Latin Manuscripts." In *Hebrew Scholarship and the Medieval World*, edited by Nicholas de Lange, 107–28. Cambridge: Cambridge University Press, 2001.

——. *Les manuscrits hébreux dans l'Angleterre médiévale: Étude historique et paléographique*. Paris: Peeters, 2003.

——. "The Money Language: Latin and Hebrew in Jewish Legal Contracts from Medieval England." In *Studies in the History of Culture and Science: A Tribute to Gad Freudenthal*, edited by Resianne Fontaine et al., 233–50. Leiden: Brill, 2011.

Partner, Nancy. *Serious Entertainments: The Writing of History in Twelfth-Century England*. Chicago: University of Chicago Press, 1977.

Patterson, Lee. *Negotiating the Past: The Historical Understanding of Medieval Literature*. Madison: University of Wisconsin Press, 1987.

Penkower, Jordan. "The End of Rashi's Commentary on Job: The Manuscripts and the Printed Editions (with three appendices)." *Jewish Studies Quarterly* 10 (2003): 18–48.

Perry, Micha. "The Imaginary War between Prester John and Eldad the Danite and Its Real Implications." *Viator* 41(2010): 1–23.

Prawer, Joshua. *The History of the Jews in the Latin Kingdom of Jerusalem*. Oxford: Clarendon Press, 1988.

Prestwich, Michael. *Edward I*. New Haven: Yale University Press, 1997.

Rajak, Tessa. *Josephus: The Historian and His Society*. 2nd ed. London: Duckworth, 2002.

Reeg, Gottfried. *Die Geschichte von den Zehn Märtyrern: synoptische Edition mit Übersetzung und Einleitung*. Tübingen: Mohr, 1985.

Rees Jones, Sara, and Sethina Watson, eds. *Christians and Jews in Angevin England: The York Massacre of 1190, Narratives and Contexts*. York: York Medieval Press, 2013.

Reeves, John. "Exploring the Afterlife of Jewish Pseudepigrapha in Medieval Near Eastern Religious Traditions: Some Initial Soundings." *Journal for the Study of Judaism*
30 (1999): 148–77.

——. "Illuminating the Afterlife of Ancient Apocryphal Jewish Literature." https://
clas-pages.uncc.edu/john-reeves/research-projects/illuminating-the-afterlife-of-
ancient-apocryphal-jewish-literature/.

——. *Trajectories in Near Eastern Apocalyptic: A Postrabbinic Jewish Apocalypse
Reader.* Atlanta: Society of Biblical Literature, 2005.

Reeves, Marjorie. *The Influence of Prophecy in the Later Middle Ages: A Study in
Joachimism.* Oxford: Oxford University Press, 1969.

Reiner, Avraham (Rami). "L'attitude envers les prosélytes en Allemagne et en France du
XIe au XIIIe siècle," *REJ* 167 (2008): 99–119.

Resnick, Irven M. "The Falsification of Scripture and Medieval Christian and Jewish
Polemics." *Medieval Encounters* 2 (1996): 344–80.

Reynolds, L. D., ed. *Texts and Transmission: A Survey of the Latin Classics.* Oxford:
Clarendon Press, 1983.

Richardson, H. G. *English Jewry under Angevin Kings.* London: Methuen, 1960.

Robinson, James T. "The Ibn Tibbon Family: A Dynasty of Translators in Medieval
'Provence.'" In *Be'erot Yitzhak: Studies in Memory of Isadore Twersky*, edited by Jay
Harris, 193–224. Cambridge, MA: Harvard University Press, 2005.

Rosenthal, Judah. "The Talmud on Trial: The Disputation at Paris in the Year 1240."
*JQR* 47, nos. 1–2 (1956): 58–76, 145–69.

Roth, Cecil. *The Intellectual Activities of Medieval English Jewry.* London: British
Academy, 1948.

——. *The Jews of Medieval Oxford.* Oxford: Clarendon Press, 1951.

Roth, Pinchas, and Ethan Zadoff. "The Talmud Community of Thirteenth-Century
England." In *Christians and Jews in Angevin England: The York Massacre of 1190,
Narratives and Contexts*, ed. Sarah Rees Jones and Sethina Watson), 184–203. York:
York Medieval Press, 2013.

Sáenz-Badillos, Angel. "Abraham Ibn Ezra and the Twelfth-Century European Renaissance." In *Studies in Hebrew Literature and Jewish Culture: Presented to Albert van
der Heide on the Occasion of His Sixty-Fifth Birthday*, edited by Martin Baasten and
Reinier Munk, 1–20. Dordrecht: Springer, 2007.

Saunders, J. J. "Matthew Paris and the Mongols." In *Essays in Medieval History Presented to Bertie Wilkinson*, edited by T. A. Sandquist and M. R. Powicke, 116–32.
Toronto: University of Toronto Press, 1969.

Schechter, S. "A Hebrew Elegy." *Transactions of the Jewish Historical Society of
England* 1 (1893–94): 8–14.

Schmidt-Chazan, Mireille. "L'idée d'Empire dans le *Speculum Historiale* de Vincent
de Beauvais." In *Vincent de Beauvais: Intentions et réceptions d'une oevre encyclopédique au Moyen-Âge*, edited by E. Monique Paulmier-Foucart, Serge Lusignan, and
Alain Nadeau, 253–84. Montreal: Bellarmin, 1990.

Schmieder, Felicitas. *Europa und die Fremden: die Mongolen im Urteil des Abendlandes
vom 13. bis in das 15. Jahrhundert.* Sigmaringen: Thorbecke, 1994.

——. "*Nota sectam maometicam atterendam a tartaris et christianis*: The Mongols as Non-believing Apocalyptic Friends around the Year 1260." *Journal of Millennial Studies* 1 (1998). http://www.mille.org/publications/summer98/fschmieder.pdf.

Scholem, Gershom. *The Messianic Idea in Judaism and Other Essays on Jewish Spirituality.* New York: Schocken, 1971.

Schreckenberg, Heinz. *Die Flavius-Josephus-Tradition in Antike und Mittelalter.* Leiden: Brill, 1972.

Schreckenberg, Heinz, and Kurt Schubert, *Jewish Historiography and Iconography in Early and Medieval Christianity.* Minneapolis: Fortress, 1992.

Schwarzbaum, Haim. *The Mishle Shu'alim (Fox Fables) of Rabbi Berechiah ha-Nakdan: A Study in Comparative Folklore and Fable Lore.* Kiron: Institute for Jewish and Arab Folklore Research, 1979.

Seidman, Naomi. *Faithful Renderings: Jewish-Christian Difference and the Politics of Translation.* Chicago: Chicago University Press, 2006.

Sela, Shlomo. *Abraham Ibn Ezra and the Rise of Medieval Hebrew Science.* Leiden: Brill, 2003.

Sela, Shlomo, and Gad Freudenthal. "Abraham Ibn Ezra's Scholarly Writings: A Chronological Listing." *Aleph* 6 (2006): 13–55.

Seymour, M. C. *Sir John Mandeville.* Aldershot: Variorum, 1993.

Sharf, Andrew. *Byzantine Jewry: From Justinian to the Fourth Crusade.* New York: Schocken, 1971.

Sharpe, Richard. *Additions and Corrections: 1997–2001.* Turnhout: Brepols, 2001.

——. *A Handlist of the Latin Writers of Great Britain and Ireland before 1540.* Turnhout: Brepols, 1997.

——. *Corpus of British Medieval Library Catalogues: List of Identifications.* http://www.history.ox.ac.uk/fileadmin/ohf/documents/projects/List-of-Identifications.pdf.

Shepard, Jonathan. "Byzantium and the West." In *NCMH*, vol. 3, *c.900–c.1024*, edited by Timothy Reuter, 605–23. Cambridge: Cambridge University Press, 1999.

Shepkaru, Shmuel. *Jewish Martyrs in the Pagan and Christian Worlds.* Cambridge: Cambridge University Press, 2006.

Short, Ian. "Patrons and Polyglots: French Literature in Twelfth-Century England." *Anglo-Norman Studies* 14 (1992): 229–49.

Simonsohn, Shlomo. "The Hebrew Revival among Early Medieval European Jews." In *The Salo Wittmayer Baron Jubilee Volume on the Occasion of His Eightieth Birthday*, edited by Saul Lieberman, 2:831–58. Jerusalem: American Academy for Jewish Research, 1974.

Slavin, Philip. "Hebrew Went Latin: Reflections of Latin Diplomatic Formulae and Terminology in Hebrew Private Deeds from Thirteenth-Century England." *Journal of Medieval Latin* 18 (2008): 306–25.

Smalley, Beryl. "The Biblical Scholar." In *Robert Grosseteste: Scholar and Bishop*, edited by D. A. Callus, 70–97. Oxford: Oxford University Press, 1955.

——. *Hebrew Scholarship among Christians in XIIIth Century England, as Illustrated by Some Hebrew-Latin Psalters.* London: Shapiro, Valentine, 1939.

——. "Sallust in the Middle Ages." In *Classical Influences on European Culture, A.D. 500–1500*, edited by R. R. Bolgar, 165–75. Cambridge: Cambridge University Press, 1971.

——. *The Study of the Bible in the Middle Ages*. Notre Dame: Notre Dame University Press, 1964.

Somenzi, Chiara. *Egesippo-Ambrogio: formazione scholastica e cristiana a Roma alla metà del IV secolo*. Milan: Vita e Pensiero, 2009.

Southern, R. W. "Peter of Blois and the Third Crusade." In *Studies in Medieval History Presented to RHC Davis*, edited by H. Mayr-Harting and R. I. Moore, 207–69. London: Hambledon, 1985.

——. *Robert Grosseteste: The Growth of an English Mind in Medieval Europe*. Oxford: Oxford University Press, 1986.

——. *Scholastic Humanism and the Unification of Europe*. 2 vols. Oxford: Blackwell, 1994–2001.

Spence, Sarah. "Felix Casus: The Dares and Dictys Legends of Aeneas." In *A Companion to Vergil's Aeneid and Its Tradition*, edited by Joseph Farrell and Michael C. J. Putnam, 133–46. Oxford: Blackwell, 2010.

Spiegel, Shalom. *The Last Trial: On the Legends and Lore of the Command to Abraham to Offer Isaac as a Sacrifice, the Akedah*. New York: Schocken, 1967.

Stacey, Robert C. "1240–60: A Watershed in Anglo-Jewish Relations?" *Historical Research* 61, no. 145 (1988): 135–50.

——. "The Conversion of Jews to Christianity in Thirteenth-Century England." *Speculum* 67 (1992): 263–83.

——. "Crusades, Martyrdoms, and the Jews of Norman England, 1096–1190." In *Juden und Christen zur Zeit der Kreuzzüge*, edited by Alfred Haverkamp, 233–51. Sigmaringen: Jan Thorbecke Verlag, 1999.

——. "Jewish Lending and the Medieval English Economy." In *A Commercialising Economy: England, 1086 to c. 1300*, edited by R. H. Britnell and Bruce M. S. Campbell, 78–101. Manchester: Manchester University Press, 1995.

——. "Lincoln, Aaron of (d. 1186)." In *Oxford Dictionary of National Biography*. Oxford: Oxford University Press, 2004. http://www.oxforddnb.com/view/article/37090.

Stern, David. "The Anthological Imagination in Jewish Literature." *Prooftexts* 17 (1997): 1–7.

Stern, David, and Mark Jay Mirsky. *Rabbinic Fantasies: Imaginative Narratives from Classical Hebrew Literature*. Philadelphia: Jewish Publication Society, 1990.

Stoneman, Richard. *Alexander the Great: A Life in Legend*. New Haven: Yale University Press, 2008.

Strack, H. L., and Gunter Stemberger. *Introduction to the Talmud and Midrash*. Translated by Markus Bockmuehl. 2nd ed. Minneapolis: Fortress, 1992.

Tabacco, Giovanni. *The Struggle for Power in Medieval Italy: Structures of Political Rule*. Translated by Rosalind Brown Jensen. Cambridge: Cambridge University Press, 1989.

Taguchi, Mayumi. "The Legend of the Cross Before Christ: Another Prose Treatment in English and Anglo-Norman." *Poetica* 45 (1996): 15–61.

Ta-Shma, Israel. "The Attitude of Medieval German Halakhists to Aggadic Sources" [in Hebrew]. In *Facing the Cross: The Persecutions of 1096 in History and Historiography*, edited by Yom Tov Assis et al., 150–56. Jerusalem: Magnes, 2000.

——. "Rabbi Moses Ha-Darshan and the Apocryphal Literature" [in Hebrew]. In *Studies in Jewish History and Literature: Lectures Delivered on the Memorial Day for the Late Prof. Yitzhak Twersky*, edited by Carmi Horowitz, 5–17. Jerusalem: Touro Graduate School of Jewish Studies, 2001.

——. "Tosafot." In *Encyclopaedia Judaica*, edited by Michael Berenbaum and Fred Skolnik, 20:67–70. 2nd ed. Detroit: Macmillan Reference, 2007.

Thomson, Rodney M. "England and the Twelfth-Century Renaissance." *Past and Present*, no. 101 (1983): 3–21.

——. *William of Malmesbury*. Woodbridge: Boydell, 2003.

Thomson, S. Harrison. *The Writings of Robert Grosseteste, Bishop of Lincoln, 1235–1253*. Cambridge: Cambridge University Press, 1940.

Tilliette, Jean-Yves. "Insula me genuit: L'influence de l'Énéide sur l'épopée latine du XII siècle." In *Lectures médiévales de Virgile: actes du colloque organisé par l'Ecole française de Rome (Rome, 25–28 octobre 1982)*, 121–42. Rome: Ecole française de Rome: 1985.

Timpanaro, Sebastiano. "Freud's 'Roman Phobia.'" *New Left Review* 1, no. 147 (1984): 4–31.

Tolan, John. *Petrus Alfonsi and His Medieval Readers*. Gainesville: University Press of Florida, 1993.

Twersky, Isadore. "Aspects of the Social and Cultural History of Provençal Jewry." *Journal of World History* 11 (1968): 185–207.

Tyson, Diana. "Patronage of French Vernacular History Writers in the Twelfth and Thirteenth Centuries." *Romania* 100 (1979): 180–222.

Urbach, E. E. *The Tosafists: Their History, Writings and Methods* [in Hebrew]. 2 vols. 5th enlarged ed. Jerusalem: Bialik Institute, 1986.

VanderKam, James C., ed. *The Book of Jubilees*. Leuven: Peeters, 1989.

Vincent, Nicholas. "William of Newburgh, Josephus, and the New Titus." In *Christians and Jews in Angevin England: The York Massacre of 1190, Narratives and Contexts*, edited by Sarah Rees Jones and Sethina Watson, 57–90. York: York Medieval Press, 2013.

Visi, Tamás. "Berechiah ben Naṭronai ha-Naqdan's *Dodi ve-Nekdi* and the Transfer of Scientific Knowledge from Latin to Hebrew in the Twelfth Century." *Aleph* 14, no. 2 (2014): 9–73.

Ward, J. O. "Some Principles of Rhetorical Historiography in the Twelfth Century." In *Classical Rhetoric and Medieval Historiography*, edited by Ernst Breisach, 103–65. Kalamazoo: Medieval Institute Publications, 1985.

Wasserstein, Abraham, and David Wasserstein. *The Legend of the Septuagint: From Classical Antiquity to Today*. Cambridge: Cambridge University Press, 2006.

Wasserstein, David J. "Grosseteste, the Jews, and Medieval Christian Hebraism." In *Robert Grosseteste: New Perspectives on His Thought and Scholarship*, edited by James McEvoy, 357–76. Turnhout: Brepols, 1995.

——. "The Written Culture of the Jews of Norman England, 1066–1290." *Parcours Judaïques* 6 (2000): 47–60.

Wetherbee, Winthrop. "Philosophy, Cosmology, and the Twelfth-Century Renaissance." In *A History of Twelfth-Century Philosophy*, edited by Peter Dronke, 21–53. Cambridge: Cambridge University Press, 1988.

Whalen, Logan E. "The Prologues and Epilogues of Marie de France." In *A Companion to Marie de France*, edited by Logan E. Whalen, 1–30. Leiden: Brill, 2011.

Whealey, Alice. *Josephus on Jesus: The Testimonium Flavianum Controversy from Late Antique to Modern Times*. New York: Peter Lang, 2003.

Wickham, Chris. *Early Medieval Italy: Central Power and Local Society, 400–1000*. London: Macmillan, 1981.

Wills, Lawrence. *The Jewish Novel in the Ancient World*. Ithaca, NY: Cornell University Press, 1995.

Wolfson, Elliot. *Through a Speculum that Shines: Vision and Imagination in Medieval Jewish Mysticism*. Princeton, NJ: Princeton University Press, 1994.

Wood, Susan. *English Monasteries and Their Patrons in the Thirteenth Century*. Oxford: Oxford University Press, 1955.

Wright, Neil. "Twelfth-Century Receptions of a Text: Anglo-Norman Historians and Hegesippus." *Anglo-Norman Studies* 31 (2008): 177–95.

Wright, Stephen K. *The Vengeance of Our Lord: Medieval Dramatizations of the Destruction of Jerusalem*. Toronto: Pontifical Institute of Mediaeval Studies, 1989.

Yassif, Eli. "The Hebrew Narrative Anthology in the Middle Ages." In *The Anthology in Jewish Literature*, edited by David Stern, 176–95. Oxford: Oxford University Press, 2004.

Yerushalmi, Yosef Hayim. *Zakhor: Jewish History and Jewish Memory*. New York: Schocken, 1989.

Young, Karl. "Ordo Prophetarum." *Transactions of the Wisconsin Academy of Sciences, Arts and Letters* 20 (1922): 1–82.

Yuval, Israel Jacob. "Jewish Messianic Expectations Towards 1240 and Christian Reactions." In *Toward the Millennium: Messianic Expectations from the Bible to Waco*, edited by Peter Schäfer and Mark Cohen, 105–21. Leiden: Brill, 1998.

——. *Two Nations in Your Womb: Perceptions of Jews and Christians in Late Antiquity and the Middle Ages*. Translated by Barbara Harshav and Jonathan Chipman. Berkeley: University of California Press, 2006.

Zerubavel, Yael. *Recovered Roots: Collective Memory and the Making of Israeli National Tradition*. Chicago: University of Chicago Press, 1995.

Zimmerli, Walther. *Ezekiel 1: A Commentary on the Book of the Prophet Ezekiel, Chapters 1–24*. Translated by Ronald Clements. Edited by Frank Moore Cross and Klaus Baltzer. Philadelphia: Fortress, 1979.

# INDEX

CPSIA information can be obtained
at www.ICGtesting.com
Printed in the USA
LVOW08*1924220317

528109LV00004B/55/P

9 781501 703072